THE SOCIAL RESPONSIBILITY OF THE SCIENTIST

The Free Press · *New York*

THE

SOCIAL

RESPONSIBILITY

OF

THE

SCIENTIST

Edited by Martin Brown

Collier–Macmillan Limited · **London**

THE FREE PRESS
A Division of The Macmillan Company
866 Third Avenue, New York, New York 10022

Collier-Macmillan Canada Ltd., Toronto, Ontario

Library of Congress Catalog Number: 75–143503

printing number
1 2 3 4 5 6 7 8 9 10

Contents

Prologue   vii

SPENCER KLAW
The Faustian Bargain   3

CHARLES SCHWARTZ
A Physicist on *Professional Organization*   19

OWEN CHAMBERLAIN
A Physicist on *Government Funding*   36

SERGE LANG
A Mathematician on *The DOD, Government,
and Universities*   51

J. B. NEILANDS
A Biochemist on *Chemical Warfare*   82

MARC LAPPÉ
A Microbiologist on *Biological Warfare*   96

JOSHUA LEDERBERG
A Geneticist on *Food Additives*   121

JOHN W. GOFMAN and **ARTHUR R. TAMPLIN**
Two Biophysicists on *Nuclear Radiation*   133

THOMAS H. BREWER
A Physician on *Disease and Social Class*   149

ROBERT C. STEBBINS
A Zoologist on *The Loss of Biological Diversity*   165

BARRY COMMONER
A Biologist on *The Ecological Crisis*   174

DANIEL LUTEN
A Geographer on *Population Growth*   184

DONALD DAHLSTEN
An Entomologist on *Pesticides*   201

RODNEY ARKLEY
A Soil Scientist on *Land Misuse*   220

ROBERT E. FEENEY
A Food Scientist on *The World Food Supply*   228

PAUL GOODMAN
Can Technology Be Humane?   247

Epilogue   267

Topical Bibliography   273

Prologue

GRIM PREDICTION: DOOMSDAY IN 30 YEARS

If Bacteriological Warfare Doesn't Get You,
The Rape Of The Environment Will

These sentiments, expressed in a San Francisco news-paper, were not those of the traditional doomsday cults but of two eminent scientists, Professors Joshua Lederberg and William Pollard. More and more scientists, especially younger scientists and science students, are coming to similar if not more vital conclusions. For example, three members of the group respon-sible for the well-publicized isolation of a pure preparation of a single gene have made the following comments on their work (in correspondence to *Nature*, December 27, 1969):

> We did not publicize our work in order to add to our own or Harvard's prestige or to make a plea for more money for basic research. In a country which makes a prodigious use of science and technology to murder Viet-namese and poison the environment, such an enterprise would be at best terribly irrelevant, at worst criminal. On the contrary, we tried to make the following political state-ment. In and of itself, our work is morally neutral—it can lead either to benefits or to dangers for mankind. But we are working in the United States in the year 1969. The basic control over scientific work and its further develop-ment is in the hands of a few people at the head of large private institutions and at the top of government bureauc-

racies. These people have consistently exploited science for harmful purposes in order to increase their own power.

The reality of the dangers we and others point out should not be minimized. Social agitation does not arise in a vacuum. . . . In Los Angeles, air pollution is often so bad that school children are prevented from taking physical exercise. Breast feeding in the United States, Sweden and Britain has become a serious health hazard because of the high concentrations of DDT and other pesticides in human milk. The American Indians, the Jews, the Biafrans, the Vietnamese, and the Palestinians are no strangers to the use of technology as an instrument of genocide. The survivors of Hiroshima and Nagasaki and the parents of thalidomide babies can testify to the horrors of the uncontrolled use of science by governments and private corporations. The list is virtually endless. We do not need to expand on it here. Let us simply point out to those who feel we have ample time to deal with these problems that less than 50 years elapsed between Becquerel's discovery of radioactivity in 1896 and the use of an atomic weapon against human beings in 1945. As to the specific issue of genetic engineering, we cannot predict the future. But who in 1896 could have foreseen the weapons of mass destruction which now threaten us all?

What we are advocating is that scientists, together with other people, should actively work for radical political change in this country. If we do not, we will one day be a group of very regretful Oppenheimers. Scientists have no right to claim a special position of intellectual leadership in this political effort. We differ from other members of society only in that our working conditions are generally more free than theirs. This is because governments and industry realize that science and technology develop more efficiently without stringent controls. As we see it, scientists are obligated to inform the public about what is happening in their secluded fields of research so that people can demand control over decisions which profoundly affect their lives. If our arguments mean that "progress of science itself may be interrupted," that is an unfortunate consequence we will have to accept. It certainly should not inhibit us from speaking out on crucial issues.

[Signed] Jim Shapiro
Larry Eron
Jon Beckwith

Jim Shapiro subsequently put aside scientific studies to devote his full time to political activism.

The case of Jim Shapiro is not exceptional, nor is the movement among young scientists limited to the United States. In France, young scientists and technicians (and some older scientists, such as the renowned molecular biologist Professor Jacque Monod) played an important role in the May–June Revolt. And today in France there are groups "consisting of radical scientists who are willing to take on the Military and Industrial Complex and its noxious effects all over the world" (personal communication from Jacque Bullot, Laboratoire De Chimie Physique, Orsay, France).

In Italy, a group called Potere Operaio has organized strikes of research workers. Potere Operaio is an Italian New Left group with the philosophy that "The State has become both the instrument of economic development and social productivity and the guarantee of the system's efficiency" (leaving the worker with no power to determine the application of the product of his labor). Thus, according to Potere Operaio (in a statement on the jailing of Francesco Tolin, the editor of the *Potere Operaio* newspaper), the worker should deny the system his labor, making the functioning of the machine–state impossible. The scientist is viewed also as a worker, a valuable technician for the maintenance of the machine. Because he is denied any right to judge whether the product of his labor should be put to use for the well-being of or for the destruction and exploitation of mankind, he should refuse to work for the system.

It is not without significance that Jim Shapiro and many other scientists, many of whom would not ordinarily be considered political radicals, have come to essentially the same conclusion. They have not come to that conclusion by way of theorizing but through their everyday experience as functioning scientists in the society. Many of them were attracted to science because of its abstract beauty and its potential for improving human existence. But when they look around the modern world of science they are faced with an ugly reality. Massive amounts of scientific know-how are applied to producing increasingly destructive weapons of war; the techniques of modern science seem almost useless in the face of the rampant destruction of the environment; many of the once promising technological solutions for human problems have backfired miserably. In short, the great promise of the "Second Industrial Revolution," that science and technology would solve most of the basic problems of mankind, has proven to be an illusion.

Because the disillusionment has taken many forms, scientists have formed special societies to discuss the problems of science and to propose solutions; have been more involved as a group in political action, both by advising and by mass action; and have set up organizations to better inform the public on technical matters. And, of course, whole branches in political science, sociology, and philosophy have been established which study only the social role of science and the scientist.

At the University of California, Berkeley, several students in biophysics, electrical engineering, genetics, math, and physics, who had become increasingly disturbed by their role as scientists in the society, formed a group called Science Students for Social Responsibility. It soon became apparent to those in SSSR that, though a great deal had been written on the social responsibility of the scientist, there was a scarcity of material which both was relevant to most urgent problems of the society and had substantial technical content. Initiating a course designed to cover in depth subjects dealing with specific pressing problems, they signed up, as guest lecturers, an impressive array of notable scientists and scholars. This well-received lecture series, which was sponsored by Professors Joe Neilands and Charles Schwartz, was given in the spring quarter of 1969 at the University of California, Berkeley. The editor of this volume was privileged to serve as Instructor.

Most of the essays contained in this volume are based on the lectures prepared for that course. They are offered here in the hope that they will throw new light on subjects of tremendous scope and importance, and will therefore aid the scientist and nonscientist alike in dealing with vital issues which well may determine the fate of mankind.

ACKNOWLEDGMENTS

My deepest gratitude goes to Joel Swartz, who first conceived of this series, and to Jon Gabel and Nikki Everts, who were instrumental in initiating and planning the course titled "The Social Responsibilty of the Scientist"; to sponsoring Professors Charles Schwartz and Joe Neilands; and to the Berkeley Physics Department Course Committee, the Course Committee of the Academic Senate, and the Center for Participatory Education. I am indebted, too, to the many distinguished scholars who served first as guest lecturers and then as contributors to the book, often under adverse circumstances. Also, I wish to thank William Woodcock of The Free Press for his constant aid and advice, and manuscript editor George A. Rowland of The Free Press. I thank Pat Schoenfield for her courageous typing efforts; and my friend Joe and my brother Jeffrey for their aid; and especially Janet for her help, patience, and encouragement.

Martin Brown
Berkeley, California
Summer, 1970

THE SOCIAL RESPONSIBILITY OF THE SCIENTIST

Spencer Klaw

was Visiting Lecturer at the University of California, Berkeley, during the 1968–69 academic year. A former associate editor of *Fortune* and a contributor to *The Reporter, Harper's, The New York Times Magazine,* and *Esquire,* he is the author of *The New Brahmins: Scientific Life in America* (Morrow, 1968).

Most scientists take the present system of funding for granted, and can hardly dream of "doing science" under any other circumstances. Yet, just 30 years ago government funding for science was unheard of in the United States. There was no Office of Naval Research, or National Aeronautics and Space Administration, or National Science Foundation, or National Institutes of Health. Research scientists either worked directly for private corporations or were allocated paltry resources by their universities. Rare indeed was the scientist who went door-to-door among the wealthy, promoting his project (The Discovery of the Century!) personally.

In 1969 the total federal budget for research and development was $16,891,000,000. Of this, $1,350,000,000 went directly to universities. As recently as 1955, the total "R and D" budget was only $3,100,000,000. The 1969 budget breaks down as follows:

1

Departments	$ Million
AEC	1,504
Agriculture	276
Commerce	81
Defense	8,194
HEW	1,211
Interior	202
NASA	4,495
NSF	257
Others	207

Notice that by far the largest sources of research money are the military and space agencies. The National Science Foundation (NSF), the one "objective, nonpolitical" science-funding agency, allocates only a tiny fraction of the total funds.

In the following article Mr. Klaw sketches government involvement in scientific funding. He opens his account with the mobilization of scientific talent for military purposes during World War II. He then describes the development of the postwar "Faustian deal" made between a wealthy military establishment interested in supporting research with military applications, and a growing body of scientists in need of research funds for basic research which they feel has nothing directly to do with such applications. It is a "deal" which, he says, has had unfortunate results—such as the dislocation of public funding toward research which may have military applications, and the agonizing conflict of the scientist who feels that his research will benefit mankind but finds that the only source of funds for such research is the military.

Is there a way out of this situation? Klaw thinks there are several ways, and his exploration of them makes for an especially appropriate introduction to this volume.

The
Faustian
Bargain

What I want mainly to talk about is the Faustian bargain that American scientists have made with their government. I don't mean to suggest by this that a scientist who accepts a research grant from the National Science Foundation has thereby lost his soul. On the contrary, it seems to me that the collaboration between scientists and government that has developed since World War II has been an extraordinarily fruitful one. I use the term "Faustian" to suggest that unless he is extremely careful about the fine print in the contract, the scientist who accepts government patronage may find himself morally compromised. Even when the fine print has been duly scrutinized and found to be free of booby traps, the scientist may retain—and I think for the good of his soul he *should* retain—a certain moral uneasiness.

This uneasiness was well expressed by a physicist with whom I talked three or four years ago. He was, at the time, helping to build and put into operation the big new linear accelerator at Stanford. He said, "In a way we are all getting money under false pretenses. You know, we go to Congress and we say, 'This is pure science. It has no practical applications that anyone can foresee. Exploring the atomic nucleus is pure intellectual adventure.' The congressmen nod. They say, 'Yes, that's fine.' But they're really thinking about Einstein, and $E=MC^2$, and about the possibility that somehow some new superweapon might come of this. And way down deep inside we know that's what they're thinking. Of course, we take the money anyway."

3

Few scientists who are doing research—and I am talking mainly about academic scientists, and scientists in other institutions who are primarily occupied with basic research—are quite as much under the gun, so to speak, as this physicist. But the fact is that most basic researchers are, in effect, wards of the federal government, on whose bounty they must depend for the privilege of carrying on their work. Here, for example, are some figures collected by Harold Orlans of the Brookings Institution. Orlans questioned some 3,000 faculty members, asking them, among other things, if they were getting federal support for their research. Here are the results for 12 leading American universities:

In the "preclinical biosciences"—I assume here we are talking about members of medical-school faculties—the percentage of faculty members getting government support was 93 percent. In physics it was 89 percent. In chemistry, 79 percent. In biology and zoology, 74 percent. Even in mathematics it was 53 percent. These figures are for 1960. But despite the recent cuts in research appropriations, I have no reason to think they would differ significantly today at universities like UC [Berkeley], or at Harvard or Stanford or Cal Tech. And many of these scientists, I should add, are also engaged in another kind of collaboration with the government. They serve as scientific advisors or consultants.

To a great many people, scientists and nonscientists alike, the collaboration I have been describing seems sinister and immoral. But I think it is important to realize that this has not always been the case. The close working relationship between government and scientist—and the assumption by the government of the role of patron of science—dates back only about 25 years. It began in World War II, at a time when what I will loosely call "liberal" or "enlightened" views about the national government were rather different from what they are today. To put it with a simplicity that would make a historian wince, the New Deal had taught people of my generation to think of the government as a powerful instrument, and an accessible one, for dealing with poverty, unemployment, exploitation, and other social evils. It is true that by 1941 some of this faith in government had been dimmed—the New Deal never really managed to make much of a dent in unemployment. But, in a different way, our faith was revived by the war. Everybody was against Hitler, and people were caught up in a great national enterprise. Scientists were like everybody else. By the hundreds and thousands they flocked into the big new laboratories like the Radiation Laboratory at MIT, established for the purpose of developing radar. And while many scientists who worked on The Bomb were later to develop haunting feelings of guilt, few felt guilty before Hiroshima and Nagasaki. If Robert Oppenheimer had refused to have anything to do with The Bomb, he would have been condemned, not praised, by the overwhelming majority of other physicists.

After the war, most of the scientists who had been at Los Alamos and the other secret laboratories went back to the universities. But things were different. The main difference was that science seemed to cost an awful lot more money than it had before the war. Changes in the technology of research had made expensive instruments and big machines indispensable in certain branches of science—and highly desirable in others. Having found the government a reasonably good patron in time of war, it was natural for scientists to turn to the government in time of peace. What the scientists wanted was what they eventually got through the programs of the National Institutes of Health and the National Science Foundation. That is, they wanted money to be allotted to scientists purely on the merit of a scientist's ideas, as evaluated by a group of his peers. It was a long time, however, before NSF was established and funded, and in the meantime scientists, with some qualms, were happy to get money wherever they could—provided it was on terms that did not infringe on their freedom, and provided the money was allotted according to scientific rather than political criteria.

They got the money: from the Air Force, from the Atomic Energy Commission, from the Army, and from the Navy. The Office of Naval Research was for several years the main support of certain kinds of basic research in American universities.

The people who got this support did so with pretty clear

consciences. They were doing scientifically important work of their own choice—work that they couldn't otherwise have done. And while they knew that the Navy was not acting out of pure altruism, many of them would have felt happy, rather than distressed, if their work had led to practical developments. After all, the feeling was, "We need a Navy—or, at any rate, we are going to have one for a long time—and it is a hell of a lot better to have a relatively efficient one."

A couple of years ago I had a talk with a mathematician who had been one of the key administrators of the Navy's research program. He was talking about the excitement and exhilaration of his job. "In those years, in the late 1940's and early 1950's, I was riding an irresistible wave," he told me. "The mathematicization, you might say, of military technology and operations. We were learning to use mathematics to optimize the use of machines and people. Many of the research programs we were putting into effect had existed for years in my mind, and I was able to move with considerable assurance, crystallizing the paths along which major efforts should be launched. In time, as my responsibilities broadened, I became less concerned with mathematics as such and became fascinated with such questions as how relevant technology can be made to emerge from the stuff of scientific knowledge and insight."

He went on to say that he had been brought up from the cradle to think that the only right thing for a scientist to do was, as he put it, "to put my six feet of immortal works on the bookshelves of history." (That's a lot of mathematics, I must say.) But he said he had found satisfaction in his work as an administrator because, and I'm quoting again, "I am aware what the alternative course of history might have been in certain instances. This does not have quite the same material existence as papers and books, but in a history-rich era such as ours, many roads meet in the wood. And to have been instrumental in helping to choose the right road, that is rather important."

Now, what are we to make of this? From one point of view he is, or was, a madman, a sort of Dr. Strangelove, gloating over his part in helping to give the Navy a bigger bang for a buck, as they used to say. But I'm convinced that that would be quite an unfair judgment, and it would, I think, cloud our understanding of events and attitudes that we must understand if we are to cope more intelligently with some of our present dilemmas. (And I say "we" because the problems that we are considering here are not exclusively scientists' problems.) The mathematician whose remarks I have just quoted is a cultivated European, who came to this country in his late teens or early twenties, a refugee from Hitler. He found himself then, in the 1940's, engaged in a crusade, as he and millions of other Americans saw it, to rid the world of fascist tyranny, and then later to see to it that Communist tyrants, such as Stalin, should not be allowed to extend their dominion.

I suspect that he, himself, would now question the validity of some of the assumptions and aims of American foreign policy, even during this period in which he was working in the Navy. I know that he has seriously questioned our policy in Vietnam—seriously enough so that these doubts were an important factor in his decision, shortly before I spoke with him, to leave the government. You may wonder why I dwelt for such a length on this man, but I did so as a reminder that it is only since 1963, the year that John Kennedy was assassinated, that so many of us have come to look on the government with such profound doubt and suspicion. Events of the Eisenhower years, particularly the vindictive persecution of Robert Oppenheimer, were deeply disturbing. But I think we felt, particularly after McCarthy's downfall, that it was only a matter of time before we would once again have an administration more to our liking.

The government, although it was temporarily in "do nothing" hands, as we saw it, was still our government in a sense which a great many of us—many of us who are by no means revolutionaries—no longer feel. The question is whether this alienation from our government, to use a fashionable term, is permanent. I think not. I think things will never, of course, be again as they were before Vietnam. As Oppenheimer said in speaking of the physicists' part in the making of The Bomb, we have known sin. I think that very large numbers of Americans now know that we as a nation can behave in just as brutal, mindless, and totally immoral a fashion as any other great nation. And we have been forced to accept the fact that we are not omnipotent, and we have lost a war. Obviously, we will never be the same again.

But I think that unless the United States is racked by revolution and civil war, the chances are that the pendulum will swing and that scientists who advise the government, or who accept its bounty, will no longer have to defend themselves so often against the charge that they are, in effect, designing gas ovens for another Buchenwald. Certainly, most scientists will have to go on depending on the government for patronage. Some faculty members, at UC and other universities, have sworn off government grants. One that comes to my mind, a man whom some of you may know, is Professor Joseph Hodges, who tells me that it was like kicking the cigarette habit and that he feels much better for it. But Professor Hodges is a statistician, and people who want to do experiments in high-energy physics, or to work in oceanography or observational astronomy, or, in fact, to do important experiments in many branches of science, will not find it quite so easy to get the monkey off their backs. Their choice is to accept government funds or to get into some other line of work.

Similarly, I suspect that the time is going to come when scientists will once again work as government advisors without feeling that they are traitorous collaborators with an occupying power. But I think that the events of these past few years have revealed some very serious flaws, both moral and practical, in the relationship that has evolved between American scientists and their government. And although I am, in effect, only a foreign visitor to a country in which most of you are planning to be lifelong residents—I mean the scientific community—I will nevertheless be rash enough to suggest what I think some of these flaws are. I also would like to suggest, in a quite unsystematic way, some ways in which I think these flaws might be remedied. These suggestions are, to say the least, tentative. But perhaps they may suggest some paths that you might wish to explore.

One suggestion is that no scientist should accept a grant or a contract for research if the consequences of that research are likely to offend his own sense of morality. A scientist cannot ignore the foreseeable consequences of his work. Nor, in my opinion, can he usefully divide himself into two separate persons, one the researcher and the other the concerned citizen. I think a scientist who does research related to biological weapons and then spends his spare time demonstrating against the Army's chemical and biological warfare programs—well, I think that's better than the scientist who does his research and then keeps his mouth shut after hours. But I would, of course, feel better if he would simply refuse to do the work. This is easy, of course, for people to say who have nice, string-free grants from NIH. It seems to me that one thing such fortunately situated scientists can do is not simply to consider the biological warfare researcher as beyond the human pale, but rather to find him a better job.

I believe that molecular biology—genetics—was to some extent kept alive in Russia, during the long night of Lysenko, by physicists who smuggled geneticists into their laboratories and set them up in business under assumed names, as it were. This procedure, known as bootlegging, is not unfamiliar, of course, to scientists in this country. Perhaps something like this might be done for civilian refugees from Fort Detrich, the Army biological warfare laboratory in Maryland.

Now I think we have to face the fact that, as an intelligent and moral man, a scientist may honestly think that in this treacherous and evil world, it makes sense for America to develop new and deadlier weapons. I think the obligation of those scientists who feel otherwise is to keep such people under fairly constant moral pressure. They must be forced to defend their position, and publicly. You may not convert a strong-minded hawk, but I think if you keep the pressure on you may save the souls of those scientists who, in one way or another, are struggling to put out of their minds the consequences of their acts. I think that this may require some change in the kind of Senatorial courtesy that holds that you don't publicly criticize a colleague's taste in research or in consulting work. I think it is reasonable to ask a colleague to account quite specifically for what he is doing in the way of research, insofar as its social consequences are concerned, because that involves you, too, as a fellow member of the same institution.

At the very least, scientists should not tolerate the kind of situation that developed, I believe, at the University of Utah. There, it was only through the accident of a laboratory fire that people in the biological sciences discovered a secret laboratory right on the campus that was fooling around with techniques for producing anthrax or some other deadly disease.

This matter of secrecy brings me to a second complaint and suggestion. I think scientists have been too easily cowed or bullied by government secrecy. This is understandable on the part of men who were schooled in security during World War II, but I think it's time for a little skepticism and perhaps even a little civil disobedience. Remember, anyway, that the man who prints classified information is breaking no law. Only the man who has been given the classified information on the condition that he not reveal it is liable. The point is that, as everyone knows, security is used to cover everything from inefficiency and larceny to the kind of mad science you might associate with Dr. Strangelove. It could be argued that even from the strict standpoint of national security, and I'm using that term in the sense that it might be used by the Joint Chiefs of Staff, we would be better off without 95 percent of our present security —that is, if we were to declassify 95 percent of all classified information. For example, I think we'd be much safer if the Russians could know for a fact just how inefficient our ABM system is.

Most leading universities, I think, no longer permit classified research on campus, or within their regular departmental structures. But it still goes on, of course, at off-campus laboratories that do research for government agencies. I'm thinking, in the case of UC Berkeley, of the UC laboratories such as Livermore and the Naval Research Laboratory in Oakland. Now it seems clear to me that universities have an obligation to lend a hand in solving urgent problems that confront the government. But they also have an obligation to themselves to help out only in ways that are compatible with the university's primary missions. And, obviously, what seems compatible today may not seem compatible next year, which means that the nature of the university's involvement must be continually watched and criticized. And if government security regulations stand in the way of this scrutiny, you may simply have to burrow underneath them. It's surprising what you can find out from *un*classified information, if you know where to look.

I'm not suggesting that scientists should have to do this on their own. Maybe what is needed is a watchdog group, an interdisciplinary effort—investigative teams consisting, say, of one biochemist, one lawyer, and one journalist.

Another suggestion I have is that the terms on which scientists act as government advisors must be radically changed. As everyone knows, we can't hope to deal intelligently with our troubles unless the government can get the advice of first-rate scientists. And as I've said, I think the time will come again when scientists will be much more willing than now to provide that advice. But it must be provided on different terms. As it is, the advisory process is shrouded with secrecy. In many cases we, the public, don't know who is being consulted on particular matters of government policy—on whether to expand an ABM, or what we ought to do after we land a man on the moon.

This is in large part the doing of the politicians who summon the advisors to Washington. If no one knows who is on an ad hoc advisory panel—and in many cases the public doesn't even know that the panel exists—it makes it much easier to deal with troublesome advice. By troublesome, I mean advice that conflicts with what the President or a particular agency head has already decided that he would like to do. Under the circumstances I have described, he can simply shelve the report with no one the wiser; or, in some cases, call together another, more pliable, panel.

I suspect, though, that scientists themselves have been much too ready to acquiesce in this sort of arrangement. One of the few I can think of who has screamed loudly about it is Philip Abelson, the editor of *Science*. Of course, a scientist-advisor's anonymity has certain advantages. For one thing, it protects him from having to admit later that his advice was disastrously wrong, since nobody knows what advice he gave in the first place. And, by protecting him from criticism, this secrecy may fortify him in the conviction to which a few scientists are prone—that is, the conviction that he is a member of an elite whose members have special intellectual qualifications that entitle them to be shielded from the vulgar inquisitions of the press and public. I recognize, of course that the President of the United States has every right to have a confidential advisor on scientific matters. But I would propose that working scientists who are called to Washington as consultants should go only if they are assured that their work, insofar as security permits, will be public—no matter what they end up advising. And I think that scientists should use their own judgment in deciding whether proposed security restrictions are reasonable or not.

I don't think that this is going to be accomplished very easily, for reasons that have to do with the science establishment. I'm referring to those scientists, numbering perhaps 250 in all, whom James R. Killian, Jr.—himself a key figure in the establishment—has characterized as "consistently influential" in government affairs. These are the scientists who have very easy access to heads of agencies, and whose advice is often sought in matters that are social and political as well as scientific and technological. Very often these are the same men who represent the scientific community, or one of its subcommunities, in the bargaining that determines how much money the government spends for research, and what that money is spent for.

Let me give you some examples of how these two kinds of power and influence are interlocked. Frederick Seitz is president of Rockefeller University. He is also a member (and former chairman) of the Defense Science Board (the Defense Department's principal scientific advisory body), and a former member of the National Selective Service Board. In the past he has served in such posts as those of president of the National Academy of Sciences (a semipublic institution which is at once an honorary society and a kind of dignified and genteel lobby for American science), and chairman of the Naval Research Advisory Committee.

Another example is Harvey Brooks. He is Dean of Engineering and Applied Physics at Harvard. And he certainly has been one of the most consulted of the consultants in recent years. Brooks is a former member of the President's Science Advisory Board. He is still a consultant-at-large to the committee. At the same time, he is chairman of the National Academy of Science's Committee on Science and Public Policy, known as COSPUP, which acts as a sort of executive committee of the scientific establishment. He has also been a spokesman for his own particular segment of the scientific community, serving as a member of the Academy's Physics Survey Committee. This committee, just a few years ago, appealed to the government for a 150 percent increase over a six-year period in federal outlays for the support of physical research.

It is possible that men like Seitz and Brooks are exceptions. But I think that, in general, the men who rise to the top in this world, the scientists who can be seen lunching with influential government officials at the Cosmos Club in Washington, are not agitators or critics. They are operators, organizers, compromisers, arrangers, experts in the creation and use of power. I suspect that my choice of words betrays my own instinctive preference for agitators over arrangers, but that's really a stylistic preference. I think we have to recognize that the setting in motion, and the governance, of large and complex affairs demands a high degree of political skill. My impression is that many scientists at the upper levels of the Establishment resemble professional diplomats. They prefer to talk privately, to build up firm relationships based on reciprocal favors. While such men are invaluable if they are on your side, and you want to get something *done,* they are not likely to be sympathetic to the notion that the advisory process should be thrown open to public scrutiny.

And so I come to the last of my suggestions. I think that scientists themselves must create a new kind of advisory and critical apparatus. I don't mean that they should refuse to serve as government advisors, provided that they can do so on more favorable terms than at present. But I think they should create an institution which will offer the government free and informed scientific advice, public advice, and supply it whether the government asks for it or not.

Just take as an example the debate over the ABM. I read that Professor Ralph Lapp did a valuable job in helping Senator Mansfield shoot great holes in the Pentagon's case. And the public has been told that virtually all American scientists who have given the matter any thought (and even those who haven't) think the ABM is not only immoral but ridiculous. How much more effective it would have been if there had been a careful analysis and study of the ABM carried out under the auspices, let us say, of two or three hundred of the nation's leading scientists, and so fully documented that it would be impossible to dismiss. It would have provided a solid platform and a public one, on which opponents of the ABM, in and out of government, could have stood. To some extent, of course, this sort of independent criticism and advice is provided by individual scientists and scholars, and is publicized in such magazines as the *Bulletin of the Atomic Scientists* and *Environment*. But to appraise a weapons system, to analyze disarmament proposals, to demonstrate the dangers of the government's over-permissiveness toward the private developers of atomic energy—all this may be beyond the powers of one man, however gifted, especially when he is spending most of his time teaching and doing research.

I think that what we need is an independent institute, modeled after the American Civil Liberties Union or the Legal Defense Fund of the National Association for the Advancement of Colored People. Or, perhaps, more precisely, modeled after the Institute for Policy Studies in Washington. The function of this institute would be to produce the kind of advice that we badly need in America. It would be produced by permanent Fellows, or Members, drawn from both the natural and the social sciences, and acting in cooperation with people from universities or other institutions serving as consultants. Some of these consultants might serve for a few days or weeks; others might spend a year as visiting Fellows. I'm certainly no expert on designing institutions. The main points are that such an institution should have the broadest possible sponsorship; that its director and staff should have great autonomy (the kind of autonomy that university faculties should have); and that it should be totally independent of the government.

Who is to pay the bill? The best way would be for the scientists themselves to put up the money. This may be a shocking suggestion, but if many thousands of scientists were to put up $50 each a year—that's about a third of what my union dues were when I belonged to the Newspaper Guild—this would produce a million dollars. And when you don't need accelerators or electron microscopes, you can do a lot of research for a million dollars. Perhaps some scientists should pay more. One of the fruits of the Faustian bargain I spoke of earlier is that many scientists now make a pretty good living. I'm not suggesting that scientists can save themselves from the clutches of the devil for a mere fifty or a hundred dollars a year. But I think it would be money well spent—and I would be happy to toss something into the pot, too.

Charles Schwartz

is Professor of Physics at the University of California, Berkeley. In 1952 he received a B.A. in physics from MIT, where he went on to receive a Ph.D. in physics in 1954. Teaching first at Stanford University beginning in 1957, Professor Schwartz transferred to Berkeley in 1960. His most recent work involves the application of computer techniques to applied quantum mechanics.

In this article Professor Schwartz gives an account of his attempts to bring to the fore, in the journals and public forums of the American Physical Society, the issues of the social role and the social responsibility of the scientist. The expected and unexpected resistance he met within the APS has led him to take an active role in Scientists for Social and Political Action (SSPA—now called Scientists and Engineers for Social and Political Action, or SESPA). SESPA was instrumental in making the ABM an issue at the APS meeting in Washington, D.C., in April of 1969. Since that time, SESPA offered to make its intellectual resources available to congressmen who seek an alternative to the official scientific advice from the Pentagon.

Professor Schwartz has been very active in SESPA at Berkeley, working especially with socially concerned graduate students in physics, chemistry and engineering who will soon have to deal with the kind of difficulties that he has encountered in the professional society.

17

In June of 1969 at Berkeley more than 80 science students and science faculty signed the following pledge sponsored by SESPA:

> I pledge that I will not participate in war research or weapons production. I further pledge to counsel my students and urge my colleagues to do the same.

SESPA is circulating this pledge internationally, along with statements by many of the original signers explaining their reasons and motivations for signing the pledge. SESPA hopes that thousands of scientists around the world will sign the pledge in the early 1970's.

Professional Organization

The university has long been pictured as a neutral institution wherein academic scientists pursue objective research. But the university is, in reality, not so isolated, nor is the scientist so neutral. The real world of the academic scientist is filled with the politics of university policy, federal funding, advisory committees, and professional societies. The young scientist who wishes to deal effectively with social problems must be equipped to deal with these institutions.

To the question "What can one person do out there?" there may be many answers. I want to discuss what the concerned scientist might do, focusing on the fact that he will go out not only as an individual citizen but as a member of a particular and powerful group: the scientific profession.

The standard answer to the question "What can I, as a member of the scientific profession and as a socially concerned —and perhaps politically active—person, hope to accomplish?" is "Nothing, because nothing is allowed." Professional societies are, almost by definition, tightly structured to promote and preserve some narrow set of self-interests. The subject of our study is the responsibility of scientists, as individuals and as a group, to some body outside—namely, the whole of humanity. Therefore, it should not be surprising that the pursuits of social responsibility and the pursuits of professional societies come into conflict. The AMA is the best-known example of this conflict, and we need not look far to find other examples.

I want to present something of a personal travelogue, relating some of my experiences while trying to create some new activity in my own professional society. You will be able to see something of what the medium is like where I have spent my professional career. On the one hand it may be described as "stiff" from lack of exercise, but on the other hand it may be seen as "fertile" because the soil has not been plowed for quite some time.

In 1967 I wrote a letter to the magazine *Physics Today,* a nontechnical professional monthly. I wanted to discuss issues of the Vietnam war with my professional colleagues at large, and thought that the letters-to-the-editor column of this magazine was an appropriate medium for such general communication. However, the editor and his superiors in the American Physical Society (APS) thought otherwise, and my letter was rejected, in spite of my appeals to elected officers of the APS.

I was sufficiently serious about the issue that I did not let it drop but instead found a way to force open discussion of the issues, at least in a second-order way. What I did was to draw up a proposal to amend the constitution of the APS; and once I had collected the required number of signatures to sponsor it, the officers of the society were obliged to acknowledge the issue publicly and allow general debate to take place. I will quote from several letters and editorials in *Physics Today,* running through the winter of 1967–68, which describe the reactions of various people at the upper echelons and elsewhere in the structure of this professional society, so that you can get an idea of what these many people were concerned about. I should explain that the constitutional amendment in point said nothing about the original issue I wanted to raise: the Vietnam war and its effects on American society and science. What I proposed was something which sounded very bland:

> The members may express their opinion, will, or intent on any matter of concern to the Society by voting on one or several resolutions formally presented for their consideration. The procedures required for this action shall be the same as those specified for amending this Constitution, with the following changes. . . .

Some friends advised me not to mix in the real political questions, but just to stick with the neutral "free speech" issue so as not to lose support, because the Vietnam question was still so very controversial. However, the two issues did become mixed up, both deliberately and unavoidably, resulting in some very interesting reactions.

It turned out that even getting the discussion started in an honest way was a bit difficult. When the amendment was first proposed it still took me many weeks of pounding on doors and tables, and of persisting on telephones, before I was allowed to print my own statements explaining what it was all about. The first two months saw only statements by the officers and the editors, giving their presentations and interpretations of the matter. They were striving, of course, to be neutral and balanced; but that was impossible since most of my complaint had to deal with the close-handed way in which they monopolized the media. Finally, however, fairness and honesty (the basic scientific virtues) did prevail, and there was a lively debate both written and oral. Here are some excerpts.

The editor of *Physics Today* wrote (December 1967, p. 128):

> A while ago the editors of *Physics Today* rejected a letter for publication that was concerned with the right or wrong of the Vietnam war. We gave as our reason that the American Institute of Physics and its publication *Physics Today* are by charter and intent devoted to physics as physics and physicists as physicists. The letter did not appear to have any special relation to either of them.

Then he gave his analysis of the proposed amendment:

> Arguments in favor of the proposed amendment deserve appreciation. Professionals in prewar Germany, for example, are frequently damned for not using their influence to stop the trend toward gas chambers. Physics is already deeply involved in the lives of nations, and its discoveries have broad technological and social implications in both peace and war. . . .

That much was a far stronger comment than any I had made; but then he went on:

> But contrary arguments also exist. One is the risk that meetings and publications now accomplishing their purposes fairly well may be badly diluted or disrupted by injection of issues not now on the agenda. . . . Another is the danger of ineptitude and arrogance. . . . They might offer a lot of bad advice. Public assertion that physicists have special competence might be an arrogance that would bring discredit to a community in place of the respect it now enjoys. . . .

Now a letter (*Physics Today*, Jan. 1968, p. 17) by Frederick Seitz, a famous physicist, president of the National Academy of Sciences, and a man who has served at top levels on many professional and governmental science boards.

> I am interested that a vote or poll is in the process of being taken to determine whether some of the AIP journals, most particularly *Physics Today*, should be opened up to debate on issues such as Vietnam and the like. It seems to me that it would be a great mistake for the American Institute of Physics, or the member societies, to be involved in such controversial matters unless they are tied very immediately to the profession of physics itself. To use our journals for very general discussion and debate means that they will lose their essentially professional character. Still further, the journals will fall into the hands of politically or socially oriented editors who will inevitably use them to support their own special viewpoints on matters far outside the field of physics. . . .

And here I quote from a letter by Edward Teller (*ibid.*):

> One may justify the discussion of public policy in *Physics Today* on two grounds. One is that physicists as a corporate unit are entitled to a medium which expresses their opinion. The other is a more ambitious claim that there are issues on which physicists have special competence and on which therefore their voice must be heard.
> As to the first point, I do not favor it because it is a

step toward a corporate state. The pressure groups which exist in our country have not been, in my opinion, a beneficial addition to our democratic institutions. To the extent that I do not agree with existent pressure groups, I would rather strengthen the basic democratic function and criticize the pressure groups which do exist. I would refrain from any step that tends to create an additional group. . . .

That may be a little hard to understand, but the British journal *Nature* commented on this statement as follows (February 10, 1968, p. 494):

> It is, of course, delightfully disingenuous that Dr. Edward Teller, who has been a one-man pressure group on defence policy for several years, should now maintain that pressure groups are a nuisance.

Teller's second point is that many physicists think they have the best advice on all issues, a matter already mentioned in the editorial quoted above.

It should not be hard to see what is bothering these men, such as Seitz, Teller, and many others at the top of the physics establishment. They have been working hard for many years to provide the government with the sort of advice from "science" that they think the government ought to have. Now we come along and threaten to open up this whole business out of the closed circuits that they have controlled, and make it an open game. This is an implied insult to their competence and an open threat to their power. Here is a letter from Herbert L. Fox (*Physics Today*, March 1968, p. 13):

> Physicists have vested interests in national policy. Physicists are solicited to advise and consent to policies of the government. Physicists' support is sought by opponents of the government. The "production" of physicists, the orientation of the physicists produced, the geographical concentration of physicists, and the wages of physicists are strongly [I say overwhelmingly] influenced by government policy. If there ever was an academic isolation of physicists, it is not so now. To take position on public issues is not a matter of choice, it is essential to our being physicists.

He is awake to some realities. Others (like Lewis Branscomb, in *Physics Today*, February 1968, p. 13) are clearly awake to other realities:

> The raising of nonscientific issues . . . could have a deeply divisive effect on the society at a time when we need unity in the face of serious declines in relative numbers of students choosing physics for study, and declining sources of support for basic research in physics. . . .

He is talking about the pocketbook, a most sensitive subject now that after a decade of unbridled expansion the physics research institutions have felt the first bruises of federal funding cutbacks. He also cites the recent phenomenon that the number of students going into physics, relative to all students entering the sciences, is declining. Two explanations are commonly given for this embarrassing phenomenon. One is that physics is relatively dead and that the real frontier of science now lies in biology. The other is that students these days think a great deal about the whole world and about humanistic problems and values; and the physicists are noted as the men who build bombs.

The letter by Branscomb, cited above, presents a number of other arguments against the amendment and then closes with this curious paragraph:

> I have circulated this letter to my colleagues in the Joint Institute for Laboratory Astrophysics and the Department of Physics and Astrophysics. Ten of them agree wholeheartedly and none of them has expressed disagreement with the views of this letter.

Clearly this man, who was director of this laboratory and has had considerable experience as a government science advisor, carries a lot of authority; for it is very rare that any physicist can claim that none of his colleagues disagrees with his views. (Branscomb has recently been appointed as the new director of the National Bureau of Standards.)

A few writers threatened to resign from the society if the

amendment should pass. Here is an interesting letter (Eugene Saletan, *ibid.*):

> To establish my credentials, I am an adamant "extremist" on the war in Vietnam. I have demonstrated against the administration's policy, have spoken at public meetings against it, have signed resist petitions, am faculty advisor to SDS, etc., etc. Nevertheless, I believe that APS should remain pure. There should be an organization of physicists whose purpose involves only physics. We have many opportunities to make public statements as physicists, and we can organize groups for such purposes. I would strongly favor such an organization. But as physicists we also need a purely professional society, one to which politics and questions of power are irrelevant. Let us join together, those of us who want to put an end to madness, but let us not do this within APS.

This is a very important attitude for us to understand. Not only the very dovish Mr. Saletan, but also some hawkish friends of mine who often travel to Washington to advise the Department of Defense and others on their science programs, have expressed this desire to maintain "physics" as a precious sanctuary where they can forget the woes of the world. This represents the thinking—or rather the emotional feeling—of a great many very good people. They insist on drawing a line, a protective barrier, around their professional society; and they emphasize that there are other ways for scientists to participate in politics—even some groups specifically for scientists as political beings. (I will talk about these other groups later on.) They defend the idea of "purity" for their professional society, and insist on a clear separation of interests and allowed activities for different institutions in the broader society.

I think we can understand the need of every man, and the greater need of the most "involved" man, to find and keep some private refuge wherein to rest and nourish his spirit, free from other distractions. However, in order to decide whether some given organization is in fact free, pure, and disconnected from the troubles of the world, is a matter for objective evaluation, not wish fulfillment; and this condition of purity may change in time. Consider, as an example, the story of clubs—bridge clubs, private clubs, country clubs. Let's say four of us get together to play bridge. We are friends and we choose at our own will whom we invite to join us. This habit is extended to larger private clubs having restrictive rules about who may join and who may not. However, when we come into the age of recognizing the problem of black and white skins in America—the present era of civil rights—then some of these habits must change. The country club is no longer viewed as the private institution it once was; it now has a larger public role to play in that the barrier of racial discrimination must be removed.

The APS was founded in 1914 to "promote the advancement and diffusion of the knowledge of physics." For three decades physics was the rather private occupation of a few men, seemingly abstract from the major concerns of the body politic; and the APS constituted a refuge where those who enjoyed physics could gather for mutual exchanges of ideas and data without other problems interfering with their "pure pursuits." But by now the role of physics in the national scene has grown into something enormously large and important. The whole rationale for physics as an isolated subject must be looked at in the context of the real world today; and I just do not see how the old myth of purity can stand any longer.

Finally, the amendment I had proposed for the APS constitution was put to a vote of the members and was defeated by almost 3-to-1. This was a great victory for the establishment. The result is now used as proof that the society is free of politics and wants to stay that way. Thus, at the 1969 annual meeting, when there was a debate on whether we should hold our next year's annual meeting in Chicago, the official line was that we were originally scheduled to meet in Chicago, and that to change that now could only be interpreted as a political response to Mayor Daley's police force—and we have already settled the question of political involvement. This matter was also finally forced to a mail ballot. Again the establishment prevailed, though only by a 4-to-3 margin.

In spite of this voting (or rather because of it), political discussion and action have become an inescapable part of recent physics meetings. At the APS annual meeting in New York in February, 1969, where leaflets, buttons, and petitions were circulated, caucuses and news conferences were held both by *ad hoc* groups and by new organizations which just happened to draw for their members upon a number of interested physicists. The APS was not officially involved in most of this, but it could hardly avoid being associated with the issues.

One petition, containing over 500 signatures, called for the creation of a new division of the Society in which questions of social implications of scientific work would be discussed. Some objected that this was just a device to circumvent the amendment that had been defeated, but proponents said they were only going to discuss problems, not take public positions. However, in spite of the strong interest expressed in this new division, the Council in charge of the APS merely referred the matter to a committee for further study.

Another proposal, more specific and well planned, had better success. The ABM question was just coming into prominence, and one man suggested setting up a big formal discussion of it at the next APS meeting, scheduled for Washington at the end of April. Lining up some well-known people, he approached the Council with a proposal for a session on "technical aspects of the ABM." Emphasizing the word "technical," he succeeded in getting their approval. Physicists are certainly competent to discuss technical features of missiles, bombs, radar, and computers; by stressing the word "technical" it was clear that we weren't bringing in politics. But of course everyone knew that ABM was primarily a political issue. Someone said, "Now let's be sure it is set up fair. You have someone very strong on your side of the debate; now make sure you get someone who is more than a hack from Johnny Foster's back room to represent the government's side of the case." (Dr. John Foster is Director of Research and Engineering for the Defense Department.)

When this debate took place in Washington, a few thousand people showed up to hear Hans Bethe and Eugene Wigner —two Nobel Prize-winning theorists—talk on opposite sides of the issue along with a pair of nuclear strategy experts, George

Rathjens and Donald Brennan. It was not a very scientific debate; each one cited his own references and gave his own interpretation of the data. They never really came to grips in their disagreements; and all too often one could see the personal political biases of the speakers dominating the technical façade. As far as the APS was concerned it was all legal and benign, although some members may have been embarrassed by it all. As far as the political activists were concerned it was almost a stacked deck, and dull at that; but at least people were there who were clearly interested in more than their own ivory towers.

What a group of us did on that occasion was to take a poll of the physicists in the audience. We passed out papers asking these obviously interested and informed scientists their opinions on the ABM. Should Safeguard be deployed or not? Would Safeguard lead to an increase or a decrease in the arms race? We counted the returns and announced to the press next day that, of over 2,000 physicists responding to our poll, 76 percent were opposed to the deployment of Safeguard ABM. Taking that poll was a very obvious and deliberate political act. I think that it was also a very proper public service for a group of scientists to find out what a large body of their fellows thought about this issue and to inform the citizenry accordingly.

So now you can see some ways in which the professional society can be led, shamed, or even dragged into the real world. All you have to do is pick up on some issue you really believe in and start talking about it. Don't think that just because you are right people will immediately give way before you; sometimes you will have to be very stubborn. The trick is to place questions so that they cannot be ignored. It is not realistic to suppose that the young and the radical can take over the professions and turn them from the selfish protective associations they are now, into the public-service organs they should be; but in this area we are so far back in the dark ages that every little bit of illumination is important.

I particularly want to encourage future members of professional scientific societies to think very carefully about their relationship to their profession when membership is granted. (Student memberships are often available.) It is very easy to put yourself in the position of the apprentice: Keep your mouth shut, keep your eyes and ears open; find out how the older boys behave, and follow suit. This is the proven way to "success." What we have learned from this new college generation is that the old formula is no longer acceptable; ills must be acknowledged and changes must be wrought. The business of "radicalizing the professions" is so new that I cannot give any formulas for success—just the suggestion that the two greatest qualities a conscientious scientist can have are honesty, and a willingness to work.

Now I will turn away from the dominant professional societies and talk about some small groups of scientists primarily concerned with the political and social aspects of scientific progress. The Federation of Atomic Scientists (FAS) was born at the end of World War II. It is dominated by physicists who were involved in the building of the atomic bomb and have felt the need to carry into the public arena their understandings and their feelings about the fullest implications of nuclear weapons. They have fought for civilian control of atomic energy and, through their journal, *Bulletin of the Atomic Scientists,* and through other educational lobbying approaches, they have worked toward world-wide arms control. Their style is polite and scholarly. In my opinion, they have lately become quiescent to the point of extinction. Most of the members can be described as older liberals who are well-off and "have a few connections up there." So when an issue comes up they are satisfied with writing a letter to their Congressman; grass-roots politics is not their bag.

The Scientists' Institute for Public Information (SIPI) follows the creed that a well-informed public is the best safety against scientific abuses by government. When they do campaign on issues they insist on speaking as scientists only about the scientific facts, and on not getting involved in the political aspects. This is a nice trick if you can do it, and they have had some success—the test-ban treaty.

The Society for Social Responsibility in Science (SSRS) is not really political at all. Its aim is to educate scientists about their social responsibilities (that is, we should not work on war research); but aside from gathering together those of a like sentiment it seems to have no vigorous program. One of its objectives is to help find new jobs for technical people who want to get out of the defense industries (a very important undertaking difficult to carry out on any meaningful scale).

The more exciting developments surround several new groups that have sprung up recently. The March 4, 1969 research strike started at MIT—an idea dreamed up by two graduate physics students who were groaning over the unhappy state of the world and the role of science—became a major event. They decided that all scientific researchers should take a day off from pursuing their immediate projects and look at the large scene of where scientific "progress" is leading us all. A large group of faculty at MIT, including almost the entire theoretical-physics group, responded enthusiastically to the project and helped to organize the teach-in of March 4. An interesting development was the split that occurred between the students and the faculty over the questions of tactics and public relations. The students were rather boisterous in their approach to press releases and the like; the faculty, more reserved, felt uncomfortable even about the title "research strike," and had it changed to "research stoppage." (At Berkeley the parallel program was billed, even more cautiously, as "A Symposium on the Use and Misuse of Science and Technology.")

As it worked out, the MIT people formed two separate but cooperating groups: The Union of Concerned Scientists (UCS), mostly faculty, and the Science Action Coordinating Committee (SACC), mostly students. As a result, March 4 programs were reproduced at about 30 research centers around the country; and a number of UCS and SACC chapters were formed. Since that March 4, the UCS people have initiated some scholarly studies in areas where science and public issues overlap, and they have produced two very good booklets on the ABM and on MIRV weapons systems. The SACC group at MIT has become even more radical with time: They have conducted demonstrations at MIT against classified weapons research on that campus, and were instrumental in bringing about some changes in the Institute's relations to this war work.

Independent of this MIT creation, but starting up at just about the same time, was a group conceived of as a "radical caucus" within the scientific profession. Scientists and Engineers for Social and Political Action (SESPA) was invented by Martin Perl of Stanford, and myself. We talked with interested friends, sent out a few hundred letters, and called for a convening session at the New York meeting of the APS in February, 1969. With 30 eager physicists packed into a hotel room one night to thrash out philosophy and plan an agenda, and with 300 attending our inaugural meeting, SESPA was launched on the platform of opposing militarism and providing young scientists with a vehicle for promoting their views on science and politics.

Since none of the several groups I have described has any real power, there is no difficulty in their working together easily on issues of common interest. The ABM controversy had been a primary focus, and during the APS meeting in Washington at the end of April, 1969 there was plenty of political activity. Leaflets and buttons were distributed on the ABM issue. A large number of physicists were organized, and briefed on how to visit individual Congressmen and talk to them about ABM. (This is called lobbying. It is a wonderful thing to try, especially if you have never done it before, but it is awfully hard to guess how effective you are.) More than 50 Senators, or their legislative assistants, were visited by physicists that week. In addition to personal opinions, there were also delivered many petitions from members of physics departments across the country expressing opposition to ABM.

In an unprecedented action, over 200 physicists were mobilized in a direct public display against the ABM: a walk to the White House, and a picketing there. A delegation from this group went in to see Dr. Lee DuBridge, President Nixon's science advisor, and delivered to him the following petition signed by 1,100 scientists:

Mr. President:

We as scientists and citizens urgently seek the withdrawal of plans to build and deploy the Safeguard ABM system.

Our concern springs from two basic sources:

1. As scientists, we are wholly unconvinced that any presently proposed ABM system can defend against a determined missile attack.
2. As citizens, we deplore the beginning of a particularly dangerous, yet ultimately futile round of nuclear arms escalation when our expanding domestic crisis demands a reallocation of the national resources.

Concurrently, another delegation presented to a group of eight members of the House of Representatives a SESPA-sponsored petition calling for open Congressional hearings on the entire military research and development program. Probably the most important single act was the taking of the poll on ABM, which I mentioned earlier. Up until this time the general appearance was that scientists were split 50-50 on the issue. This was because at every committee hearing there would be a balanced presentation—two experts for and two experts against Safeguard. Thus our announcement that the poll showed 76 percent opposed was a new and concrete piece of information.

All these activities in Washington received good news coverage and served, I think, not only to voice scientists' technical opinions about Safeguard, but also to demonstrate the deep concern many scientists have about broad public affairs.

The ABM is, however, only a rather small issue in itself; its significance on the political scene is that there has been a breakthrough in the manner in which the Pentagon does business with the Congress; and since so much is involved with fancy weapons technology, the scientists have a very key role to play. In the past, all the technical advisors have been exclusively in the employ of the Defense Department or the executive branch generally. If some scientific advisory group makes a recommendation on some weapons proposal (as has been the case with the negative opinion on ABM for many years past) this is only advisory, and it is strictly confidential. Thus, when countervailing forces (military, industrial, political interests) win out, what comes to the Congress for approval is a single package. It is then very difficult for even the most critical Congressman to have the technical resources to question the proposal of the Pentagon experts.

Actually, we (SESPA) sent each Congressman a brief discussion of this problem, along with the offer that we would try to provide him with a personal scientific advisor so that he can keep up with many new problems in technology which he will have to decide upon. I don't think we were taken very seriously, and I am sure that a few of us cannot answer all questions, but it is a beginning in the direction of opening up for broader public study many of these important questions which too easily become the private dominion of a few experts who are often deeply entangled in politics of their own.

In acting as a scientific advisor, spokesman, reformer, agitator, or whatever, there is always this crucial decision of how to distinguish between purely scientific judgments and those which involve some amount of personal and political beliefs. Most traditionalists insist on not only a clear separation but a complete negation of the political side. They argue that your politics are no better than anyone else's (which is true), and that by mixing the two you will dilute your effectiveness as an objective scientific observer. It is also claimed that this mixing-in of politics will dilute or destroy the "holiness" of science.

I think it is easy for any honest scientist to present his views in a way which clearly labels those things which are objective scientific facts and those which involve judgments of a personal or political nature. (It is also important to note that often this is not done, and quite deliberately.) In explaining a complex matter to a scientifically naive audience one must not only state the facts but also interpret them. In this process of interpretation many nontechnical aspects will be involved, and the honest man can point out his own biases. Of course, the greatest safety lies in an open process of discussion, review, and debate, wherein all the technical and nontechnical aspects are made clear in the blending.

As far as preserving the "holiness" of science, what does

this really mean? I think this is part of the myth that "science" is something above and beyond ordinary human affairs. This myth, promulgated by the successful gadgeteers and empire builders who have so nicely ridden with the explosion of money and power in the science establishment since the last war, needs to be destroyed. It is the essence of the responsibility of the scientist that he is dedicated to science as the servant of humanity, not as its master. Thus the latest slogan among young scientists is: "Science for the People."

Owen Chamberlain

is Professor of Physics at the University of California, Berkeley. The recipient of a B.A. from Dartmouth in 1941 and a Ph.D. in physics from the University of Chicago in 1949, he has been a staff member at Berkeley since 1948. He received a Guggenheim Fellowship in 1957. In 1959, he shared the Nobel Prize in physics with Emilio Segrè for the discovery of the antiproton, the oppositely charged counterpart of the proton. Since that discovery it has been generally accepted as fact that for every electrically charged particle, such as the proton, there can exist an oppositely charged particle, its antiparticle, the antiproton. Professor Chamberlain, making use of polarized proton scattering targets, has been studying the scattering processes of such particles.

In this essay, Professor Chamberlain tells of his involvement in the Manhattan Project during World War II and reveals how the events of that period shaped the methods of governmental science funding. He also discusses current government funding practices, especially on the university level, and the difficulties that sometimes result from such practices.

Government Funding

I am writing about this topic in large part because in 1967 I got involved, almost accidentally, with a subcommittee of the Academic Senate Policy Committee (Berkeley Division, Academic Senate). This subcommittee was assigned the task of looking into the nature of government support of research—into the questions of whether there were classified contracts involved in the government support of research on the UC Berkeley campus and whether there was research in military weapons areas and perhaps in a number of areas that the faculty might find morally objectionable. I shall cover mainly two brief periods of time: the period of my involvement with the development of the atomic bomb, and the past few years of government involvement in research.

In the summer of 1941 I entered UC Berkeley as a beginning graduate student in physics. The war was very much in the air. I had no indication whatever during the first semester that there were any secret research projects on the campus. In December of 1941 there was Pearl Harbor, and by New Year's day of 1942 I had gone to Professor Lawrence—who, I had heard, was looking for young physicists to help in some defense project—and volunteered my services, not actually knowing at that time what this project was all about. I was fortunately assigned by Lawrence to act as a helper to Professor Segrè. It turned out to be more of a learning process than many of the assignments that my fellow graduate students were given, some of whom got much more into the area of very technical things that you could call plumbing; and I would say the particular project that

Professor Segrè was working on was closer to a physics study. For an account of this period you might refer to the Smythe Report, entitled "Atomic Energy for Military Purposes," a non-secret version of many of the things that went on in the Manhattan Project. It was published in 1945, shortly after the use of the first nuclear weapons. [See bibliography.] Here I will give you only a brief résumé of it.

Atomic fission had been produced by Segrè and Enrico Fermi in 1934, but it was not until 1939 that it was identified as such, and its significance recognized, by Otto Hahn and Lise Meitner. She recognized that the uranium atom, when struck by a neutron, splits into lighter "daughter" atoms with a loss in mass and a consequential enormous release in energy—about 200,-000,000 electron volts per atom. Additional neutrons are also released which may go on to collide with new uranium atoms and cause a "chain reaction." It was immediately recognized by several physicists that a process which enabled such a swift and violent release of energy had great potential military significance.

In the course of this period there was extremely little government support of basic research. According to the Smythe Report, in February of 1940 the Army put $6,000 into material for this research. I believe that was the first military involvement in this project. In the course of the year 1940 something like $100,000 had been estimated as the cost of finding out whether a controlled chain reaction could be made in a nuclear reactor. By the end of 1941 some $300,000 worth of projects had been approved, but the amount actually spent was much less than that. Through June of 1942 the reactor project had used only about $40,000 of government money.

Most of the early work was done by individual scientists who were supported by their university salary with some help from graduate students but not very much help from hired technicians. The early work, the work that really started in this country sometime in the middle of 1939, was kept secret by a completely voluntary process. There was no government regulation of it. It was kept secret by a decision among scientists to have a committee of scientists who would act as secondary referees on papers that were to be published. Thus any articles that the editors of the physics journals thought should not be published, for reasons of secrecy, were sent to this committee, members of which would consult with the author. As far as I know, in every case they obtained the author's cooperation in simply not publishing material that might have a direct bearing on the possible military application. This voluntary secrecy was in effect before there was any sizable government commitment to support the project.

The situation at that time was that Nazi Germany had made its character clear, by its march across Europe and in particular through its invasion of Poland. Under these circumstances, and because there was a potential military use of fission, there was a general feeling that it was to everybody's interest in this country to see that any military project in Germany did not accidentally get help from people here. There also was a feeling at that time that U.S. involvement in the war was imminent. But it was a war approved of by me, by my friends, and, by and large, by the citizens of the United States. There was at that time not at all the same feeling that we tend to have about the Vietnam war at the present time—a thing on which we, as individuals, are, to say the least, very much split. The situation then was very different. There was virtually unanimous support for the British–French side of this conflict.

The work on the so-called "Uranium Project" proceeded with gradually increasing government involvement. By January of 1942, as I have mentioned, I had already started work on that project. I acted mainly as a technician. I think I had worked on the project some nine months before I understood what the purpose of the project was. In July, 1943, when I'd been involved in the project about a year and a half, our whole group moved from Berkeley to the new location at Los Alamos. The Los Alamos Project was intended, in essence, to design the atomic bomb. The materials were being produced elsewhere. The idea was that at Los Alamos we should figure out how to put an atomic bomb together.

Word that the chain reaction in a reactor made with uranium and graphite had been successfully operated in December,

1942, spread like wildfire though the project. Although the secrecy was remarkably well maintained on a voluntary basis, as time went on and the project moved to Los Alamos we began to encounter stricter government regulations. We were then called the Manhattan Project, and our director was Dr. Robert Oppenheimer—who did a very, very good job.

In the course of the next couple of years the materials were gradually assembled—some by the enrichment of uranium isotopes, some by the production of plutonium from a nuclear reactor. In July of 1945 there was the first test of a nuclear explosion in Alamogordo, New Mexico, and in August the use of the two nuclear weapons over Japan, at Hiroshima and Nagasaki. And I might say, in case some of you might have doubts, that it was perfectly clear to us at Los Alamos that this weapon would be used against Germany if it were ready in time. It was not ready in time to be used against Germany—V–E Day had already occurred by the time the atomic bomb was tested—but it was ready in time to become rather instrumental in halting the war with Japan.

We at Los Alamos had no idea how great would be the effectiveness of the atomic bomb. We knew that with 20,000 tons of TNT you could do, on paper, a little bit less than you could with 20,000 tons of TNT distributed more advantageously over a region. That is, the concentrated explosion of a nuclear weapon shouldn't do as much physical damage as would an equal amount of TNT, because its effectiveness is somewhat diminished by being very concentrated. Before the bombs were dropped we had little idea of the effect they would have on Japanese morale. We were actually very much surprised that the atomic bombs were so effective in precipitating the Japanese surrender.

At the beginning of the early wartime period, whereas there was some federal support in agriculture and there was some federal support in the biological sciences, federal support of scientific research in the area of the physical sciences was next to nothing. For instance, construction work on the 184-inch cyclotron at the Lawrence Radiation Laboratory in Berkeley was at first supported mainly with funds from the Rockefeller Foundation. There were some other sources, such as the Research Corporation, but there were no federal funds invested in the 184-inch cyclotron before the war. During the war period, federal support of this military application—the making of the atomic bomb—became quite sizable: President Truman stated that it was a two-billion-dollar project before it was through. I take it that the rate of spending must have been around one billion dollars per year near the end of World War II. But federal support of basic science—at least of the physical sciences—came only as an aftermath of a situation in which an atomic bomb emerged from nuclear-physics research.

Early nuclear-physics research was conducted almost exclusively in universities—in universities throughout the world. Remember that fission was discovered in Germany by Otto Hahn. Word of it came by way of Denmark through Lise Meitner and through physicists traveling and writing letters to each other. Curiously, the impetus for the United States to get involved was almost exclusively the result of the presence of foreign scientists in the United States, mainly scientists who had fled from the situation in Europe and from Nazi Germany. Einstein was very important in bringing to the attention of President Roosevelt the possibility of the military use of atomic energy—the atomic bomb. (The famous "Einstein Letter," however, was actually written by Leo Szilard.) It is doubtful whether U.S. scientists acting alone—without the participation of European scientists–could have acted so quickly or so persuasively to obtain direct government involvement in the making of an atomic bomb.

Following World War II there was a recognition that the government, and in particular the Department of Defense, had an interest in maintaining some liaison with the physical sciences. The idea was that a new development similar to the atomic bomb might soon crop up again. Actually, there have been, for the military, a fair number of benefits from contact with research physicists, chemists, and practitioners of many of the other sciences and mathematics. But most of these benefits have been indirect. Some have come through summer studies by professors who have looked into military problems from a scientist's point of view. For instance, a group of physicists could be asked what the ways are in which one submarine might track another submarine. You might find them coming up with some methods not already being exploited by the military.

You also find cases where it's just advantageous to have somebody who comes from the outside as a consultant take a new view of things. Very often the academic types who do consulting jobs for the military simply act to give a fresh look at the situation. There have been, I think, numerous cases where there were blind spots that academic types recognized and cautioned about.

By and large, the contact of the military and the government with the academic researchers is a fairly general one in which the government hopes to learn things from academicians. The academic types, I think, sometimes welcome the idea of a little travel or some financial support in the summertime. Also, many scientists simply welcome the opportunity to pay attention to the question of the military preparedness of the United States which they, for the most part, generally approved.

This situation has grown gradually without undergoing frequent review. The field that I work in at the Lawrence Radiation Laboratory, and have kept pretty close to (to the exclusion of almost everything else) since the early 1950's, is particle physics. Particle physics is very expensive because it involves the use of expensive accelerators. It is supported almost wholly by the federal government, primarily by the Atomic Energy Commission. One wonders, of course, to what extent the support of this field, basic research in particle physics, was derived from the fact that it was part of the Atomic Energy Commission's program. It could have been assumed by congressmen to have potential applications in parallel with some of the other interests of the Atomic Energy Commission, which included the making of nuclear weapons. After all, the Atomic Energy Commission is in charge of making nuclear weapons for the military. I am sure there was a period in which congressmen asked physicists about the potential applications of fields such as particle physics, and were assured that, indeed, there were no applications immediately obvious. There were no real hints of applications soon to come from particle physics research other than those that had already been recognized from an earlier period. These were the nuclear reactor and another very important derivative, the artificial radioactivity of all the elements in the Periodic Table (which has led to great diagnostic tools in chemistry and in biology).

These applications were known long ago. The question in more recent years has been: What were the expected applications of particle physics? The answer is pretty much: None, with the possible exception of some secondary things in which particle physics might have helped somewhat, such as the development of digital computers.

There was a period when congressmen tended to say: Well, the professor is very humble and doesn't want to claim that he has an application up his sleeve, but we know that there are military applications not too far off; otherwise the Atomic Energy Commission wouldn't be supporting the work. I think that period has pretty well passed now, and Congress recognizes particle physics as basic physics research, which does not mean that there is any particular application. It's aimed, rather, at finding out what the basic rules are that govern matter. There isn't at present any hint of an application of much practical consequence for military or any other purpose in particle physics. It's a matter of following one's curiosity. Perhaps the only excuse I know for putting as much expenditure into particle physics as we do is that no one knows how to make those investigations for any less money and effort than they are now costing. It seems like a very natural human endeavor to try to discover the basic rules that govern the matter that all of us are made of.

The situation now, I think, is that congressmen view basic research much more realistically. Of course they support it, first and foremost, on a prestige basis: They don't want the United States to fall behind other countries in any area of endeavor, and there's something to be respected in a good, strong, basic-research establishment which produces prestigious scientific discoveries.

Now, let us take UC Berkeley as an example of government funding of research. According to the June 5, 1967 report of the Berkeley Academic Senate on University Research Policy, the Radiation Laboratory in Berkeley showed a budget of $40,000,000 per year, with $21,000,000 of it assigned to particle physics. The other areas were biology and medicine, chemistry and chemical engineering, and engineering. The situation at the Radiation Laboratory is rather anomalous because at least the particle-physics part is one of the most expensive research areas. It's not quite as expensive as the space effort, but other than that I would say that it's the most expensive research area that I'm aware of. The cost for each physicist involved is unusually high for research fields.

In the College of Letters and Science, research (mainly in the physical and biological sciences) is 74 percent federally funded. The importance of the dependence on federal funds was dramatically demonstrated by the stir generated when the National Science Foundation abruptly announced in the middle of the 1968–69 academic year that there was going to be a sudden and unexpected 20 percent decrease in National Science Foundation funds. This put the campus in quite an uproar and placed many of the research projects involved at a very great disadvantage because they had already gone though most of the school year. They had already lost the flexibility which they would have had at the beginning of the year to allocate their funds. Funds had been committed to people for salaries. A sudden decrease meant either breaking these commitments or completely stopping the purchase of any equipment. It was very disruptive to many research projects.

It is most important that we realize that we are so dependent on federal funds that even a small decrease in them raises havoc among the research projects. In the physical and biological sciences, the support is 90 percent federal. This added up to something like $14,000,000 per year in the period 1965–66. If we look at the social sciences, we find that the support is

31 percent federal, this representing $1,600,000. Notice that this is only about one-tenth as much as the figure for the physical and biological sciences. Looking at the humanities, we find that the support is 40 percent federal, but that this is only $80,000—or about one-half of 1 percent of that allocated to the physical and biological sciences. This shows one of the obvious effects that federal support of research is having on the university: The physical and biological sciences are being overemphasized.

Of the total federal support of $31,000,000 for the Berkeley campus, only 15 percent comes from the Department of Defense —that is, from the Army, Navy, and Air Force. Another 15 percent comes from the AEC and NASA. The remaining 70 percent comes from other sources, such as the Department of Agriculture, the National Science Foundation, the Public Health Service, and the Department of Health, Education, and Welfare. So, looked at in these terms, it doesn't appear that the military has too great a total input. Of course, military spending will be concentrated in certain areas, and in certain areas the military contracts will certainly represent much more than they seem to here. On the other hand, many of the military research contracts support basic research and are handled in a very satisfactory way from the scientist's point of view. Most of our cosmic-ray studies have been supported by the Navy for many years.

The situation at present doesn't seem to be, from my point of view, too unhealthy. Although there is a tremendous dependence on federal support, there are no classified projects on the Berkeley campus. (There are, however, some classified projects off campus that certain professors work on, especially during the summer. And of course some consulting activities involve classified work.) Once in a while at the Radiation Laboratory something temporarily requires a cloak of secrecy. It sometimes happens that a part of the chemistry building at the Radiation Laboratory becomes a classified area for a period of perhaps two weeks when some special material is being dealt with, such as the debris from a nuclear explosion. Such a sample would be treated as secret because knowledge of its detailed constitution might lead to knowledge about the construction of nuclear weapons. But the purposes of these research efforts are not classified. This security procedure is what we call "occasional reference to classified materials" or, for that matter, to classified data. True, there is a storage room at the Radiation Laboratory for secret documents, but on most days of the year that's the only room to which there isn't general access for anybody who has a good reason to go to the Laboratory.

Back to federal support: What are its consequences? In general, the availability of funds tends to influence the research projects undertaken. It's much more comfortable to undertake a program if there is money available to do it well, so that there's a tendency for the availability of support to steer things in certain directions; certainly to steer things in the direction of the physical and biological sciences as opposed to the social sciences or the humanities.

To what extent is there a tendency to have a kind of indirect political interference in people's lives through government support? I would analyze it this way: I don't think there's much of a problem on campus, though I must say that this sort of interference can be a very subtle thing. It may be that I have to look more into the question of how the younger professors feel on the campus—whether they are a bit inhibited in their public expressions on political matters because of their reliance on government support. I don't know how great this inhibition is, though I know that it can be there even when the dependent person is not fully aware of it. It can occur in indirect ways. For example, if I'm asking the chancellor's support for some pet project of mine—maybe it's the Special Opportunity Scholarship Program—it makes it harder for me to come out against some other project which the chancellor himself is supporting.

It is just part of human relationships that different subjects get mixed up with each other. The same thing can happen with government support, particularly if the people that you are going through for support are very sensitive. You may have friends in the AEC office in Washington who are going to the

Bureau of the Budget and asking for, say, some supplemental funds at midyear review for the Radiation Laboratory to carry on certain vital projects. These same people who have to go to the Bureau may be very upset if some of the Radiation Laboratory people out here are very strongly outspoken against some government policy, perhaps the ABM or the Vietnam war. There can be circumstances in which somebody makes a big splash in an anti-Vietnam-war way, and people start to inquire from Washington: "Does he work for the Radiation Lab?" or "What kind of people have we got out there?"

So there can be some pressures. I must say that I haven't felt very much pressure myself, but then, I've operated from a somewhat protected position in which I can get away with a few things. I don't think my expression of views on public issues was ever completely stifled, but I may have been a little hesitant to make my views completely open and public and to get the maximum publicity if I felt that it was going to hurt the Radiation Laboratory in its ability to keep its full government support. The point is, I would feel badly if I lessened the support for some of my fellow physicists. So, there's certainly a question about whether federal support doesn't to some extent stifle one's expression on public issues.

Frankly, I think a little stifling is almost inevitable—which brings me to the pressure from our California State Legislature. The Legislature has a lot to say about particular courses that we offer—for example, the course in which Eldridge Cleaver gave a majority of the lectures. How are we going to avoid this? If the university is going to have support through the state government or through the federal government, how are we going to avoid a certain degree of government pressure? Our communication with the government occurs through more than one channel—partly through the public press or public pronouncements, and partly through business channels—and the channels are going to get mixed up with each other as long as we depend on government funds. And we can't *do* without those government funds! About all we can hope to do, in my view, is to try to set up a somewhat more insulating arrangement between the federal structure and the university. They've attempted to do this in Great Britain, I think somewhat success-fully, by having funds to support research go through a national committee that dispenses funds to the various universities.

I believe that government interference in our affairs does exist, but that it is minimal. I don't know how we're ever going to avoid interference completely. It's simply very hard, if not impossible to achieve complete independence under the present system.

Serge
Lang

is Visiting Professor of Mathematics at Princeton University, on leave from Columbia University, which has been his home base since 1955. Professor Lang received his B.A. in Physics from the California Institute of Technology in 1946, at the age of 18. After serving in the Army in 1946–47 he became a graduate student in philosophy at Princeton University, but after one year switched to mathematics and received his Ph.D. in that subject in 1951. He then remained one year at Princeton University as an Instructor, and one year on fellowship at Princeton's Institute for Advanced Studies, before spending two years as an Instructor at the University of Chicago. From 1955 to 1970 he taught most of the time at Columbia University (he was Visiting Professor of Mathematics at the University of California, Berkeley, in 1968–69). In the Fall of 1970 he returned to Princeton on a one-year teaching assignment.

Professor Lang is the author of fifteen mathematics books, half of which are texts at the college or graduate levels and half of which are research monographs, covering a broad scope of mathematics. He is presently a member of the Council of the American Mathematical Society, and one of the representatives of the Society to the National Research Council.

In this essay Professor Lang discusses the cases of

several mathematicians, in the U.S. and U.S.S.R., who have encountered political intimidation, to varying degrees, after having publicly voiced political and moral positions at variance with official government policy. He also gives a general discussion of the effects of Department of Defense funding of academic research, and the granting of, or sometimes rescinding of, such funds, for political reasons. In the case of the United States, he shows, the controversies generally have centered around mathematicians' opposition to the war in Vietnam.

The
DOD,
Government,
and
Universities

My political activities began in 1965, when I got worried, to the point of being frightened, by the political and social developments in the United States and the world. The degeneration of certain aspects of our lives, trends within the universities, the encroachment of the Department of Defense (DOD) within the universities, the militarization of society, began to appear sufficiently serious to me that I thought I would try to understand better what was going on, and perhaps do something about it.

I have played two roles. One is informative. I have tried to make others politically and socially aware of these trends which frightened me. In the other role, I have taken an editorial position from time to time, and I think I can separate the two fairly well. I shall describe the mechanics of DOD support of universities, the way it happens, its political implications—not implications that I invent myself, but implications which have come out in concrete cases—and occasionally express my opinion concerning recent developments. In the last part, I shall deal with the academic and human problem which faces us all. The first part has been substantially rewritten from the original delivery of my talk, because the verbal style which I thought appropriate to the lecture is not appropriate for the permanent record. The last part, on the other hand, is taken from the tape of the lecture with essentially no change. I have expanded considerably the thoughts expressed in this last part, and the documentation which led to them, in a forthcoming book.

51

I also gave a prelude to the whole thing, which I have decided to keep here so that no misunderstandings can arise. I expect that there will be divergent views concerning the national interest, or different philosophies of life, cultural divergences between people. One of the basic sources of troubles in any society is the inability of a sociopolitical group to have proper sensitivity for the values and interests of others, and this is especially serious and dangerous when it is practiced by the people who run things, who have institutional power. This leads to political controversies, but I wish to emphasize that, at least as far as I am concerned, such controversies do not involve personal animosity. I wage my political battles on the basis of issues, not personalities.

* * *

Ever since I began giving lectures on topics other than mathematics, and have had to deal especially with university administrators, I have written down the following phrase on the blackboard:

ALL UNIVERSITY ADMINISTRATORS
ARE WELL MEANING AND DEVOTED

You can replace the name "university administrators" with the name of anyone else—in the government, outside the government, professors, students, anyone you wish. And you will have a true statement. I'm placing emphasis on that because never do I question the motivation of anyone. It is a waste of time. First because everyone is well motivated, and second because as you start arguing about motivation, you will be taking away from the substance of the issues, and you will *make yourself less effective*. I regard it as a political and human mistake to question motivations. Now, even though everyone is well-meaning and devoted, it doesn't prevent some from also being stupid or misinformed, and that, unfortunately, is very often the case. Besides, university administrators are caught between their strictly academic responsibilities, and pressures from above (trustees, the public, fund raising, etc.). On the whole, I have found them failing in their representation of university interests to the nonacademic constituencies. I once wrote a paper of 20 pages to document this assertion, and concluded that university administrators needed encouragement and support at the academic grass roots to strengthen their position in the face of pressures from above. Here is not the place to go into this particular problem any further, but since university administrators are occasionally mentioned in what follows, I felt that I should make some comments on them. Finally, I never apply a broad evaluation of a group to any single person with whom I happen to deal, and I always evaluate an individual on his own merits.

TERMINATION OF A DOD CONTRACT

During the past 16 years two well-known professors, L. LeCam and J. Neyman, of the Statistics Department at Berkeley, have had contracts with the Army and the Office of Naval Research (ONR), for the support of their unclassified research in statistics, which has been published in standard journals. In letters dated September 3 and September 10, 1968 they were notified by the Army and Navy that renewal of their contracts was being questioned or terminated, the reason given being that these professors had signed the following advertisement in the January and August, 1968 *Notices* of the American Mathematical Society:

> MATHEMATICIANS: Job opportunities in war work are announced in the *Notices* of the AMS, in the Employment Register, and elsewhere. We urge you to regard yourselves as responsible for the uses to which your talents are put. We believe this responsibility forbids putting mathematics in the service of this cruel war.

The Army letter stated:

> . . . the results of your efforts have been utilized by the Army in various activities related to the current conflict in Vietnam including your regression procedures as applied to ammunition and ballistics problems. . . . While you as individuals have every right to your own opinions and

convictions, your present position vis-à-vis that of the Department of Defense must place you in a most uncomfortable, and perhaps untenable, situation; continuance of this relationship could well serve as a source of embarrassment to you. In view of this unfortunate circumstance, a mutually acceptable decision to terminate our present association when your present support expires appears to be consistent with both of our positions. . . .

The ONR letter stated:

Before proceeding further with your recent renewal proposal entitled "Statistical Study of Problems of Weather Modification," we would appreciate an indication of your intent and desire with regard to continued support by this office.

Similar letters were sent to other mathematicians who signed the same ad. (Four others, it seems.) The case was reported in *Science*, 20 September 1968, and also in the *Washington Post*, same date.

When asked about the utilization of their research in the Vietnam war, Professors LeCam and Neyman answered respectively as follows: "I don't know what they are talking about"; and "I did war work during the Second World War. For 16 years, I have not done any war work. I prove theorems, they are published, and after that I don't know what happens to them." Professor Neyman also told me that he hoped the ad would appear again, and that he would sign it.

Depending on to whom one talks, one gets the reactions to the Army and ONR letters: "What did you expect?" or "This is a shock, and is totally unexpected." I have had both reactions from two top administrators at Columbia University. In fact, the Army and ONR letters come at the end of a period during which obnoxious trends and drifts developed at an alarmingly increasing rate. I shall summarize some relevant history in an appendix. In the present atmosphere, I believe one should not have been surprised at the Army–ONR letters, which however constitute the first clear and unambiguous instances of political review of contracts in the light of the political statements of the recipients.

After increasing publicity (e.g., in *Science* and the *Washington Post*), and a mounting number of phone calls from members of the scientific–academic community to Washington (DOD, NSF, Presidential science advisors, etc.), the case developed as follows. The Army telephoned that the letter of September 3 should be disregarded, and that if an application for renewal was sent it would almost certainly receive a favorable answer. Neyman telegraphed the ONR:

> Your sentiments are understandable. While announcement in AMS *Notices* reflects my feelings on the Vietnam war, my intentions are to proceed weather modification studies promising benefits for Nation and humanity and would welcome continuation of ONR support. . . .

The ONR answered:

> I am pleased to advise you that Office of Naval Research is proceeding with the necessary contract actions to extend your contract.

After several weeks of hesitation, LeCam decided to apply for renewed support and got it. The other four mathematicians in a similar position also confirmed their desire to continue with DOD support, and received it.

For the moment, the case is typical of the unstable equilibrium of forces between the scientific–academic community, and the DOD (subject to pressures from Congress or other public sources). It shows that the DOD does not want a confrontation with that community, and can back down in a specific case when the threat of a serious uproar makes itself felt, as was obviously happening after the letters of September 3 and September 10.

Nevertheless, the intimidating effect of the incident is not negligible. Two months after these cases were publicized in *Science* and other places, I was informed by a junior faculty member at one of the campuses of the University of California (not Berkeley) that a senior professor who holds an Air Force contract for the support of mathematics told the young man that he would put him on the contract, which would result in a summer stipend, providing that he promised not to sign any controversial political statements. The young man refused— good for him—but we have here a good example of the intimidation which results from the LeCam–Neyman case or similar ones (e.g., the Smale case, see below).

THE FOSTER MEMORANDUM

On the other hand, also in response to the threat of a public uproar, John S. Foster, Director of Defense Research and Engineering, issued a memorandum on 18 September, 1968 indicating policy to be followed in making grants to persons whose political opinions were causing concern to the Defense Department. The memorandum, reproduced below, is also indicative of the present balance of political forces. In particular, its first proviso, to "review . . . contracts for quality and productivity" in cases where "the situation is uncertain" (with respect to "nontechnical issues," a euphemism for political issues), confirms that political considerations are being taken into account under present policy. One can judge the deterioration of the situation by asking a simple question of those who now receive DOD contracts: Do you feel as free in expressing your political opinions and as comfortable about DOD support now as before the LeCam–Neyman case, and/or the Foster memorandum? The answer is obviously *no*. Specifically, the Foster memorandum strongly raises the possibility of rejection of contracts with quality considerations being taken as an excuse even when it is a political consideration which motivates the rejection. Furthermore, how is one to react to the requirement that principal researchers should "consult on appropriate DOD problems" to receive DOD support?

There is another point which should be emphasized about the Foster memorandum—namely, "when the situation is uncertain (meaning that politically controversial statements have been made by somebody with a DOD contract), review all such contracts for quality and productivity." This makes it quite clear that the guy who is not top rank is going to have to watch out

18 September 1968

MEMORANDUM FOR THE
Assistant Secretary of the Army (R&D)
Assistant Secretary of the Navy (R&D)
Assistant Secretary of the Air Force (R&D)
Director, Advanced Research Projects Agency
Director, Defense Atomic Support Agency

SUBJECT: Consideration of Non-Technical Issues in Research Contract Management

Recent concern regarding the views taken on nontechnical issues by the principal investigators under certain DOD contracts warrants our careful attention. In general, I believe we must be confident about the willingness of principal researchers to receive DOD support, consult on appropriate DOD problems, and bring to our attention any findings relevant to national security. Thus I ask you to take the following steps in instances where the situation is uncertain:

1. Review all such contracts for quality and productivity.
2. Do not emphasize non-technical issues in your evaluation of the desirability of terminating or renewing research contracts. These are subtle issues which require careful, consistent, and sensitive treatment. Clearly, some members of the R&D community have disagreed with governmental decisions while they contributed significantly to the country.
3. Request principal investigators to re-examine their intent and desire to receive continued DOD support. To ensure a consistent DOD-wide policy, please consult with the office of the Deputy Director (Research and Technology) in my office on any such written requests to your contractors.
4. Take all necessary actions to preserve our mutually beneficial relationships with the academic research community during this period when there are potentially divisive pressures.

—s/John S. Foster, Jr.

much more. On the basis of the experience I have had over the past several years, I really think that is the way things have operated. There is a difference between the absolutely top people in a scientific field, and those who are not quite that good. I believe that the intimidating effect is very much less on the very top men than it is on the others. That is one of the reasons why a lot (or even most) of the professors at universities like Berkeley or Columbia have not been aware (or have refused to become aware) of this type of political–economic blackmail. When they say that they don't know about it, I think that they are in good faith. That does not mean that they are not at fault in having closed their minds to a situation which should be obvious to them. Whenever anything happens to people like LeCam, Neyman, or Smale, we can always count on the mathematical community and on the scientific community to rise strongly in their defense, although one can also find some who say that they should shut up because they affect the amount of money we can get out of the government. Still, the natural reaction is to defend them, because they are famous enough and good enough. But those in lesser positions have no such chance. It is very difficult to rise in defense of a name which nobody has heard.

THE FULBRIGHT–RICKOVER VIEW

Many persons have warned for a long time that political pressures were associated with DOD contracts, albeit in a more subtle form, and had issued warnings against them. Student groups were by no means the only organizations or persons to have done so. Admiral Rickover himself, in testimony reported in *Science* (2 August 1968, testimony released on 19 July before the Senate Foreign Relations Committee), stated:

> President Eisenhower mentioned the industrial–military complex . . . I have mentioned the military–scientific complex. I think this is the really dangerous one. . . .It may be difficult to regain control of the DOD. Yet if its empire-building is not restrained, it may become the most powerful branch of the National Government. This surely was

not intended by the Founding Fathers; nor, I feel sure, is it the will of the American people. . . . I believe Department of Defense research sponsorship is partly responsible for the troubles on our campuses. . . .

Admiral Rickover also opposed the Themis Project (a DOD program to spread federal research dollars to relatively underdeveloped academic institutions; see "Appendix: A Brief History," below) for two reasons:

> . . . one, it gets the hand of the Department of Defense into our universities; and two, it draws the people who should be teaching away from their proper work.

And for those who think that opposition to the DOD's interference in the universities is somewhat subversive, or necessarily contrary to the opinions of our elected representatives, I add *Science's* report that: "The Senators seemed sympathetic to Rickover's opinions."

In fact, Senator Fulbright, in a speech to the Senate, 13 December 1967 (also in *Playboy*, July 1968), stated:

> The bonds between the Government and the universities are no more the result of a conspiracy than those between government and business. They are an arrangement of convenience, providing the government with politically usable knowledge and the universities with badly needed funds . . . a contribution, however, which is purchased at a high price. That price is the surrender of independence, the neglect of teaching, and the distortion of scholarship. . . . The corrupting process is a subtle one: no one needs to censor, threaten or give orders to contract scholars; without a word of warning or advice being uttered, it is simply understood that lucrative contracts are awarded not to those who question their government's policies, but to those who provide the government with the tools and techniques it desires. The effect . . . is to suggest the possibility . . . that academic honesty is no less marketable than a box of detergent on the grocery shelf. . . . When the university turns away from concerning itself with techniques rather than purposes, with expedients, rather than ideals, dispensing conventional orthodoxy rather than new ideas, it is not

only failing to meet its responsibilities to its students, it is betraying a public trust. . . . It seems likely that the basic cause of the great troubles in our universities is the students' discovery of corruption in the one place, besides the churches, which might have been supposed to be immune. . . .

Thus spoke Senator Fulbright.

PUBLIC SUPPORT OF UNIVERSITIES AND RESEARCH

Support of unclassified and "pure" research by the DOD dates back from the late forties when there were no operating agencies in our democratic institutions specifically intended for that purpose—the NSF was still in a foetal stage. However, continued support by the DOD is explainable in different terms, well put again by Admiral Rickover (hearings, Senate Foreign Relations Committee, 28 May 1968):

> I think the problem you have here is that the DOD is able to get large funds for doing basic research while this is not possible for other Government agencies. I once had a discussion with Secretary of Defense McElroy on that subject, and . . . he said it is important that basic research be done in the United States. As I remember his words he said it was not too important that the Defense Department do it, but that the work should be done, and since the Defense Department has the funds to pay for the work, it is therefore being done by them. . . . It gets the money because the word "defense" has in itself an element of urgency. Whatever is asked in its name somehow acquires the connotation of a life and death matter for the nation.

One can also go beyond Rickover: Caught in the habit of a rhetoric which deplores "socialism," the people who run things in this country are nevertheless very happy about DOD projects which supposedly prop up the local economy, while being justified by so-called patriotism. A Mendel Rivers gets reelected consistently because of his ability to bring in the military pork barrel, and becomes one of the most powerful men in the United

States government, through what is no doubt a natural political process, but is nonetheless extraordinarily dangerous for our democratic future.

At the same time, agencies like NSF are starved for funds. For instance, in 1965, of 16.1 billion dollars federal support for research and development, 7.3 billion came from the DOD, 5.3 billion from NASA, 1.5 billion from AEC, 2 billion from HEW, and the remainder from miscellaneous agencies. Figures are rounded off, and it is significant that the total support for NSF is so small as to be thrown into the miscellaneous, which can be counted in terms of millions, not billions! (Committee on Government Operations, House Report 1158, October 1965.)

Not only that, but Congress has often subjected the NSF to sudden, arbitrary, and retroactive limitations. Specific example: Professor LeCam pointed out that on July 3, 1968 a document from NSF authorizing $78,800 for his grant arrived in Berkeley. This authorization followed several months of discussion, and assurances that his grant would not be subject to further cuts. Commitments were then made, but on August 14, 1968 he and his colleagues were notified that they could not spend more than $33,000 for the year. This was less than what had already been spent. As LeCam wrote me:

> Since what happened in fact is a breach of contract on the part of the federal government, there is no recourse. . . . We have absolutely no complaint against NSF. . . . In view of this situation, we have decided to continue requesting support for basic research from other agencies, including the Army Research Office. We have been told that as far as this Office is concerned, the request will be granted. . . . The tax monies which come to us from the Federal Government either through the Army Research Office or through NSF are used essentially for the same purpose, which we hope is valuable, namely to help us and above all graduate students to advance basic knowledge in our field.

The situation is worse than ever, partly because of the Vietnam war, whose political and financial pressures have caused mammoth cuts in NSF budgets (by the Spring of 1969 the cut in that year's budget already had reached 20 percent), entailing a corresponding curtailment of activities in universities throughout the nation.

It is scandalous that projects which are recognized as useful for the nation and humanity can be properly supported in our society only under cover of the military. The ambiguity inherent in DOD contracts must be stopped, and I believe that universities should now refuse to administer DOD contracts. At the same time, it is urgent and essential that they should make strong representation to Congress and the body politic to provide them with adequate support from agencies like NSF, whose stated policy is that its grants are independent of the political opinions expressed by the recipients. The danger of a single agency in Washington administering this support is obvious, and therefore this support should be forthcoming under a system providing suitable competition, in accord with the basic philosophy of this democracy. This could be achieved by some decentralization at the state and regional level, by suitable federal tax rebates channeling tax money directly to education and research, by encouraging the private foundations to expand their support both of research and fellowships, to counteract federal abuses of power (now evident in the political constrictions imposed on scholarships, for instance).

FACING POLITICAL–ECONOMIC BLACKMAIL

It is a general problem for this society to decide whether to make the award of educational or research grants dependent on the political shutting up of the recipients. This is precisely the present state of affairs in the U.S.S.R., and I personally regard it as totally undesirable. In that country, the scientists are well paid and well housed, and have reasonably good working conditions (relative to the rest of the population) *at the cost* of keeping politically silent. (For a recent example, cf. the Volpin case, *Notices* AMS, June 1968.) They have moved into this position from that of Stalinism and Lysenkoism, and hence regard it as an improvement. I regard our moving into this position in the United States as a political catastrophe.

The general problem is not whether the universities should

accept dirty money or not. Major Barbara found out long before I did that all money is dirty. However, the situation concerning government grants has been deteriorating steadily and rapidly since the latter mid-sixties, sufficiently so that in 1967 I gave up my NSF grant to reinforce my position in speaking out against what I regarded as obnoxious trends (cf. my letters to the editors, *Science*, 17 February 1967, and *Notices* AMS, August 1968). This decision had both advantages and disadvantages (leaving out entirely the consideration of personal finances). On the one hand, it strengthened my political position somewhat, because it is unfortunately true (although it should not be so) that some people would listen more carefully to what I had to say if I took this action. On the other hand, it could weaken my position, since some people could infer that to speak out, one should give up one's grant, an implication which I reject completely. After consulting with friends on this question, to clarify the implications of my action, I decided to give up my grant on an *ad hoc* basis, thinking that the advantages outweighed the disadvantages in my personal case. Because of block support, students and colleagues who were associated with me on the grant still kept the grant, and I did not see any reason why they should give up what I regarded as legitimate support for worthy educational and research purposes. However, I reaffirm the principle that having kept this grant, they have exactly the same right as I do to protest obnoxious practices or trends when they deem it appropriate to do so. This affirmation is definitely necessary at present: In 1966, at Berkeley, subsequent to my having signed some protest document pertaining to the military involvements of the university, no less than the executive Vice Chancellor told me: "We had a good laugh here in the office when we saw that you and some of your friends signed this document. We looked you all up and saw that you were all on government contracts." I regard this expressed point of view as a grave failure in administrative responsibility, but experience shows that important persons in university administrations and in the government subscribe to it.

In determining priorities, when faced with a choice between scientific achievement and intellectual–political freedom,

I believe that we should choose the freedom. I believe that the universities are due for a period of retrenchment, during which they will have to give renewed priority to their educational functions, and their functions as centers of free thought. It would be a human abomination to be so cynical at this time as to surrender without raising our voices in protest. We were born free (at least some of us were). We must fight for our political and academic freedom publicly and relentlessly, in the hope that we can preserve it.

Appendix: A Brief History

After 1945 the ONR, and to a lesser extent Army Ordinance, were already supporting scientific research on a fair scale. The AEC existed for a specialized type of support, but in the early fifties there were no operating agencies in our democratic institutions specifically intended for the purpose of general scientific support—the NSF (National Science Foundation) was still in a foetal stage. Certain highly placed officers in the DOD, and especially ONR, decided to make some of the monies appropriated by Congress for the DOD available to support pure unclassified research in the universities, as a long-term investment for the country and/or the DOD. A story, perhaps apocryphal, relates that the ONR long ago had been offered the atomic bomb project but had turned it down, and was so sorry afterwards that, ever since, it had been eager to support pure science so as not to miss the boat the next time around.

It should be emphasized that I am speaking here of the support of pure research, principally originated by professors, definitely not classified, and of the type which is generally regarded as legitimate within a university. This type of work should be distinguished from the "illegitimate" type (classified work, biological warfare research), on which there is now a consensus that it has no place within the university, even though instances of it have occurred during the past years.

At the very beginning, some voices warned that there was some ambiguity concerning this support, and questioned how free was the money thus provided. The need of this money on the part of professors (partly in the form of research stipends, at a time when salaries were very low, and partly to pay for hardware in the experimental sciences), and the need for a development of science in the country created a *de facto* situation in which this ambiguity was allowed to stand.

One can get a rough idea of the low financial operations of universities at that time by the following figure: In 1955, four years after my Ph.D., as an instructor at the University of Chicago, I was making $4,200 a year!

Over the years, many contracts and grants were shifted to NSF. During the period from 1950 to about 1966 the money, whether from military agencies or NSF, was always granted seemingly without any requirements on the professors other than a proposal for the research projects, refereeing, and a yearly progress report. The refereeing was always done on criteria of excellence. No other criteria seemed to be applied, as far as the professional levels were concerned.

OBNOXIOUS TRENDS

About three years ago, certain obnoxious trends became apparent and developed at an alarmingly increasing rate. There was Congressional and Presidential pressure on the DOD and NSF to spread the support of research on the basis of "geographic distribution," in itself quite commendable, but which in practice turned out to be partly pork barrel, and partly was used as a means of extending the DOD's influence into the universities, thus gradually changing the original idea of supporting "pure research." Testimony at Congressional hearings on research and development is very illuminating (on S. Res. 110, July 11, 17, 18, 1967, Part 3, see especially p. 655 *et sequ.*).

Project Themis

A number of articles in *Science* magazine have reported this trend. Project Themis is an example in which, as reported by *Science* (7 April 1967), "there is a frank fusion of two sets of goals, one having to do with the universities, one having to do with DOD." And Donald MacArthur, deputy director of the

Directorate of Defense Research and Engineering which is running Themis, stated:

> ... the scientific content of these programs [those of Themis] must be oriented toward areas of science and technology in which a strong mutual interest is shared by the Department of Defense and the university. . . . Thus a further objective of these programs will be to foster closer relationships between the university scientists and engineers who are in daily contact with real military problems.

About 50 new university projects were planned under Themis for 1970. The Themis Project was vigorously opposed by one of the local chapters of AAUP (University of Montana), which stated in a memo:

> Our academic institutions have a vital but different concern in the free development and criticism of scientific knowledge, social institutions and artistic expression. . . . For academic institutions to achieve their goals, it is essential that they function in an atmosphere of independence as complete as is humanly possible. . . . We are seriously concerned at the encroachment by the Department of Defense and other military agencies in financing academic research. . . .

Because of budget cuts and academic pressures, the Themis project is now discontinued.

Waging "Peacefare"

At another time (17 November 1967), *Science* reported that "a study group appointed by the National Academy of Sciences has advised the Department of Defense to increase its support and use of research in the social and behavioral sciences. The Department "must now wage not only warfare but peacefare as well," the panel states in its report. "Pacification, assistance and the battle of ideas are major segments of the DOD responsibility. The social and behavioral sciences constitute the unique resource for support of these new requirements and must be vigorously pursued if our operations are to be effective."

Center for Naval Analyses

In 1968, in what I regard as a major development in the subversion of universities by the DOD, Rochester University entered into a contract of $8,819,000 with the Center for Naval Analyses (similar to IDA), in which the contract allocated 5 percent of the budget to the support of "fundamental unclassified research" at the Rochester campus. The main part of the contract effort covered a program on problems in naval warfare in the broadest sense, including operational and logistic aspects. Thus support of pure unclassified research became here tied for the first time as a *percentage* of straight services for warmaking. The AAUP chapter at Rochester protested this contract vigorously, in a memorandum dated 9 May 1968.

The CNA contract also provided a good example of how top university administrators and a few professors can involve the university in a major DOD enterprise without the rest of the academic community being informed. As the AAUP memo stated:

> In an institution which can devote two years to careful consideration of honorary degrees, careful evaluation of the CNA proposal would not have been out of place. It is useful here to observe the manner in which the University Senate was informed about CNA. We do not have permission to quote from minutes of October 2, 1967, when the President reported to the Senate on the contract. He made a brief statement outlining the arrangement, mentioning the previous history of CNA management, and indicating that some of the faculty had been involved in the decision. The minutes contain no report of prior debate on the question, no mention of documents bearing out the notion of faculty support after consultation, and no suggestion that the contract itself is an available reference.

After many delays, great reluctance, and prolonged attempts to turn the AAUP representatives away from getting the contract, a copy was finally handed to them. However, in their memo they state:

> As an experiment in bureaucracy, we addressed a request to the Contracting Officer of ONR. His reply, received after three weeks, informed us that "extra copies . . . are not available," and registered his assurance that we are "free to examine this document" in the hands of Mr. McBride [Director of Research Administration].

It is really terrible when one has to deal on that basis within a university! And the case is typical of what has been going on for years. The student movement of course has been in the vanguard of the protest against the encroachment of the Defense Department in the universities, but except for isolated voices (like those of Fulbright and Rickover), was misunderstood by the public at large and met little sympathy in our society until 1969, when it seems that significant changes of attitudes began to appear. For instance, *Look* magazine ran a series on the defense establishment, and in one section, called "The University Arsenal" (p. 34, 26 August 1969), related how a meeting between students and trustees

> . . . turned very nearly into a rout, as the trustees' answers became progressively inadequate and evasive. At one point, Hewlett [of Hewlett–Packard] denied a charge that FMC manufactured nerve gas. The students presented evidence; Hewlett countered that his source was the president of the corporation. Finally he admitted FMC *had* been making nerve gas up to six months earlier.

And, further in the article, *Look* reported:

> Jerry Dick, a young physicist and father of two, is opposed to the Vietnam war. In February, at a meeting sponsored by the Stanford chapter of the AAUP, Dick heard Stanford Research Institute President Charles Anderson argue that no researcher was forced to take on any project he found morally objectionable. Dick stood up: "Sir, I was pressured into doing chemical-warfare research." That candor, he learned later, nearly cost him his security clearance. . . . When I found Jerry Dick, he'd been fired.

Political–Economic Blackmail

Whether in the case of IDA, CNA, SRI, or whatnot, one repeatedly meets top university administrators and trustees who lie blatantly, act secretively, and contribute to the running of organizations indulging in political–economic blackmail. The case of Jerry Dick is a good example, and under the pressure of the Vietnam war, this blackmail has been substantially increasing, also in connection with government contracts or grants. As reported in *Science* (5 April 1968): "Mathematician James Simons was fired by IDA on 29 March because of his refusal to engage in military-related research—a refusal which grew out of his opposition to the Vietnam war, even though Simons had indicated his willingness to work on IDA's nonmilitary projects." (Simons is now chairman of the math department at Stony Brook, by the way.) Of course the Simons case is not, strictly speaking, a university case, but it gave strong hints on the way the wind was blowing.

The case of Stephen Smale provides a good example within the university. On August 5, 1966, Smale was subpoenaed by HUAC, presumably because of his overt dissent with U.S. policy in Vietnam. The subpoena could not be served because Smale was on his way to Moscow to attend the International Congress of Mathematicians, where he had been invited to deliver a major address and to receive one of the Fields Medals. The *San Francisco Examiner* headlined this event: UC PROF DODGES SUBPENA [sic], SKIPS U.S. FOR MOSCOW. On the last day of the Congress, Smale held a press conference, in which he simultaneously criticized U.S. policy in Vietnam, actions of HUAC, Russian intervention in Hungary ten years before, and the lack of "the most basic means of protest" in the U.S.S.R. Smale was then attacked publicly from various quarters, notably by Rep. Roudebush (R.–Ind.), member of both the House Science and Astronautics Committee and HUAC. When the time came for the renewal of Smale's grant in Summer 1967, Rep. Roudebush attacked again, and said he would seek a Congressional veto if the NSF approved the grant. An aide to Roudebush in September 1967 said that "the Congressman looked into Smale's background and he's about as pink as they come. . . . We have already been in touch with Senator Gordon Allott and he has agreed to veto the grant." (However, an aide to Senator Allott said that no firm decision had been made.)

After attempting to blame Smale's management of the grant (characterized as "relatively loose" and "not conforming to appropriate standards" by the chairman of the National Science Board, Philip Handler), NSF, acting under what it regarded as serious pressures, attempted to cut Smale's grant in various ways—split it up, and so on. (For full details, cf. the complete story in the *Notices*, AMS, October 1967, January 1968, February 1968.) *Science* reproduced the allegations of NSF. The mathematical community stood firm behind Smale. Forced to answer only the "journalistic account of NSF accusations rather than the accusations themselves," in a letter to *Science* (never printed), Smale took on the points raised in *Science* one by one and refuted them. The *Science* reporter then initiated his own investigation of the facts, concluding:

> On the basis of material that NSF has recently made available from its own files, two very disturbing facts are now clear: NSF is unable, or at least unwilling, to provide any documentary evidence to support its allegations of impropriety or substandard performance on Smale's part in the administration of his government grant; but even more important, at the time NSF made these allegations, it was in possession of documentary evidence which clearly contradicted the allegations, or showed them to be based on trivial and technical departures from ambiguous regulations.

After that, Smale got his grant, in an essentially satisfactory form.

Of course, it is the stated policy of NSF that its grants are independent of the political opinions expressed by the recipients. Needless to say, the DOD has no such stated policy. The Smale case shows how NSF can panic under pressure which ultimately is shown to be basically inconsequential. On the other hand, the scientific community should be aware that when it moves sufficiently strongly, on a firm basis, following its customary practices of accuracy and honesty, a given situation involving political factors can be resolved in an essentially satisfactory manner—at least so far. But the residual feelings of discomfort and intimidation cannot so easily be eliminated.

Political Criteria

A number of cases have come to light in which political criteria have been used to screen personnel for governmental scientific organizations. The most famous is perhaps the black-balling of Franklin Long for the directorship of NSF, because of his known opposition to the ABM system. *Science* also reports rigid security criteria for employment in HEW, involving the political opinions of candidates and their attitudes on the Vietnam war. For instance, one physician, Henry S. Kahn, was denied a Public Health Service (PHS) commission apparently because he had taken part in an antiwar demonstration, and because he had (with many others) signed a letter suggesting a memorial to Negro author W. E. B. DuBois (*Science,* 18 July 1969). Senator Brooke took interest in the case, and wrote to Secretary Finch:

> . . . I am myself a member of a committee formed to raise private funds for a memorial to DuBois in his hometown of Stockbridge, Massachusetts. . . . There are certainly grave questions about the desirability and constitutionality of governmental practices by which anonymous officials use secret information and undisclosed criteria to deny someone a job in a nondefense-related field. Dr. Kahn's case prompts a nagging suspicion that some applicants may be rejected for federal appointment because their beliefs or their efforts in behalf of legitimate causes are deemed contrary to government policy.

Science also reports "several cases of doctors who had not been denied a commission outright on the basis of the HEW security check, but who had been delayed past the PHS cut-off date, thus effectively depriving them of a PHS commission." And when *Science* tried to get information from a Mrs. Yolles, who supervises the PHS commissioning process, they report that ". . . Mrs. Yolles discussed these matters for a few minutes with *Science*, but then declined to answer further questions on how the HEW security check system affected PHS commissioning. After the initial discussion, Mrs. Yolles would not make herself available even for the purpose of ascertaining why she was unwilling to answer questions on this subject." Secretary Finch seems to have been unaware of such practices, and apparently has taken steps to correct the situation.

Universities Treated as Service Centers

Even more importantly, *Science* (21 June 1968) reported action by the Senate "to whip rebellious colleges and students back in line" by "denying NASA grants to institutions that bar Armed Forces recruiters from their campuses." Columbia was mentioned specifically because of the resolution of the college faculty taken early in 1968 after General Hershey's obnoxious directives to draft boards. Senator Carl Curtis, who had proposed the amendment to the Senate bill, said in support of his amendment: ". . . Institutions have an obligation, patriotic in nature, and in the interests of our country to cooperate with programs of the U.S. Government. . . . I do not believe that very many universities will continue this practice (of barring recruiters) if Congress takes this action."

As far as I am concerned, there is absolutely no reason why different agencies of the government should act in consort and collusion of this type. It is perfectly conceivable that at different times, one agency of the government may be involved in desirable policies from the point of view of a university, which may wish to deal with one and not the other.

The Humphrey Statement

One has to resist the view expressed so revoltingly by Hubert H. Humphrey, when as Vice President he said:

> I know many times I read in the press there is a little rebellion on some campuses about government research projects, projects in universities. I don't know whether I ought to say this or not, but I'm a rather free-wheeling man.

I feel if you don't want the money, there is another place for it. I sort of feel that if the university wants to exclude itself from the life of the nation, then it will most likely find itself living a rather barren life. . . . I hope that our universities and our Government can work together. I hope that there will not be a breach because if there is it will not be the Government that suffers, because the Government can set up its own laboratories. I don't think that is very smart. I think that the Government ought to work with the private sector. . . . But if a nation is denied that then it has to have some way to protect itself.

(Excerpts from a statement made at the meeting of the Panel on Science and Technology, House Committee on Science and Astronautics, 24 January 1968; also quoted in *Science.*)

I believe that, far from excluding themselves from "the life of the nation," our universities should exclude themselves from the death of the nation. Humphrey's remarks have been all the more frightening since they have occurred in a context in which many influential persons have viewed the universities as service centers for the "government," and have tended to treat professors as civil servants. Such views are expressed on the Senate floor increasingly frequently, especially in connection with proposed legislation to introduce more and more restrictions on government grants, DOD or NSF.

THE HUMAN AND ACADEMIC PROBLEM

Now I'll go on to the human aspects of the situation.

I think the basic problem we have to face is intimidation. It's very easy to be intimidated. Our economic well-being is one source of intimidation. There is the social pressure for conforming, for not creating waves, for going along and getting along with those who surround us. There is the fear of getting on FBI lists, of being harassed or watched.

But, in a less crude form, you might say: What's the use? The amount of effort required to get any sort of result politically, socially—it's just absolutely fantastic. That's one aspect of intimidation, the knowledge that you will be drained emotionally, physically intellectually, for very long periods, to achieve what? Little relief, big relief, permanent, nonpermanent? Certainly never permanent. It's a constant fight.

What is our responsibility? I don't know. Probably there is no answer, valid for all of us, for all times. It depends on how bad the situation is at any given moment. It depends on how much hope you can have for curing the evils of the situation. It depends on how bright you are. It depends on how many graduate students you have. It depends on how old you are, how many children you have, how big a family you have to support. It depends on how repressive the established forces are.

There are certain things we can still do in this country without any courage, which would take a considerable amount of courage to do elsewhere. I have a leaflet which tells of just such a case in Moscow—of the confinement of a Russian mathematician, Volpin, who was put in an insane asylum. A very large number of mathematicians signed a protest letter against that, and it took considerable courage. I'm glad to say that I recognize many of my friends' names on that list. The letter said:

> The forcible commitment of a talented mathematician, in full possession of his powers, to a psychiatric hospital for the seriously ill, and the conditions to which he has been subjected . . . are extremely harmful to his mental and physical health and to his dignity as a human being. In view of the humane purposes of our laws, . . . we regard this action as a gross violation of medical and legal standards. . . .

Ninety-five mathematicians signed this petition, ranging from members of the Academy of Sciences and Lenin Prize winners, to Corresponding Members of the Academy, professors, doctors of science, research associates, candidates for doctorate degrees, assistants, and so on. There was enormous pressure on these guys. Some of them had two positions, dual positions, one at the university and another one. They lost one of these positions. There was economic pressure. Some were thrown out of the Communist Party, which over there is sometimes a routine thing to be in.

A group of American mathematicians then wrote a letter of concern to the Soviet Embassy, asking for a clarification of Volpin's status. Nine of the most outstanding mathematicians in the Soviet Union wrote a garbage letter claiming that Volpin "has been under medical observation for mental illness for several years . . . and is under the care of first-class specialists." This shows you the type of pressure put on the scientists, because two of these nine mathematicians were among the 95 signers of the original protest letter. On the other hand, it is very encouraging that only two switched under pressure. Actually, the case ended by Volpin being released shortly afterwards, and that's encouraging, too.

What we're trying to do here in this country is prevent us from meeting that fate, where you wind up in an insane asylum if you start saying things that are not pleasing to the government. I think that over there, they have moved in the right direction with respect to their position on Lysenkoism and Stalinism. Stalinism means that if you do anything that is displeasing to the establishment, you end up either dead or in a concentration camp. Lysenkoism means that if you have some theory in the sciences, and the theory does not correspond to the ideology of the people who run things, then the theory is false, and you don't have to test it out. They have gone from that state to the stage characterized by the Volpin case. But things are still pretty bad, and the intimidation process still goes on very commonly.

Here we start from the opposite end, and, in a way, it's much more depressing to see us move toward a worsening situation, because we've known better. We were not born under Stalinism or Lysenkoism, and I don't want us to get there. I don't even want us to get to the point where we will have Volpin cases, but just for that we have to fight because that's the way we're drifting at the moment.

After all, freely expressing our opposition to certain policies of the President of the United States a few years ago did cause the President to say that we were "Nervous Nellies . . . breaking rank and turning on our leaders." That's a pretty horrible thing to say in a democracy, and a President is really acting like a political thug when he says that, or when he says: "Now there are many, many, many who can recommend and advise and sometimes a few of them consent. But there is only one that has been chosen by the American People to decide." And he almost got away with it—in fact, he got away with a lot, and he started so many trends which are not reversible.

But what each one of us individually does, I don't know. You see, if I have to worry about lectures, gather information, get articles duplicated, read *Science* magazine regularly (the political section, which I reccommend), keep up with proceedings in the Senate, fight for the Smale case, collect the mails on the LeCam–Neyman case, read what Admiral Rickover has to say in testimony to the Senate Foreign Relations Committee, get involved in affairs of my own university, find out what projects are there, what's going astray—I can't do mathematics. I can't do what I like to do and what I'm really best qualified to do, because of lack of time and lack of energy—and I have more than most. But it requires a certain amount of concentration, and if I have to concentrate on this type of garbage, I can't concentrate on mathematical theorems and on educating students. It's a genuine choice—you cannot do both. At least you cannot do both in a really substantial way. Just to give a lecture, for instance (and most of the preparation is done long before the delivery), I still have to order all the reprints, get things organized, and so on. But I can't spend too much time. If I spend too much time, I cannot return to the scientific activity. [I made available to the audience large quantities of reprints of a dozen or so documents mentioned in the earlier part of the talk.]

After two years away from my field I was at the limit of what was possible for me to do and still go back to mathematics. That's why, after Columbia blew up in the Spring of 1968, I decided to take a leave away from my own university and go someplace where I was emotionally unattached and I could keep up with mathematics. This I succeeded more or less in doing. But it's a very serious problem. The guys in the DOD, or the administrators—they have 24 hours a day just to screw things up. It's their job to administer, not mine, and any time I step

out of my normal activities and into counteradministration, because I think they've failed, it is a tremendous burden on me. I
do not enjoy it. Like any intellectual activity, I make it as interesting as I can, but it is nothing compared to the excitement, the beauty, and the interest provided by a beautiful
mathematical theorem. And in addition to that, my mathematical results and those of my colleagues have some permanent value. At best, like those of Euclid or Archimedes, they will
still be enjoyed three thousand years from now, but to act in a
political situation just to make sure that the next day you have
some modicum of free speech never has permanent value.
Because once I've taken care of that day or the next week or
the next year, I'll be out of the picture and somebody else will
have to take over just to take care of the next year after that.

And yet, I find it unbearable to live under conditions of
political repression, so I have to reconcile two contradictory
desires. One is to do my beautiful mathematics, and the other is
to preserve working conditions, living conditions which are acceptable philosophically, intellectually, humanly. It is a disastrous situation to be in, but we will never find again, for the
foreseeable future, the situation which we had until a few years
ago in this country. Of course, you can get into a situation like
that of Stalinist Russia, where people like mathematicians had
absolutely no other choice but to withdraw completely into their
mathematics without touching the outside world in any way.
There, it became a question of pure survival. There is nothing
they could do to improve the situation. When it has degenerated
to that point, when it is clearly utterly hopeless, then withdrawal is the only possibility. We are not in that situation now
in the United States. We are seeing some results from some
efforts to correct the abuses of power, abuses in political blackmail. Some Senators, some public figures are speaking out who
would never have dared do it a few years ago. But very few.

The one constituency which is the freest from political and
economic blackmail is the constituency of young people, students, in high school, college, and immediately out of college.
Economically they are fairly independent, and psychologically
they are fairly free of the commitments of their elders. Com-

mitments can be of many kinds. I have a commitment to mathematics. One can have a commitment to family, to one's job.
The kids are free of most of these commitments. They can and
do take risks, but they can afford to more than older people.
And in the movement throughout the world, the movement of
these kids, you find some very common features. They all
respond to a situation created by people who run things, who
hold *de facto* power, no matter what form of government exists;
it has nothing to do with Communism or Capitalism. It has to
do with big complex sociological structures, an excess of technology, the natural drift of power to a few, who have created
a situation which is to me extraordinarily frightening, because
those who run things are repressive socially, politically, cul-
turally, whether in Prague or Budapest or Vietnam. They are
repressive in different ways. You can read in the newspapers
what happens in Prague or Moscow. Or you can read what
the American Army Major said about a Vietnamese village:
"We had to destroy it to save it." And you can see pictures of
American soldiers setting fire to a Vietnamese village, or napalm-
ing it to death. The Nazis used to do that, because some German
soldier got sniped at—the wanton destruction of whole villages,
like Ouradour. Or you can read "How U.S. 'Know How' Is
Ruining a Viet Industry" (headline in the San Francisco Chronicle, March 18, 1969), about how the Americans ordered the
rubber trees cut down in Tay Ninh Province—and rubber is the
only viable industry in the province. We cut down 150,000
rubber trees—because American convoys have been sniped at.

That's the American way when applied to the Vietnamese.
But we have also the American way applied to Americans. Like
the draft:

> Even though the salary of a teacher has historically
> been meager, many young men remain in that job, seeking
> the reward of a deferment. . . . The psychology of granting
> wide choice under pressure to take action is the American
> or indirect way of achieving what is done by direction in
> foreign countries where choice is not permitted. . . . De-
> livery of manpower for induction . . . is not much of an
> administrative or financial challenge. It is in dealing with

the other millions of registrants that the System is heavily occupied. . . ."

This quote is not from a leaflet by SDS. It is from a memorandum from the Selective Service Orientation Kit, entitled "Channeling."

So far, the American way has not yet napalmed Americans (except by mistake in Vietnam). But it has beaten, gassed, arrested Americans, both Negro private citizens and students, and the repressive violence is getting worse.

So what have the kids to look forward to? Having their lives directed and channeled by a vast bureaucracy, getting blown to bits by atomic bombs and missiles, burned into a black crust by napalm, paralyzed by nerve gases like the 6,000 sheep in Utah a few years ago, polluted out of existence by fumes and oil, ruined by taxes used to carry out all of this, and repressed in the process by the police and the Army. Is it any wonder that they try for something else? That they protest in schools, that they protest in the streets?

The way I see it, the kids form the only substantial political force with the drive, the energy, the persistence to stand between us and the ultimate catastrophe being brought about by the people who run things. Their movement has been mostly free from ideological dogma—I hope it stays that way. It gets replenished every year, and whatever excesses may have occurred, so far they are negligible compared to the excesses of those in institutional authority.

The future is theirs much more than it is mine. I wish them luck.

J. B.
Neilands

is Professor of Biochemistry at the
University of California, Berkeley. He received his B.A.
from the University of Toronto in 1944, his M.S. from
Dalhousie in 1946, and his Ph.D. in biochemistry from the
University of Wisconsin in 1949. Before beginning his long-
term affiliation with Berkeley in 1952, he spent a year as an
instructor of biochemistry at the University of Wisconsin.
A former National Research Council Fellow and Guggenheim Fellow, Neilands is co-author of *Outlines of Enzyme
Chemistry*, and editor of *Structure and Bonding*. He has
published about a hundred research papers on enzymology,
iron metabolism, and bioinorganic chemistry. He has also
published several articles on CBW in Vietnam. Among
numerous professional societies of which he is a member
are the American Association for the Advancement of Science, and the Society for Social Responsibility in Science.

Professor Neilands has been chairman of the Berkeley
Faculty Peace Committee, and president of the American
Federation of Teachers #1474. He was a member of the
third investigating committee of the International War
Crimes Tribunal, testifying before the Tribunal in May
1967. He is at present chairman of the Scientists' Committee
on Chemical and Biological Warfare on behalf of the
Scientists' Institute for Public Information.

Chemical
Warfare

This essay, which furnishes a certain amount of technical information on chemical agents in use in the Vietnam war, also estimates the magnitude and purpose (or intent) of their use, and the relationship of this program of chemical warfare to international law. It unabashedly offers some suggestions for appropriate action on the part of the scientific community.

NAPALM

Napalm was first compounded by Professor Louis Fieser of Harvard University during World War II. The word was coined from the names of *na*phthenic and *palm*itic acids. Although subsequently it was found that the crude ingredients used by Fieser were not especially rich in palmitic acid, the original name has persisted, and in fact is applied to all formulations of gelled gasoline.

Many casualties from napalm probably arise from asphyxiation. This is a consequence of the fact that burning napalm sucks all of the oxygen from the atmosphere and, because of incomplete combustion, gives rise to carbon monoxide.

In a letter to me dated September 26, 1966, Fieser states: ". . . We certainly had no thought of use of napalm against non-military personnel. . . ." It is now accepted that napalm is dropped on open hamlets, incinerating civilians in their huts. The use of napalm by the Air Force alone has accelerated on the following scale: 2,181 tons dropped in 1963; 1,777 tons in

1964; 17,659 tons in 1965; 54,620 tons in 1966. By March of 1968 the total dropped by the Air Force had reached 100,000 tons. (Of course the Navy also drops napalm bombs, and the Army uses napalm in flame-throwers). Some years ago a type of napalm with superior adhesive qualities was developed. This form, napalm B, consists of 50 percent polystyrene, 25 percent benzene, and 25 percent gasoline. Dow Chemical has been sole supplier.

White phosphorus is the classical ignition substance for napalm. Elementary phosphorus does not occur in nature; on exposure to air it ignites spontaneously. As a munition, phosphorus can be delivered via either bombs or shells. The maximum allowable concentration of white phosphorus in air is 0.1 mg/m³. Doctor A. Behar, a French physician, writes:

> Phosphorus has the particularity that inside the wound or burn, it burns slowly. On occasion this slow combustion lasts up to 15 days. At night can be seen the greenish light produced by the material that continues burning the flesh and bones. Besides this, accompanied by the wounds and the profound burns, the victims suffer a severe intoxication produced by the augmentation by three or more times the quantity of inorganic phosphorus in the body.

According to a manual of civilian defense: "One thing to remember about these phosphorus bombs is to be sure that the solid particles that are in the air do not touch your skin. They cause terrible burns. . . ." Evidently this weapon has been and is being directed at human targets: A ranking Special Forces officer has been quoted as saying, "We killed them one by one with grenades, with direct hits with Willie Peter [white phosphorus artillery shells], or with napalm."

CHEMICAL AGENTS

Chemical weapons presently in use in Vietnam, as announced by official U.S. sources, may be classified either as herbicides or as antipersonnel gases.

Herbicides

In late 1942 Dr. E. J. Kraus, chairman of the Botany Department at the University of Chicago and an expert on plant hormones and growth regulators, suggested to committees of the National Academy of Science that "the toxic properties of growth-regulating substances for the destruction of crops or the limitation of crop production" might be of military significance. The U.S. Army then set up a large program on herbicide research at the recently established Camp Detrick; by the end of World War II more than 1,000 different chemicals had been tested. In June, 1945, the Army was prepared to recommend the use of ammonium thiocyanate as a defoliant in the Pacific, but the idea was rejected by higher civilian authorities on the basis that if we used this chemical, we would be accused of conducting poison gas warfare.

Following a field test of the butyl esters of the phenoxyacetic acids at Camp Drum in New York, the government of South Vietnam asked the U.S. Army to apply defoliants for control of guerrilla forces. Preliminary tests carried out in Vietnam between July, 1961, and April, 1962, demonstrated that the esters of 2,4-D and 2,4,5-T were capable of killing most of the plant species in that country. Thailand, having similar vegetation, was used as a test site for development of other sprays; simultaneously, the Army conducted tests in Texas and Puerto Rico. A 70-mile stretch of Highway 15 out of Bien Hoa was sprayed in early 1962, and a high Vietnamese official said: "Tests have shown that manioc and sweet potatoes die four days after having been sprayed. These are the two most important food staples for the communist bands in the mountains." The first operational spraying of herbicides for crop destruction in known Viet Cong strongholds was carried out in late November, 1962.

The first group of C-123 cargo planes, equipped with tanks and spray nozzles, arrived at the Tan Son Nhut airport on November 29, 1961. From this modest beginning, "Operation Ranch Hand" has escalated to a level which requires the better part of $100 million annually for chemicals alone. Table 1 shows estimated areas sprayed through September, 1967. In the first nine months of 1967, about 15 percent of the area treated was crop land.

Table 1
Estimated Area Treated with Herbicides in South Vietnam in Acres per Year

Year	Defoliation	Crop destruction	Total
1962	17,119	717	17,836
1963	34,517	297	34,814
1964	53,873	10,136	64,009
1965	94,726	49,637	144,363
1966	775,894	112,678	888,572
1967	1,486,446	221,312	1,707,758
1968	1,297,244	87,064	1,384,308
1969 (First half)	797,200	38,800	836,000

Three main types of herbicides have been used, viz., phenoxyacetic acids (2,4-D and 2,4,5-T), cacodylic acid, and picloram. Table 2 gives some characteristics of these substances.

Table 2
Herbicides Used by U. S. Military Forces in Vietnam

Chemical name	Common name	Code name	Target
2, 4-dichlorophenoxyacetic acid	2, 4-D	orange	general defoliant
2, 4, 5-trichlorophenoxyacetic acid	2, 4, 5-T	orange	general defoliant
Dimethylarsinic acid	cacodylic	acid blue	rice
3, 5, 6-trichloro-4-amino-picolinic acid	picloram	white	broadleaved crops

The phenoxyacetic acids are the favorite herbicides for Vietnam; in 1967 and 1968 the Department of Defense commandeered the entire U.S. production of 2,4,5-T, amounting to some 13 or 14 million pounds. If applied once, the phenoxyacetic acids probably will not kill trees; if applied repeatedly, trees may be killed. In the soil these agents may or may not be rapidly degraded to harmless products. The greatest threat from their massive application in Vietnam is that they may denude the land, alter the ecology (including that of the soil), and possibly change the climate. Up to half of the dry weight of many soils may be microorganisms—bacteria, fungi, other organisms—and much of this life exists in a rhizosphere fed by organic substances excreted by plant roots. Total destruction of the vegetation could lead to extensive soil erosion. Much of the soil of South Vietnam is lateritic, and unless it is covered by plant growth it could become baked into a rocklike consistency (laterite) and irreversibly lost for agricultural purposes.

The presence of 2,4-D and 2,4,5-T in the environment presents a direct hazard to human health. The toxicity of 2, 4-D and 2,4,5-T has been seriously underestimated. Bryce Nelson reported in the Fall of 1969 that one of the main herbicides used in Vietnam, 2,4,5-T, would be restricted in its domestic uses as of January 1, 1970, because of its potential teratogenic (birth defect-producing) effect. The action against the herbicide came from the White House after Bionetics Research Laboratories, Inc., reported to the National Cancer Institute that the offspring of laboratory animals fed 2,4,5-T showed 100 percent birth defects. The other phenoxyacetic acid, 2,4-D, was said to "require further study." Almost immediately it was stated that the restriction would not apply to the use of 2,4,5-T in Vietnam (Los Angeles *Times*, October 30, 1969; *Sunday Times* of London, November 30, 1969; New York *Times,* December 7, 1969). In the Summer of 1969 several Saigon newspapers disclosed a sharp rise in the incidence of monster births and linked this phenomenon to the defoliation operation. The newspapers were ordered out of business by the Thieu-Ky government (San Francisco *Chronicle*, December 1, 1969).

Dow Chemical Company, one of the manufacturers of the phenoxyacetic acid herbicides, was apparently taken by surprise by the government's order restricting the use of 2,4,5-T. The company soon circulated word that the toxic principle in 2,4, 5-T was not the herbicide but an impurity introduced during manufacture. They stated further that improved procedures of preparation would reduce the toxic contaminant to negligible levels. The U. S. Department of Agriculture then obligingly agreed to continue to license 2,4,5-T while further tests were in progress. Those results, which were brought in during April, 1970, proved that even highly purified 2,4,5-T could be teratogenic. Three Departments–Agriculture; Health, Education and Welfare; and Interior—then issued regulations severely restricting the use of this herbicide. At the same time, the Pentagon announced that "orange" would no longer be used for defoliation in Vietnam.

Cacodylic acid is being used to kill rice in the Viet Cong areas. It contains 54.29 percent arsenic. Actually, the LD_{50} in dogs is about 1 g/kilo, which means that it is a fairly toxic substance. United States government authorities have stated that it is no more toxic than aspirin. Nothing is known about the fate of this substantial amount of arsenic introduced into the biosphere. Once reduced from the 5+ to the 4+ or 3+ charge state, arsenic becomes much more toxic. Demethylation of cacodylic acid renders it ten times more poisonous, and biochemical systems are known which are capable of this reaction.

Picloram, the third main herbicide applied in Vietnam, is similarly hazardous. In one test, only 3.5 percent of the administered dose vanished from the test plot in 467 days. It thus retains phytotoxicity for a very great period, possibly decades. Picloram, which is also manufactured by Dow Chemical, is not authorized for use on a single American crop.

Obviously, total destruction of vegetative life results in the elimination of all animal life as well. No one can say what Operation Ranch Hand will ultimately do to the ecology of Vietnam. One study was made of possible consequences, but without any field work in Vietnam. The Department of Defense then sent one plant scientist to Vietnam, but he stayed for only one month, ventured no more than a few yards out of camps, and made no attempt to examine the crop destruction program. The latter (Operation Ranch Hand) amounts to the use of starvation as a weapon. (Admiral William Leahy, in response to a suggestion made in 1944 that biological agents be used to destroy the Japanese rice crop, said such activity would ". . . violate every Christian ethic I have ever heard of and all of the known laws of war.")

Antipersonnel Gases

On March 22 and 23 of 1965, the New York *Times* and other news media made the first report on the use of antipersonnel gases in Vietnam. White House Press Secretary George Reedy called the gases "riot control" agents and said President Johnson was not consulted on their use. There was an immediate worldwide reaction. Secretary Rusk stated that the gases used in Vietnam were not banned by the Geneva Protocol of 1925, and he implied they would be used only in "riot control" situations. A State Department source was quoted as saying: "The Geneva Protocol of 1925, prohibiting the use of 'asphyxiating, poisonous, and other gases,' was never ratified by the U. S. Senate. So, the U. S. is not bound by it. But the State Department does not consider the use of riot-control gas in Vietnam as a violation of this agreement anyway."

A British statesman intimately familiar with the history of the Geneva Protocol, Philip Noel–Baker, has commented: "I find it difficult to understand how anyone can argue that the Protocol permits the use of 'harassing' gases and herbicides" (New York *Times*, December 9, 1969). The Political Committee of the General Assembly of the United Nations has approved a Swedish resolution which declares that the Geneva Protocol applies to the use of "any chemical agents." The vote was 59 positive, 35 abstentions, and 3 negative. The latter votes were cast by Australia, Portugal, and the United States (New York *Times*, December 11, 1969). The vote was rejected by the State Department on the grounds that there were too many abstentions (New York *Times*, December 12, 1969). The British government, which abstained, was believed to be under pressure from the U. S. to vote "no" or, at the very least, to abstain (London *Observer*, November 30, 1969).*

Secretary McNamara once released data on CN, CS, and DM, the three gases he said were chosen for use in Vietnam (see Table 3). The amount of CS gas requisitioned by the U. S. Army for Vietnam escalated from 367,000 pounds in 1964 to 6,063,000 pounds in 1969. These figures, which are from the

---

* Subsequently the UN adopted by a vote of 80 to 3 a resolution which declared in part that "any chemical agents . . . which might be employed because of their direct toxic effects on man, animals or plants are contrary to the generally recognized rules of international law, as embodied in the protocol."

Congressional Record, H 4775, do not indicate if agencies other than the U. S. Army procure additional amounts of CS. According to several press reports this gas, and perhaps CN, are in routine military use in Vietnam (San Francisco *Chronicle,* September 29, 1969; New York *Times,* December 6, 1969).

Table 3

Characteristics of Antipersonnel Gases Admitted To Be in Use in Vietnam (32)

Agent	Code	Effect	LCt_{50} (mg/min/m^3)
Chloroacetophenone	CN	harassing, lachrymation	8,500
o-chlorobenzalmalononitrile	CS	harassing, nausea	large
Diphenylaminochloroarsine	DM	harassing, nausea	30,000

By late 1965 it was not difficult to find news items such as: "Marines Use Tear Gas in Caves to Oust Vietnamese Civilians." The "riot-control" use had given way to underground application. An air pump, called a "Mighty Mite," was devised for pumping the gas into tunnels. A compilation of press reports indicates that these gases are in massive use in various ways in Vietnam. Since the 1965 announcement on CS, CN, and DM, we have obtained no information on possible deletions from or additions to this list of gases, certainly CS is used in vast amounts.

Thus far there has been no detailed accounting of the number of casualties arising from the use of gas, but the total must be a substantial figure. In one operation an Australian soldier was killed by a combination of smoke and "nonlethal" gas even though he was wearing a mask. And a Canadian doctor who spent several years at the Quang Ngai Hospital in South Vietnam has written:

> During the last three years I have examined and treated a number of patients—men, women, and children —who had been exposed to a type of war gas, the name of which I do not know. The types of gas used make one quite sick when one touches the patient, or inhales the breath from their lungs. After contact with them for more than

three minutes one has to leave the room in order not to get ill.

The patient usually gives a history of having been hiding in a cave or tunnel or bunker or shelter into which a cannister of gas was thrown in order to force them to leave their hiding place. Those patients that have come to my attention were very ill with signs and symptoms of gas poisoning similar to those that I have seen in veterans from the First World War treated at Queen Mary Veterans Hospital in Montreal. The only difference between the cases was that these Vietnamese patients were more acutely ill and, when getting over their acute stage, presented a similar picture to that of the war veterans.

Patients are feverish, semicomatose, and severely short of breath; they vomit and are restless and irritable. Most of their physical signs are in the respiratory and circulatory systems. . . .

The mortality rate in adults is about 10 percent, while the mortality rate in children is about 90 percent. . . .

An article in the Saigon *Post* of October 11, 1967, titled "U. S. Tear Gas Use Saves Lives of Viet Innocents," provoked this response from an eyewitness:

About three and one-half months ago I was involved in an attempt to be of assistance to some 6,000 new refugees that had been created in Quang Ngai Province by a forced evacuation of an area under Viet Cong control. . . . I took two of them, a 10-year-old boy and a 12-year-old girl, by far the most seriously ill, and drove the eight miles back to Quang Ngai. Emergency measures proved fatal for the boy; he was in the morgue the next morning when I went to the hospital. He died from an overdose of tear gas. The victims reported that about 20 women and children did not even make it out of the cave. . . .

There have been unconfirmed reports that agent BZ, an "incap" (incapacitator), has been released in Vietnam. As far as I know, these reports have never been documented and verified. However, in late 1968 a chemical trade journal announced that plans existed to manufacture 2.16 million pounds of an "irritant," presumably CS, so gas is an important munition in the Vietnam war.

APPLICABLE LAWS

The Hague Convention of 1907, signed and ratified by the U. S., declared in its Article 25: ". . . belligerents do not have unlimited right concerning the choice of means of doing harm to the enemy." After World War I there was universal horror about the effects of gas, and this led to the Geneva (Gas) Protocol of 1925. The text of the substantive part is: "Whereas the use in war of asphyxiating, poisonous, or other gases, and of all analogous liquids, materials, or devices, has been justly condemned by the general opinion of the civilized world. . . ." This was originally ratified by 42 nations, and subsequently was by many more; it was signed but never ratified by the United States.

By the 1930's there was a common agreement among nations, or at least an understanding, that the laws and customs of war had been well codified. Then came the Nazi atrocities, followed by the tribunal at Nuremberg. While aggression, or a crime against the peace, was recognized as the most flagrant violation of international law, Nuremberg took note of two other types of crimes: (1) "Murder, ill-treatment, or deportation to slave labor or for any other purpose, of civilian populations of or in occupied territory; murder or ill-treatment of prisoners of war or persons on the seas; killing of hostages; plunder of public or private property; wanton destruction of cities, towns, or villages; or devastation not justified by military necessity. . . ." (2) "Murder, extermination, enslavement, deportation, and other inhuman acts done against any civilian population . . . in connection with any crime against peace or any war crime." These were the war crimes proper, and the crimes against humanity, respectively. Another relevant statute is the Genocide Convention adopted by the General Assembly of the United Nations in 1946. The following articles are pertinent:

Article I
The contracting parties confirm that genocide, whether committed in time of peace or in time of war, is a crime under international law which they undertake to prevent and punish.

Article II

In the present convention, genocide means any of the following acts committed with intent to destroy, in whole or in part, a national, ethnical, racial, or religious group, as such:

  a. Killing members of the group
  b. Causing serious bodily or mental harm to members of the group
  c. Deliberately inflicting on the group conditions of life calculated to bring about its physical destruction in whole or in part
  d. Imposing measures intended to prevent birth within the group

Article III

[Enumerates the acts to be punishable]

Article IV

Persons committing genocide or any of the other acts enumerated in Article III shall be punished, whether they are constitutionally responsible rulers, public officials, or private individuals.

To what extent are citizens and soldiers of the United States bound by these agreements? The Constitution, in Article VI, C1.2, states: "This Constitution, and the Laws of the United States which shall be made in Pursuance thereof; and all Treaties made, or which shall be made, under the Authority of the United States, shall be the supreme Law of the Land; and the Judges in every State shall be bound thereby, any Thing in the Constitution or Laws of any State to the Contrary notwithstanding." The responsibilities of military personnel are enunciated in Section II, Par. 498 of the Department of the Army Field Manual: "Any person, whether a member of the armed forces or a civilian, who commits an act which constitutes a crime under international law, is responsible therefore and liable to punishment. Such offenses in connection with war comprise: (a) crimes against peace, (b) crimes against humanitiy, and (c) war crimes...."

We have already noted that the United States claims that the Vietnam antipersonnel gases are not covered by the Geneva Protocol, and that even if they were, this country is not a party to the agreement. But the U. S. supported a United Nations resolution in 1966 which asked all states to adhere to the Protocol. Furthermore, the Protocol explicitly outlaws *all* gases, without exception. Even in the absence of ratification, the U. S. can be charged with crimes "recognized as such by common, public demand, and by the existing laws of humanity" (Nuremberg judgement).

President Richard M. Nixon announced at a White House news conference on November 25, 1969, that the Geneva Protocol would be resubmitted to the Senate for ratification. It was made clear that "tear gases" and herbicides would be excepted from the proposed ban on chemical and biological weapons. Only biological agents, and certain incapacitating chemicals, would be prohibited under the U. S. interpretation of the Protocol. Until the matter has been debated and clarified in the Senate the numerous loopholes in the U. S. position renders it difficult to say if the President's gesture is, as he claims, an "initiative toward peace" or a public-relations ploy (New York *Times*, November 26, 1969).

It is interesting to compare this body of international law with a statement attributed by *U. S. News and World Report* (February 15, 1965) to Ambassador Henry Cabot Lodge: "As far as I'm concerned, the legal aspect of this affair is of no significance. . . ."

CONCLUSION

By the massive and unrestrained use of herbicides and antipersonnel gases in Vietnam, the United States is in violation of numerous international laws, including those pertaining to genocide.

The land of Vietnam, in the south, has been drenched with herbicides on a scale unprecedented in history. Certain of the agents used (cacodylic acid and picloram) have not been and would not be approved for similar use in the United States. No one can forecast what effect these herbicides will have on the human population, the total ecology, and the future agricultural productivity of the soil.

By maiming and killing civilians, most of whom are children under five, pregnant and lactating women, or the aged and the infirm, with antipersonnel gases in confined spaces, the United States is guilty of crimes against humanity. Furthermore, such use of antipersonnel gases has tended to legitimize chemical warfare.

Responsibility of the American Scientist

Existing scientific associations being compromised beyond redemption, the onus has been upon scientists to form a specific organization which will educate the public on the facts of (a) chemical warfare abroad, as in Vietnam, and (b) research on chemical warfare agents, such as is conducted at such military installations as Detrick, in most universities, and in the colonies —the islands and Latin America. Such an organization, named "Scientist's Committee on Chemical and Biological Warfare," was set up at the Dallas meeting of the American Association for the Advancement of Science in December, 1968. Professor E. W. Pfeiffer of the Zoology Department of the University of Montana and I are serving as Executive Secretary and Chairman, respectively.

The Geneva Protocol should be ratified by all nations, and attempts should be made to secure international agreements for the elimination of research on chemical and biological weapons.

Marc
Lappé

is Assistant Research Immunologist at the Cancer Research Genetics Laboratory, University of California, Berkeley. His work concerns the immunology of tumors—how the natural immune response of the body might be utilized to fight cancer tumors.

Dr. Lappé received his B.A. from Wesleyan University in 1964. He did his graduate work at the University of Washington and at the University of Pennsylvania, receiving from the latter in 1968 his Ph.D. in experimental pathology. He has also studied at the Weizman Institute in Israel, at the Rockefeller University in New York, and at the Jackson Laboratory in Maine. Several of his published papers on cancer immunology have appeared in *Nature,* in *Journal of the National Cancer Institute,* and in *Cancer Research.*

Biological
Warfare

During the past 50 years civilization has witnessed the gradual perversion of advances in those biological and chemical sciences to which it has historically entrusted the promotion of human life—medicine, agronomy, pharmacology, and biochemistry. Insidiously, biological and chemical substances have been transformed into weapons of mass destruction. This process has resulted in the appearance of an entirely new concept of warfare: the use of chemical and biological (CB) weapons to disrupt the balance of life processes, both within and outside the body. It is ironic that just as an urgent worldwide ecological awareness begins to appear, a new science arises to pose the threat of worldwide ecological catastrophe. This new science forms the basis of the chemical and biological warfare (CBW) program of the United States. It can aptly be called "the science of public death."

Who is responsible for the burgeoning of this new class of "death sciences"? Can we affix the blame solely on the military establishment? Or have scientists themselves contributed to this degradation of the life sciences? By monopolizing research funds, the Department of Defense has been able to co-opt scientists and influence the direction of their work on an increasingly large scale. Indirectly, the military has been able to subvert basic research done to further human ends and turn it to further military ends. The fate of much of the work done in the new field of aerobiology demonstrates how readily basic research can be subverted by the military. Originally developed for the study of airborne diseases like staphylococcus and pneumonia, this science has become the backbone of the military's biological warfare (BW) program. (The science can be said to have originated in 1934 in this country with the concepts of Wells concerning disease transmission via "droplet nuclei." The original impetus for aerobiology came from the military, which had been plagued by outbreaks of "barracks strep" in the post-World War I years.)

Historically, the scientist himself has contributed to the perversion of his work through loyalty to parochial patriotism rather than to the higher ethical tenets dictated by his professional code and by world law. I wonder how many of the 14 medical doctors working for the Army's biological warfare program at Fort Detrick are adhering to the Hippocratic Oath, which states:

> I will use treatment to help the sick according to my ability and judgment, but never with a view to injury and wrongdoing. Neither will I administer a poison to anybody even when asked to do so, *nor will I suggest such a course.* [Emphasis added.]

Similarly, I wonder how the introduction of BW into combat situations will affect the traditional role of corpsmen and Army doctors when the Code of Ethics in Wartime of the World Medical Association explicitly states:

> It is deemed unethical for doctors to weaken the physical and mental strength of a human being without therapeutic justification, and to employ scientific knowledge to imperil health or destroy life.

To make painfully real the consequences of forsaking basic ethical standards in the service of patriotism, one need only recall how nerve gases were introduced prior to World War II in Nazi Germany. In the course of developing a more potent insecticide, Gerhard Schrader chanced upon the formula for an organophosphorous compound with profound inhibitory effects on nerve transmission. Schrader's first impulse was to inform the then (1936) rapidly expanding German military of the war potential of his compound. His discoveries later provided the Nazis with an "economical" agent (Zyklon B) for murdering prisoners at Auschwitz as they stood in sealed "shower rooms" holding stone bars of "soap" and were showered by the gas. (Like the other gases later produced by I. G. Farben, where Schrader worked, the first was named after a common German soap product, "Tabun." Perhaps this name reflected the German obsession with purity.) Schrader's early invention became the first member of the anticholinesterase nerve gases that now occupy a prominent position in our chemical warfare arsenal.

Chemical weapons are now well incorporated into the military establishment. In fact, essentially all of our stocks of nerve gas (most of which, incidentally, were produced prior to 1958) are now in the hands of military technicians. Biological weapons, on the other hand, are still in the innovative stage, and as such continue to require the support of imaginative scientists. In 1890, Alfred Nobel predicted that it would be mindless technicians who would make "germ warfare" the logical conclusion to mankind's history of warfare. One can only hope that scientists will refuse to become amoral technicians and thus will prove his prediction false.

Opposition to CBW is complicated by the fact that it is in the nature of CB weapons to be developed and used covertly. Indeed, the very fact of secrecy of development almost insures the covert use of CB weapons. And, in the shroud of secrecy surrounding CB weapons, no one would be able to trace with certainty the source of a CB attack. It is this element of CBW which places these weapons in a category apart from those of both conventional and nuclear warfare.

In 1946, as an allegory of the consequences of the cult of silence imposed on nuclear physicists prior to Hiroshima and Nagasaki, Frederic Joliot–Curie conceived a short story called "The Secret War." In it he imagined the consequences of similar circumstances were they to accompany the development of biological weapons. He envisioned entire countries ravaged by successive crop failures of unknown origin, epidemics of human disease mimicking naturally occurring illnesses but infinitely more devastating, and widespread declines in livestock and even in human fertility. Thus, Joliot–Curie pictured a situation in which the economy of a country could be insidiously eroded by an unseen enemy without any overt declaration of war. As we will see, the U.S. would currently be able to conduct such a "war" against almost any country it chooses.

What can individual scientists do to avert what Joliot–Curie foresaw? How can we stem the tide of chemical or biological munitions now being developed? What is the responsibility of the scientific community to those munitions which have left its hands? Before such questions can be answered, one must have a clear overview of the scope and realities of the problem.

I plan to provide such a perspective. In the following pages I will trace the history of the development of CBW, assess the effectiveness of and prospects for the use of chemical and biological weapons, determine which military objectives these weapons fulfill, estimate their potential hazards, present the current government policies about CBW, and assess the current attitude of scientists on CB use. Having done this, I will consider the scientist's role in affecting a change in government policy.

HOW WE GOT INVOLVED: RUSSIA'S PUBLIC HEALTH PROBLEMS BECOME OUR BW ARSENAL

The most reasonable interpretation of Russian and American BW efforts during and shortly after World War II was that in both countries initial efforts were prompted by fear that Germany was developing BW. (Camp Detrick, the U.S. BW facility, was opened in 1943, the same year that our Office of Strategic Services informed Congress in secret session of the German BW program.) The decision to escalate the BW program toward the development of biological weapons for offensive use was based on faulty intelligence about the Russian capability after World War II.

Essentially all of our intelligence about Russia during the post-World War II period was from expatriate Russians living in this country who led us to believe that Russia had a major offensive BW capability. Our "hard" intelligence consisted only

(1) of numerous public statements by Russian military men, both during and after the war, indicating that Russia was anticipating the use of biological weapons in future conflicts, and (2) of the fact that she had captured the Japanese detachments which had helped develop the Harbin BW installation in Manchuria.

However, it is clear now from a reading of the history of that time that the vital decision to embark on a major CBW program (1959–61) stemmed from decisions made amidst the general aura of Cold War paranoia which pervaded the fifties. We interpreted the Russian-supported claims of China that we had used BW agents in North Korea in 1952 as an indication that both of those countries intended to develop BW weapons behind a smokescreen of world public opinion condemning the United States.

The U.S. public learned of our CBW program through the Army Chemical Corps' "Operation Blue Skies" in 1959. I reviewed the Army training films of that era: They made amply clear the "fact" that Russia had a BW program, and stressed the ease with which "other" countries might develop their own. (One film depicted a man in Eastern European dress opening a vial containing some lethal virus mailed from abroad; the next frames showed immense copper kettles at a brewery, suggesting how any virus could be grown in enormous quantities at little expense. The main point of the film was how easily BW could be used to sabotage our country—a rubber boat lands with a handful of men who set up an aerosol* spray system; a waiter dumps biologic agents into the ventilating system of a hotel; a plumber pours poison into a major water main, and so on.) But this interpretation has never been confirmed by our intelligence agents. To this date we have been unable to locate a biological test facility inside Russia, and of course such a facility is a prerequisite for conducting offensive biological warfare. (The U.S. has at least four such testing facilities: The Dugway Proving Ground in Utah; Fort Greeley in Alaska; Eniwetok Atoll in the Pacific; and certain open-water sites in

* Here "aerosol" means a cloud of droplets containing biological-warfare agents.

the Pacific.) Our intelligence has also been unable to identify any significant activity in the country at large to indicate that Russia is testing munitions which might contain biological agents.

Why, then, did we cling to our belief in a Russian threat great enough to stimulate our CBW program? There are at least two distinct possibilities: (1) We misread as "offensive capability" the expertise the Russians had developed in the course of treating four decades of epidemic disease; and (2) We felt that the fact that a portion of the Russian population had been immunized against certain exotic diseases gave them a BW potential against our population. There does not appear to have been, or to be, a "credible" threat of CBW attack from the Soviet Union. In fact, estimates of the real risk of Soviet BW attack are so low that the DOD does not feel that any unusual civil defense preparations, such as the stockpiling of antibiotics, is necessary.

It can only be generally concluded that we were so convinced of a real threat of Russian BW attack that we chose to research the weapons that we knew she was familiar with. A more alarming possibility is that someone conceived the idea of playing havoc with diseases that we knew were endemic to her countryside. In this way we would be able—*à la* Joliot–Curie—to covertly increase the incidence of naturally occurring diseases. Note that the second alternative constitutes a better rationale for developing an offensive BW capacity than does the first.

A similar review cannot be applied to the history of development of our chemical warfare capability. It was clearly the need to broaden our offensive options in the 1960's that prompted President Kennedy to approve the development of a CB weaponry by the Army.

WHAT THEY CAN DO:
THE CB BOMBS REPLACE THE A-BOMB

There is great danger that recent publicity focused on biological warfare against future populations may numb the public to the reality of the *present* warfare. The widespread mass-media image of CB warfare (entire populations succumbing to exotic diseases) provides an inadvertent smokescreen for the Army's highest priority CB effort: the destruction of crop plants.

This facet of the U. S. military program has the formal approval of the Senate. In the course of the debates which raged around the CBW issue in the Senate in 1960 as the result of an attempted censure of CB weapons, various advisory committees presented purportedly "hard" information concerning the necessity of maintaining a strong CBW capability. Among these reports was one which claimed that "anticrop agents are good examples of tactical weapons." That we have no inhibitions against using this "good tactical weapon" is clear from the Army's training manual, in which "the law of land warfare" states:

> The Hague regulation banning "poison or poisoned weapons" does not prohibit measures being taken ". . . to destroy, through chemical or bacterial agents *harmless to man,* crops intended solely for consumption by the armed forces (*if the fact can be determined*)." [emphasis added.]

The extent to which the Army has taken measures to destroy through chemical agents crops intended solely for consumption by enemy armed forces in South Vietnam is truly staggering. One measure of the extent of our "carefully limited operation to disrupt the enemy's food supply" (which, according to John S. Foster of DOD, had "not affected in any single year as much as 1 percent of the annual food output of South Vietnam") is the rice production statistics in that country. In 1964, South Vietnam exported 48,700 metric tons of rice; in 1968 she had to import 700,000 tons. By the latter year, the U.S. Army had sprayed an estimated 500,000 acres of cropland with herbicides. *In addition* to this program, the Army has sprayed *fully 16 percent of the entire forested region* of South Vietnam with defoliants *at least once.* A battery of three different combinations of defoliating and herbicidal chemicals, which Army Training Manual TM 3–216 states possess "high offensive potential for seriously limiting production of crops and defoliating vegetation," have been used in complete disregard of international law, which prohibits the indiscriminate destruction of food crops. (See the Hague Regulations regarding the destruction of nonmilitary food crops cited above.)

The military's response to the short-lived public outcry against its defoliation program was unofficially contained in the following statement from former General Jacques Rothschild, who wrote in the April 14, 1967 issue of *Science:*

> The plea for discontinuing the use of defoliating chemicals seems the most illogical. In every war, depriving the enemy of food and supplies has been an essential part of the action. Blockades have been used and widely accepted for the purpose. [In war] the scorched-earth policy has been normal. . . .

American intelligence services have long recognized the military value of anticrop activity, particularly in what we have come euphemistically to call "limited wars"—i.e., wars against insurgents in small countries. In the early Vietnam years, crop destruction was conducted almost exclusively on a trial-and-error basis, but since then the military has sponsored numerous feasibility studies to establish the exact requirements for efficient crop destruction. (Some of the typical studies are listed in a brochure from the Research Analysis Corporation, "Study of Biological and Chemical Attacks on Crops," "Covert Attacks on Food Crops," and "The Impact of Chemical Attack on Guerrilla Food Crops.")

Although the Army's anticrop program is kept under tight security, ominous signs have appeared sporadically over the years. For instance, the Distinguished Service Award (the Army's highest civilian medal) was presented to a Fort Detrick researcher for her development of a new variety of rice blast (a fungus disease of rice).

And recall the "top secret" NATO plan uncovered by *Ramparts* magazine that gave the NATO commander the authority to use herbicides against guerrilla food crops in the event of hostilities in Eastern Europe. The plausibility of the *Ramparts* allegation is reinforced by the testimony of Swedish Colonel

Stig Wennerstrom, the man who went on trial in 1964 as an accused double agent for Russia. Wennerstrom testified that he had uncovered evidence that the U.S. had plans to use biological anticrop agents against the major Russian wheat fields in the Ukraine and Kuban regions. While this evidence was largely discounted during the trial, I have corroborated Wennerstrom's testimony. In conversation with a former Army intelligence officer, I was able to verify that during the early 1960's both Army and Air Force Intelligence placed extremely high priority on targeting "crop intelligence" in Eastern Europe. This "intelligence" was not so much economic in content as concerned with ecologic considerations, such as precise location, growing season, variety, and disease susceptibility of cereal and corn crops.

This country maintains a continual surveillance of major food crops in Russia and China, with particular emphasis on their susceptibility to known blights, rusts, blasts, and smuts. The Army Biological Laboratory at Frederick, Maryland, has an extensive translating service which culls the Russian and Chinese literature for data on the status of their respective agricultural services. The Army Biological Laboratory's ostensibly random search of the literature takes on a frightening cogency once it is recognized that biologic warfare against food crops requires precise information about density and distribution of target plants, their susceptibility to disease, their growing seasons, and the general ecology of the region in which they grow.

The following are representative articles screened by the Army labs as they appeared in the U.S. Department of Commerce's "Research and Development Reports" and "Chemical, Biological, and Environmental Surveys":

China	*Russia*
1. "The introduction of Improved Varieties of Winter Wheat: Peking 6 and Peking 8"	1. "Fungus Diseases of Leguminous Crops"
	2. "Smut and Other Corn Diseases"
2. "Research on the Special	3. An Analysis of the Growth

Features of the Appropriate Sowing Periods for Winter Wheat"
3. "The Circumstances and Progress on the Breeding of Rust Resistant Wheat"
4. "Problems, Treatment and Prevention of Paddy Rice Bacterial Disease in Kuangtung Province"
5. "Ecology of the Scrub Barrens of Central Asia"

and Degeneration of Wheat Stem Rust in 1964"
4. "Description of Wheat Susceptibility to 'Loose Smut' "
5. "Aerological Characteristics of the Atmosphere Over Armenia"
6. "Influence of General Atmospheric Circulation Processes on Wind Power in Moldavia"
7. "Natural Fluctuation of Temperature and the Dormancy of *Puccinia glumaren*" (yellow wheat rust)

The fact that these translations are done by the Army *instead* of the Department of Agriculture leads to the obvious conclusion that the information is primarily of military and not of agricultural interest. This conclusion is reinforced by noting that the military includes in its selected articles those necessary for estimating Russia's and China's abilities to *control* crop disease. For example, the Army Biological Laboratory has prepared translations of articles on "Predicting Epiphytotics [epidemics] of Grain Rust" (Russian); "A Course to Improve the Crop Protection Service" (Russian); "Anti-smut Activity of Some Chemical Compounds" (Russian). All of these articles deal with the problems of plant quarantine and crop protection from disease in Russia. The Army labs have also provided their military patrons with information to help them estimate whether or not anticrop attack would be detected. They routinely translate articles like "Mold Fungi in the Air of Moscow," "Identification of Plant Fungus Diseases New to the Soviet Union," and "Comparative Evaluation of the Effectiveness of Bacteriological Traps . . . for Determining the Concentration of Bacterial Aerosol." (Note that the last article would also apply to BW attempts to generate human disease.)

Scientists like those responsible for the UN CBW report

downgrade the risk of anticrop warfare because an aggressor nation might never be sure the disease would not spread and endanger its own crops. The Army is well aware of the problems of plant epidemics. America's program of crop seed control and distribution makes it possible to anticipate the plant pathogens to which our crops would be resistant. Our risk in anticrop warfare with biological agents has been assiduously evaluated. The Army sponsored a study at the University of Pennsylvania's Institute for Cooperative Research to estimate the ecological variables in the spread of wheat stem rust in order "to provide protective equations for disease development."* Surveillance of the success of any given anticrop attack would be assured by a system of spy satellites equipped with infrared cameras which can detect minute foci of plant disease anywhere on the planet through changes in the normal absorbence characteristics of healthy vegetation.

From a military viewpoint, how effective could a biological attack on an enemy's food supply be? The answer is "very effective." An Army training manual reminds its readers that in Asian countries operating without U.S. assistance (e.g., providing hybrid rice resistant to many plant diseases), as much as 30 percent of the annual rice crop is lost to paddy-rice bacterial disease. Were an epidemic of rice blast superimposed on this situation, a UN report conservatively estimates, 70 percent of a country's rice crop would be lost. Similar estimates for the introduction of wheat rust into an unprepared country show that as much as 80 percent of the wheat crop could be destroyed in a single attack. One has only to realize that a *doubling* of both wheat and rice production would be necessary to adequately feed today's world population, to further realize what a devastating impact anticrop warfare could have. The end-product of a crop destruction would be famine of unprecedented proportions. No longer, as in the past (during blockades), could civilian populations rely on their own ingenuity in

* The Army's interest in *offensive* use of wheat rust is underscored by their subsidy of a large-scale investigation at Minnesota University's Institute of Agriculture on the "aggressiveness" of wheat rust spores. The study included a systematic attempt to increase the infectivity and virulence of wheat rust spores with radiation and chemicals.

growing crops—recall the Liberty Gardens. As Harvard nutritionist Jean Mayer has observed, "To destroy crops—with herbicides or in any other way—is . . . to employ a weapon whose target is the weakest element of the civilian population." Thus, the use of anticrop agents strikes at the deepest moral fabric of society.

What are the real prospects for the widespread use of biological anticrop agents? In 1944, when presented by the Army with the possibility of destroying Japan's rice crop with biological agents, Admiral Leahy stated that such an undertaking "would violate every Christian ethic I have ever heard of and all the known laws of war." Apparently, our military leaders in Vietnam have changed the laws of war. The only remaining obstacle to an escalation of their ecological abuses, then, would seem to be the removal of any military personnel who may still cling to "Christian ethics"—and, given the current tone of Pentagon pronouncements, this step is not beyond the taking. When confronted with ethical criticism of the Army's aerial herbicide spraying program, a Pentagon spokesman replied:

> What's the difference between denying the Viet Cong rice by destroying it from the air or by sending in large numbers of ground forces to prevent the enemy from getting it? The end result's the same; only the first method takes far less men.
> —Benjamin Welles, "Pentagon Backs Use of Chemicals," New York *Times,* September 21, 1966.

In the end, then, apparently it will simply be a question of *feasibility,* and not one of morality, which will guide the military in its decisions to wage biological warfare against crops. Given the intrinsically greater stability of anticrop agents to human pathogens (only the former are currently being stockpiled at the Pine Bluff Arsenal), it is more than likely that anticrop biological warfare will be practiced well before antihuman biological warfare. The result, however, will be the same: the systematic destruction of the civilian population through starvation and disease.

CBW: ACE IN THE HOLE AGAINST
REVOLUTIONARY THREAT

Chemical and biological weapons systems are being developed for use in wars of counterinsurgency and in "limited wars," and as such they will be used against underdeveloped countries. This hypothesis is based on purely military considerations: Underdeveloped countries are intrinsically more susceptible to CBW attack than are countries like Russia and the United States. Underdeveloped countries tend to have ineffective methods of maintaining surveillance against epidemics (witness the devastating cholera epidemic which ravaged Ethiopia for months a few decades ago, before world health authorities discovered it). This is usually the result of inadequate public health, veterinary and agricultural services. The recent UN report on CBW warns that *any* country with such inadequacies would be highly vulnerable to a "systematic, covert plan to increase the incidence and spread of *normally* occurring diseases." It follows that, under similar circumstances, an overt BW attack would tend to be more devastating in an underdeveloped than in a developed country.

Chemical warfare against an underdeveloped country's food crop would also tend to have a disproportionately damaging effect. Since most such countries are dependent upon a single staple crop, often grown in a localized region (e.g., the Mekong Delta), chemical anticrop agents, like their biological counterparts, could be applied with telling effect with a minimum of military expertise. As will be shown later, crop destruction and jungle defoliation *per se* increase the likelihood that endemic diseases will spread out of control. (For example, a defoliated forest is replaced by secondary growth which may favor the rapid increase of rats and other rodent populations.)

Such a situation has already occurred in South Vietnam. Bubonic plague has long been endemic to Southeast Asia, but it was not a major health problem in South Vietnam prior to U.S. involvement there. In the five years preceding widescale U.S. intervention, there had been only one province which had reported cases of plague. By the end of 1966, however, fully 22 of the 29 provinces in South Vietnam had reported plague outbreaks. From January 1 to August 5, 1966, 2,002 cases were reported, including 116 deaths. By 1968, more than half the cases of plague reported in the world were coming from South Vietnam. (Unofficial estimates give 13,000 cases.)

Plague vaccine produced by the Cutter Laboratories in Berkeley, California, and tested by the Navy Biological Laboratory in Oakland, California, was first used sometime after 1962 to immunize all incoming servicemen. (There is good reason to believe that the principal reason why Khe San was never overrun was that the enemy suffered a major plague epidemic while U.S. forces were protected from contagion by the vaccine.) A limited amount of the vaccine is employed to protect members of the ARVN and an unknown proportion of the "friendly" civilian population.* The extent to which we have denied protection against plague to civilians in VC-controlled areas remains undetermined. However, to whatever extent it has occurred, this practice is biological warfare by default.

The Defense Department's interest in CBW as a counterinsurgency weapon is obvious from the kind of studies it sponsors. Recall the "feasibility study," entitled "The Impact of Chemical Attack on Guerrilla Food Crops," completed by the Research Analysis Corporation. (Another of their studies with a revealing title is "Evaluation of Counter-Insurgency Requirements in South East Asia.")

In the final analysis, the proof that we are considering CBW as a counterinsurgency weapon can be found in defense documents from major contractors. Like the Research Analysis Corporation, the Traveler's Research Center (a branch of the Traveler's Insurance Company), is primarily concerned with new military options afforded by CBW weapons. Their brochure succinctly sums up my contention:

> The Center's interest in this field [chemical and biological weapons systems] stems from our desire to assist the U.S.

* In fairness to the U.S. it must be observed that the South Vietnamese have insisted on using their own vaccine, which is probably ineffective.

in acquiring effective, humane, incapaciting (nonlethal) systems for coping with proliferating limited war and counterinsurgency.

Of course, when the Traveler's Center states that it intends to help the U.S. in "coping with proliferating limited war and counterinsurgency" it is speaking about the use of CBW in counterinsurgency operations in underdeveloped countries.

As I noted earlier, CB weapons readily lend themselves to covert use. As such they have become a potential tool of "special forces" and "advisors" in those underdeveloped countries in Latin America and Asia where revolutionary movements threaten "American security." In fact, according to the New York *Times*, January 24, 1969, the Army has trained 550 foreign officers in CBW techniques at Fort McClellan, Alabama, and is currently training officers from Korea, the Philippines, Thailand, and Saudi Arabia. In any discussion of the possibilities of CBW disarmanent, it would be injudicious to overlook the fact that chemical and biological weapons are America's "ace in the hole" for stemming the tide of revolution in underdeveloped countries around the world.

OUR CW STOCKPILE

Our preparedness in the field of chemical weapons is made clear even by unclassified listings of weapons and munitions. The Army admittedly maintains large stockpiles of gas-loaded munitions ranging from 105-mm to 8-inch shells. These munitions are constantly being updated for combat readiness. One can determine the extent of these stockpiles by the contents of a proposed shipment of "obsolete" and "surplus" chemical munitions. Included in a railroad shipment which ran afoul of incensed Congressmen were 12,000 tons of "surplus" munitions filled with GB (the original Nazi "sarin") and 5,000 tons of mustard gas. GB is lethal to 50 percent of all personnel exposed to as little as 40 drops (2,000 mg) through their clothing; inhalation doses are less than 1/100 of the contact dose. Among those munitions labeled "currently unserviceable" were 1,000-

pound GB bomb clusters containing 76 cluster bombs each; M-55 rockets loaded with GB; and numerous 1-ton mustard gas containers. The total weight of the munitions, including concrete casings, was approximately 27,000 tons. (The Nazis were unable to synthesize more than half a ton of GB gas over the entire period from 1936 to 1944. We completed stockpiling GB in 1957; the 12,000 tons of GB-filled munitions simply represent the surplus of that production.) This shipment was to have filled 809 railroad cars. Until a hue and cry went up from Congress, this shipment was to have been dumped in international waters, as were the four or so which preceded it.

Some of our more functional weapons loaded with gas include ground-to-ground missiles like the Sergeant; air-to-ground missiles like the Weteye (part of the TV-guided "eye" series); guided missiles of the ICBM class; land mines; and various multiple-fraction cluster-bomb types. The World War I concept of disseminating gas by ground-based generators has been largely abandoned except for the tactical use in Vietnam of wind generators for dispersing CS gas.

It is not difficult to prove that we presently have the capacity for conducting CBW in conjuction with military operations. We have developed and updated both chemical and biological agents, estimated their most likely immediate effects, stockpiled them, and developed means of delivering them. A large unanswered question concerns their possible long-term effects. And it is here that the answers stop coming.

CB WEAPONS:
AGENTS FOR ENVIRONMENTAL DISASSEMBLY

A basic element—in fact, the *sine qua non*—in the design of chemical and biological agents is too often overlooked. All CB agents are designed to persist and work in the face of environmental forces which might tend to degrade them. These weapons as a class are constructed to be as nonbiodegradable as possible; they are intentionally stabilized against physical decay.

The disastrous ecological result of this design criteria is

illustrated by the Army's defoliation program in Vietnam. This program, run under the absurd code name "Operation Ranchhand" (its motto: "Only we can prevent forests"), was conducted in complete disregard of potential ecological effects. It was not until about three years after the program started that the Army sponsored a study from the Midwest Research Institute. Even then, however, the entire report was compiled from a literature review, in the absence of any on-the-site inspection. Nevertheless, in April of 1969 the Army cited this report in defense of its contention that herbicides and defoliants "are harmless to the soil and to life and have no residual effect on the soil, being effective [for] no more than one growing season."

Such a statement is a blatant distortion of the truth: Even the most selective and seemingly "innocuous" of the battery of chemicals we use in Vietnam—2,4 D (2,4 Dichlorophenoxy acetic acid)—has been shown to be poisonous to lower organisms. One of these, *Daphnia,* a small arthropod which forms the major food source of many aquatic organisms, occupies a pivotal position in fresh-water food chains. A second chemical in extensive use in South Vietnam—2,4,5 T—has recently been implicated as a teratogen.* While there has been as yet no evidence that fish have been adversely affected by herbicide usage in Vietnam, a *Science* report by Fred H. Tshirley has indicated that herbicides are detrimental to other species in the aquatic ecosystem. For example, large areas of mangrove forest have been killed outright by the application of defoliants. Professor Tschirley estimates that 20 years will be necessary for regeneration of the mangrove forest to its pre-1962 condition. Because it has been impossible to know how much of the 16 percent of the treated forested area of South Vietnam has been sprayed more than once, the greatest damage to tropical forests cannot be adequately estimated. Trees that may have survived one spraying are likely to succumb to another. The principal hazard of our defoliation program is that it may destroy the intrinsic regenerative capacity of the forest itself. Should this happen, the native forests would probably be irreversibly re-

---

* Teratogen: a substance which produces birth defects.

placed by bamboo. Once this occurred the entire ecology of the area would be transformed, because bamboo halts the natural progression of forest regrowth.

An even grimmer picture of the ecologic situation in South Vietnam has been painted by Professors E. W. Pfeiffer and G. H. Orians, who inspected Vietnam for two weeks in April, 1969. The most ominous observation of their trip was that during a 60-mile voyage down one of the major rivers of South Vietnam they failed to sight a single bird, with the exception of a few fresh-water fishing species.

The intrinsic danger of the ecologic disruption accompanying defoliation is that animal vectors (carriers) of human disease may invade the newly created secondary forest or grassland. In Southeast Asia, where rodent-carried diseases like typhus and plague are endemic, this eventuality is frighteningly real. Both rodents and their insect parasites—like mites and fleas, which are the proximal vectors (immediate carriers) of the disease for humans—become much more numerous in secondary forest and grassland than in the primary forest. Scrub typhus has become a major health problem in other Southeast Asian countries where agriculture or extensive logging have affected the normal pattern of vegetation.

THE ATTITUDE OF THE SCIENTIST: HEAR NO EVIL, SEE NO EVIL...

The majority of scientists are likely to feel that it is outside their professional domain to make the moral or ethical judgments needed to take a stand on CBW.

I base this statement on the history of scientific response to this type of issue. One valuable sample of scientific opinion was obtained in a poll conducted in 1967 by the magazine *Industrial Research.* When asked if they felt that the United States was justified in employing chemical weapons for its military operations in South Vietnam, a large sampling of scientists in American industry responded to specific instances of chemical weapon use in the following way:

Type of Use	Yes	No
For use in crop destruction	65%	35%
For use in defoliation of "combat areas"	81%	19%
For use as nonlethal, antipersonnel weapons	79%	21%

When asked if they thought the U.S. would be justified in using lethal CB weapons, only 65 percent said "No," and in fact 20 percent said that the use of lethal weapons would be justified "in certain cases." Fully 89 percent supported the U.S. research and development program for CB weapons, agreeing that such weapons should be developed and tested "even if they are not intended to be employed." When asked if the U.S. should make a firm declaration of restraint from the use of CB weapons, more than 60 percent said "No."

Several incidents are useful illustrations of the attitudes of scientists toward the CBW problem. At the end of 1967, a handful of the members of the American Society of Microbiologists (ASM) attempted to extricate their organization from their advisory role to the Army Biological Laboratories at Fort Detrick. The debate which followed at both the national and local levels brought out much of the latent sentiment of microbiologists across the country.

At the Northern California Chapter of the ASM, the issue was joined when members proposed a sense resolution (an informal means of applying moral persuasion) to disband the ASM's Advisory Committee to the military. The more liberal view among those who supported the continuation of the Advisory Committee emphasized that it would enable the organization to keep a "finger-in-pot" for influencing military decisions on CBW. However, most of the opposition based their objections to the proposed disbandment on the grounds that it contained implicit statements of an "ethical" nature which were outside the rightful province of a professional scientific society. For example, one member declared, in a letter to the local organization, that she felt it was undesirable to "shroud the organization with moral or political views." Another stated the case for the opposition succinctly: "[the resolution] commits our members by a majority vote to an implied ethical and moral position which has no place in a professional society."

The resolution was defeated at the local level. However, at the 1968 national meeting of the ASM, Salvador Luria used his prerogative as outgoing president to dissolve the Advisory Committee anyway. His own sentiments were that the association of the ASM with the defense establishment was ethically incompatible with the proper roles and functions of a scientific society. The fact that Luria chose to use such moral and ethical grounds for dissolving the committee outraged the society's membership. In a special plenary session, the membership overruled Luria and reestablished the Advisory Committee.

A second major debate raged around the propriety of the American Institute of Biological Scientists' jointly sponsoring two symposia honoring the twenty-fifth anniversary of Fort Detrick in 1968. In spite of forceful opposition from some of the members, the general membership of AIBS supported the decision to sponsor the symposium. In stating their case (see the letter by Allen, Emerson, Grant, Scheiderman, and Siekovitz in the June 21, 1968 issue of *Science*), the opponents had maintained that all research activities pertaining to CBW are immoral and that no life scientist should honor a laboratory dedicated to the perversion of the life sciences. In response to such statements, one member replied in a letter in *Science* that "morality is a sometime thing" and that "to take a moral stance . . . is perhaps the last refuge of a scoundrel."

The few protests by scientists against the use of defoliants in Vietnam have been met by a flurry of criticism from fellow scientists. When three members of the Board of the AAAS took the position that the use of defoliants should be stopped because of unknown ecological hazards, they were promptly repudiated. Professor A. Carl Leopold supported the use of defoliants in South Vietnam in a *Bioscience* editorial, stating that such agents "are a military device of an unprecedented degree of harmlessness." (Results of tests begun in 1966 by the National Cancer Institute have since been released implicating 2,4 D as a "potentially dangerous" and 2,4,5 T as a "probably dangerous" agent: Both agents were found to produce birth defects in mouse fetuses.)

From the strict logic of a scientist it was possible for

Leopold to make such a statement. That is to say, in 1967 there was no evidence to show that 2,4,5 T was harmful, but at that time only the *direct* toxicity of herbicides had been intensively studied. From the pragmatic logic of a militarist, it was still possible to make such a statement even *after* the teratogenic effects of 2,4,5 T (and possibly of other herbicides, such as 2,4 D and cacodylic acid) had been revealed by the National Cancer Institute. Defoliants continue to have the same military value that they did prior to their testing in pregnant animals: they can destroy vegetation which blocks the line of sight of a pilot on a bombing run, as well as life-giving food sources for "hostile" civilians. As such they will continue to be used in South Vietnam. The general military attitude toward a "scientific" appraisal of potential health hazards is perhaps best summarized by a military pragmatist like former General Jacques Rothschild: "If the U.S. is involved in a killing war initiated by aggression, we should not forego the advantage of the use of weapons based on our advanced technology." (Letter to *Science*, April 14, 1967.)

Astonishingly, scientists in the Nixon Administration have continued to underwrite the military's use of teratogens like 2,4,5 T in South Vietnam. And Lee DuBridge, President Nixon's White House Science Adviser, has responded to the National Cancer Institute's warning by indicating that the Defense Department need not stop its use of 2,4,5 T as long as it confined applications to areas "remote from populations." (*The New Republic,* January 10, 1970, p. 19.)

It is the scientist who has provided America with its advanced technology. But as long as he continues to believe that his professional standing prevents him from making moral judgments on the political implications of his work, he is doomed to be a technician in the service of military pragmatists.

ADDENDA

On November 26, 1969, President Nixon announced that the United States would curtail its research and use of CBW weapons. I subsequently released the following statement:

Even a careful reading of Nixon's November 26 statement on chemical and biological warfare leads the uninitiated to the erroneous conclusion that this proclamation disengages us from our CBW effort. We feel this is a dangerous misconception.

Nixon declared that we "renounce the first use of incapacitating chemicals." The U.S. has been using at least one incapacitating chemical (CS-2 lung gas) and possibly two (DM gas), in Vietnam for the last five years. Requisitions for CS-2 gas (and lesser amounts of its predecessors —CS and CS-1) came to 6,063,000 pounds in 1969 (Congressional Record, July 12, 1969, H4775). A White House spokesman obfuscated this contradiction by indicating that Nixon excludes "tear gases" from his statement. Apparently CS-2 gas is now considered such a "tear gas." Is it possible in this age of double-think to simply give an asphyxiating gas (CS-2) the same designation as a previous lacrimator (CS) and thereby convert it into a "tear gas"?

Nixon urges the Senate to ratify the Geneva Protocol of 1925. Note that this Protocol not only included incapacitating gases but also so-called "tear gases." (See Congressional Record, May 21, 1969, E4207.) Evidently, if we ratify the Geneva Protocol, it will be on our *own* terms and not those intended by the original drafters.

Similarly, Nixon declares that he associates the U.S. with the "principles and objectives" of the United Kingdom Draft Convention; yet, Nixon's own statement clearly exempts the U.S. from any ban on chemical and, by implication, biological anticrop agents. Anticrop chemicals have been sprayed over 16 percent of the forested area of South Vietnam, helping to change Vietnam from an exporter to an importer of rice. One defoliant (2,4,5 T) has been linked to infant deformities in Vietnam. The actual U.K. Convention expressly condemns use of biological (and by intent, chemical) anticrop weapons (British Convention, Article I). The existence of growing stockpiles of biological anticrop agents both here (Pine Bluff Arsenal) and abroad (Thailand) clearly belies Nixon's stated intention that we renounce "all . . . methods of biological warfare."

Finally, there is the "loophole clause" in Nixon's statement which permits the U.S. to continue biological research under the guise of a defensive program. (We might recall that the *existing* offensive biological warfare program was originally justified by precisely this rationale!) Two of the measures mentioned as part of this defensive program are "immunization" and "safety measures." In the Congressional Record of April 21 (H2862), Dr. John S. Foster of the Department of Defense declared that public immunization against biological weapons is "logistically impossible" and would be "generally injurious to health." The Department of Defense clearly has not considered public safety to be threatened by any foreseeable enemy use of BW. How does this fact jibe with Nixon's statement on the need for BW defense research?

If the U.S. is to gain the moral confidence of the world, Nixon's statement on CBW must be a credible statement. To be such, we feel that it must also include the following:

1. That, realizing public safety against BW can only be insured by strong international agreements, we renounce all research in the field of biological warfare.
2. That our renunciation of biological warfare *expressly* include anticrop agents.
3. That we adhere to International Law (The Hague Convention) and ban the use of herbicides on civilian food crops.
4. That in accord with the intent of the Geneva Protocol we renounce the use of "tear gases."

On February 21, 1970, in accord with President Nixon's statement on CBW, a Congressional Subcommittee headed by Representative Henry S. Reuss (Dem., Wisconsin) recommended that the Army close its open-air testing facilities at Dugway, Utah. The Army responded by stating that testing of chemical (and presumably biological) weapons would not be discontinued since such tests "may be necessary to ensure the development of a strong deterrent capability." (San Francisco *Chronicle*, February 23, 1970.)

In August, 1970, the Senate was presented with two bills which would have banned the use of defoliants. Both were defeated.

Joshua Lederberg

is Professor of Genetics and Biology, chairman of the Department of Genetics, and director of the Kennedy Laboratory of Molecular Medicine, at Stanford University. He received a B.A. from Columbia College in 1944, and a Ph.D. from Yale University in 1947. He also holds honorary degrees from the Yale, Columbia, and Wisconsin universities.

Professor Lederberg has pursued a distinguished research career in genetics and in the chemistry and evolution both of unicellular organisms and of man. He was awarded the Nobel Prize in 1958 for studies on the organization of the genetic material in bacteria. He writes the nationally syndicated Washington *Post* column "Science and Man."

In the following article Professor Lederberg deals with dangers that might arise from the thousands of chemical food additives used in the United States. He suggests that biological scientists might do much to increase our knowledge of the possible harmfulness of these substances, and proposes that scientists consider themselves "vigilantes" in working to protect the general public health. It is of interest to note that he included the artificial sweetener cyclamate on his list of strongly suspected substances in his article, which was prepared *before* the government announced the ban on that substance.

The National Academy of Science estimates that 2,000 chemical substances are used as food additives. In order for a food additive in use before 1958 to be listed on the "generally recognized as safe" (GRAS) list of the FDA and be free of government regulation, the manufacturer merely must state that he considers the product safe; no laboratory testing is required. To remove the substance from the list the FDA may either go into court with laboratory evidence that the substance causes cancer in animals, or furnish compelling evidence of its injuriousness to man. Only two food additives, one of them cyclamate, have ever been removed from the GRAS list. The fact that the FDA, due to woeful understaffing and a serious lack of proper laboratory facilities, is incapable of testing very many questionable food additives, makes Dr. Lederberg's "vigilante" proposal all the more relevant.

Food
Additives

Many of the brilliant intellectual talents of our era are closely engaged in investigations of nature whose long-term impact cannot be overestimated, and which cannot be impeded without great risk to the basic values embodied in the definition of man as "the rational animal." Nevertheless, many scientists are concerned over dissociation of their intellectual effort from the manifest and urgent problems of contemporary life. All too often, however, when they attempt to deal directly with major problems, they are frustrated by the slow pace at which national policies respond to the challenges of—for instance—peace, population, and pollution. The very scope of these challenges also tends to minimize the utility of the scientists' own individual expertise. In fact, on many issues the basic scientist holds little advantage over the average concerned citizen.

Without demanding these expressions of civic conscience, we suggest that many scientists could advantageously use their creative imagination to seek ways in which their special expertise could be applied to the possible solution of more obscure, if smaller, problems, or to the discovery and anticipation of insidious new ones. A biochemist, for example, may be uniquely aware of the toxicity of an environmental contaminant; a physicist might see parallels between his own theoretical work and the conditions for forming or dissipating smog; and so on. The individual creative mind can best determine its own locus of highest efficacy. Groups of scientists may be able to refine the anticipation of technical shocks—like synthetic substitutes for commodities imported from underdeveloped countries, or techniques of surveillance manipulation and intrusion on personal privacy—in time to plan for their amelioration.

In many sectors, small areas of science have been exploited as the foundations of major burgeonings of technology. Take for example the internal-combustion engine: We daily suffer from the consequences of the disharmony rampant in that technological growth—for instance, in the profligate poisoning of air with lead, nickel, and other smog-causing delicacies. Sensitive minds have reacted with a revolutionary movement that would seem to be aimed at taking us all back to the paleolithic age, a move that from the start is utterly unrealistic in terms of both the sacrifice of essential economic benefits of technology (food, shelter, health) and the loss of the kind of education and culture that thrive on economic surplus. It is also unrealistic in terms of the powerlessness that a savage culture would exhibit in comparison with the positive forces that technology can create. The net effect of the retreatist idea seems to be an alienation of life goals that threatens the very continuity of our culture. This is manifest, on the one hand, by the dropping-out and turning inward of the "counter-culture" movements; on the other, by a reinforcement of the illiberalism of the middle-class majority, exhibited in taxpayers' revolts against the support of education, of research, and indeed of all forms of social progress in the public sector.

I do not propose that the major blame for this conflict be heaped on the shoulders of the abstract scientist. However, it is evident that too often his abstraction has been a contributory factor—e.g., the denial of problem-solving techniques, or even of the existence of certain problems if they are beyond the reach of the methods of objective verification and reproducibility that are the core of the scientific method. In fact, I must condemn those social scientists who blindly have aped this kind of illusion of rigor much more than the physical scientists who have furnished the successful models of this approach in their own sphere. On the other hand, the scientist can still make an important contribution by exhibiting the success of compassionate rationality in seeking solutions to urgent human problems. For instance, the basic question of race-genetics should not be whether one race is genetically inferior. It should be whether we can isolate specific factors (genetic or environmental) that hinder successful acculturation, with a view to finding the remedies. In this light, the facts that at least 5 percent of blacks are heterozygous for an abnormal hemoglobin (the sickle cell trait), and that a great many poor children—black, brown, and white—are mentally retarded as a consequence of dysnutrition during fetal life, loom immensely larger than do scholastic debates about statistical studies of racial differences in genes "for intelligence." Everything we know about developmental genetics already tells us how milieu-dependent such genetic factors must be in any case, which deflates what little scientific interest inherently attaches to such debates. The other extreme, a passionate but unfactual insistence that individuals or racial groups are likely to be born with no significant difference in their biological adaptation to their present environment, is equally destructive to the actual solution of important problems.

I suggested earlier that a scientist could well apply his special knowledge in a kind of vigilance over contemporary affairs, to seek out specific opportunities where special knowledge suddenly becomes particularly relevant. If he investigates specific situations, he may be surprised how often he knows much more about a facet of some technical misapplication than almost anyone else: There are very few areas of technology where we begin to know enough to be justifiably complacent. The rule is that the basic work has never been done.

This widespread lack of basic work was dramatized for me recently when I realized that the safety of chlorine, as used in the sanitization of drinking water, swimming pools, utensils, dressing poultry, and so on, had never been carefully scrutinized in the United States since the chlorination of water supplies was first adopted 60-odd years ago. Today a large proportion of the drinking water in this country is chlorinated—a public-health measure which is undoubtedly the major bulwark against epidemics of typhoid fever, dysentery, and cholera. It would undoubtedly be conservative to say that millions of lives have been saved by its promulgation. In fact, concentrated urban settlement would be impractical without chlorination or some equivalent means of removing polluting bacteria from domestic water.

Chlorine was used for the treatment of sewage as early as 1835 (long before the work of Pasteur and Koch proved that infectious disease was an attack upon the human body by living microbes), the rationale being the dissipation of foul odors which were, for many years, blamed for contagion. Chlorine was first introduced into an American waterworks at Jersey City, New Jersey, in 1909, in response to potential contamination by sewage from nearby towns. The city demanded that the water company either install expensive filtration equipment or pay for diversion of the sewage. After considerable litigation the court found that the chlorination process was both safe and effective for the production of potable water.

It is difficult to reconstruct the arguments that would support, by contemporary standards, the safety of chlorination. Over the years a few tests of acute toxicity have shown that chlorinated water can be safely drunk in concentrations of 50 to 100 parts per million, by comparison with the 1 to 2 ppm generally required for water purification. And, during World War I, chlorine (under the name "Dakin's solution," the only available disinfectant for contaminated wounds) did what was generally considered a splendid first-aid job. But the only serious contribution to the subject that I could find did not appear until 1968, and that was by a German scientist, Dr. H. Drückrey. Drückrey, of the Max Planck Institute for Immunobiology at Freiburg, reared laboratory rats for seven successive generations on drinking water supplemented with 100 ppm of chlorine. The treated animals showed no obvious pathology, and no shortening of life-span as compared to that of the controls.

This is an impressive demonstration, but one which should have been made at least 50 years earlier because many theoretical suspicions concerning human uses of chlorine remain. For instance, no modern methods have been applied to test the claim that chlorine is rapidly dissipated when it reacts with organic material in the body's fluids. We have no clear picture of where, how, or how quickly chlorine is converted into chlorine ions within the body, nor of intermediate products of that conversion. These days, what with the help of radioactive tracers, it should not be very difficult to find out.

What little we do know of the chemistry of chlorine reactions is portentous. It *should* at times react with nitrogenous groups from various sources to form substances which eventually reach and react with DNA, the genetic material of body cells—though probably only when used in badly contaminated waters needing heavy doses of chlorine.

Nobody knows for sure, because the reactions of chloride with DNA have been remarkably little studied. What we have found out along these lines in our laboratories is this: We have confirmed that chlorine reacts very readily with DNA, and that it also inactivates purified DNA very rapidly. The data suggest that this inactivation process is actually the mechanism by which chlorine performs its intended function of killing bacteria and viruses. We also have considerable evidence, not yet completely conclusive, that chlorine causes mutations in the DNA of bacterial and yeast cells exposed to it.

This laboratory work does not necessarily mean that chlorine is a genetic hazard in man. It is conceivable that it is completely neutralized by -SH groups and other groups in proteins in the body fluids and in cell sap before it can react significantly with the DNA of tissue and germ cells. But this is no more than a reasonable supposition, and it might not be exactly right. We need more intense biochemical studies of the fate of chlorine introduced into the body. It is even more surprising that we have no epidemiological comparisons of districts which have, versus those that have not, intensely chlorinated their water supplies over periods of years.

In any case, the theoretical arguments, not yet experimentally resolved, about chlorine are at least as impressive as those about toxic residues, which have prevented radiation from being used for the sterilization of foods and water. However, radiation is an environmental factor to which there has already been almost too much scientific and public hypersensitization, at least by comparison with chemical environmental factors.

Very similar remarks could be made about a host of environmental factors. Rather than dwell in too much detail, I will offer a challenge to other scientists to read such references as "Water Quality Criteria," and food additives handbooks which contain long lists of compounds about whose biological effects little is generally known. One solitary reader might have the essential clue. As a teaser, I am providing a list (Table 1) of a few items which have caught my attention from the armory of food additives—substances which are intentionally added to foods and about which I believe reasonable questions can be asked concerning their effects on human health. These additives are not used out of malice; they are part of our economy of food technology, and they should not be condemned if they actually present no hazards. Do we know? And if we are unsure, how should the burden of risks be allocated?

Effective vigilance demands of the scientist more than his goodwill and energy. He must educate himself, more than in the past, about the social and technological realities he has overlooked. He also must find an institutional framework which will sustain the autonomy of his critical thinking—thinking which may eventually be imperiled by systems of research support confined to the contracting of specific results. That framework should also make some accommodation, in its system of prestige and rewards, for the contributions of critical vigilance as well as for those of topical analysis.

I am all too certain that many fellow scientists will discover

Table 1
A Selective Listing of Chemicals Used in Food Processing

acetal	hydrogen peroxide
acetone peroxide	nitrosyl chloride
allyl isothiocyanate	peracetic acid
axodicarbonamide	phenylethanol
benzoyl peroxide	sodium methyl sulfate
cyclamates	sodium nitrite
diethylpyrocarbonate	stannous chloride
ethylene oxide–methyl	sodium hypochlorite;
formate fumigant	chlorine; chloramine–T;
formaldehyde	chlorine dioxide

SOURCE: NRC publication No. 1274. (Items selected by J. Lederberg.)

their own special nightmares, on the basis of their personal expertise, when they review the long lists of approved additives. Of course, I realize that if the FDA had to give adequate scientific assurance about the absolute safety of every additive, we might starve to death while the necessary research was being done, and again when new insights into sources of peril emerged. Nevertheless, the food industry and the scientific community, as well as the government, should be sharpening their focus in dealing with these vital problems.

We should also think of more flexible legal and regulatory approaches to these problems. Abbott Laboratories* should not be charged with insincerity for having asserted its confidence that cyclamates were safe, but the cold, hard, retrospective fact is that the main risk was being borne by millions of consumers, not by the corporation. On the other hand, a government agency probably would have little to lose in responding to public arousal by banning a product before all the evidence was in.

Perhaps existing laws could be altered to provide for unconditional liability for the eventual hazard of a product when the FDA has certified a bill of particulars, for example about bladder cancer or mutation. An outfit like Abbott Laboratories would then have to back up its confidence by affirming its willingness to share the costs of ill results stemming from risks which prove to be not wisely taken on behalf of its customers. It might also be required to post an insurance bond, a move which would require the approval of what would most assuredly be an eagle-eyed and conservative insurance underwriter. In the long run this insurance (paid for by the consumer, any way one looks at it) would indirectly pay for important research on hazards, and for the development of safer alternatives—as well as encourage broader discretion by the purveyors of unproven products.

Protecting our genes from environmental damage is crucial

---

* Abbott Laboratories, it must be noted, dealt entirely correctly and prudently with transmitting the laboratory data on the basis of which cyclamates were eventually banned. These remarks are addressed to statements made by the management at a time when the safety of cyclamates was merely controversial.

for two reasons. One is parental concern for the health of children both living and planned-for. The other is the social burden of handicapped and retarded children who need not only our compassion but our material resources and the best of our technical skills. Furthermore, no self-respecting individual can be totally indifferent to his responsibility as a vessel of the species—as a trustee of a role in human evolution that answers to the most profound religious instincts.

Research geneticists are beginning to speak up more and more pointedly about their concern over genetic hazards. Not too many years ago, I was able to compartmentalize my own thinking to such a degree that I did not immediately grasp the relationship between an abstraction, like the statistics of "lethal mutations" in fruit flies, and the human impact of malformation in the newborn. The current generation of young scientists is less likely to miss such connections. However, we all have a basic responsibility to go beyond an emotional expression of concern, and to use it to energize the search for authentic scientific measures of potential hazards, and for means to neutralize them.

Unfortunately, just as many academic scientists have rediscovered the importance of relating basic science to human needs, the political establishment, which controls the purse strings, has turned away—perhaps in bafflement or resentment —from the difficulties that a truly careful use of scientific thinking uncovers about the world we make for ourselves. Unfortunately, nonresearch on (for example) new viruses arising in nature may conceal them from being promptly seen, but it will not make them disappear from the real world. Nor will it change the facts—only our insight into them—about the importance of viruses, or food additives, or drugs, as agents of genetic damage.

We biologists have still not done the job that badly needs to be done to assess the really important hazards of environmental chemicals in such areas as cancer, teratology (embryo damage), and mutation. We know that these effects are often associated with one another, so that when cyclamate derivatives are proven to break chromosomes, we should already be alert to cancer potential. We may still make costly mistakes for lack of basic knowledge of chemical effects on cells.

We have a few fundamental tools today, especially in genetic studies of cultured human cells, that might begin to clear things up. We can also be looking more closely at the fundamental chemistry of DNA. For example, a somewhat surprising report that LSD forms chemical complexes with DNA in the test tube (see T. E. Wagner in *Nature* magazine, June, 1969) adds weight to claims that LSD breaks chromosomes. Even more recent work, indicating that the tryptamines, a whole class of related compounds which occur naturally in the brain, also react with nucleic acids, may unify these findings. After all, we have still to work out how these agents can affect brain function at all in such low concentrations, and nucleic acids in brain cells may well be their targets.

A group of geneticists and cell biologists, headed by Dr. Alexander Hollaender, retired director of biological research at the Oak Ridge National Laboratory, has organized a new "Environmental Mutagen Society" to help further the scientific understanding of these difficult problems. Such a group will fill a vitally useful function if it does nothing more than provide a channel for mutual communications among a wide range of separate disciplines: the DNA biochemist ordinarily does not have his attention directed to matters like outbreaks of chromosome diseases of newborns.

It is not likely that we will—and certainly we do not wish to—learn very much about genetic hazards from observations of catastrophes in human populations. We have a great deal of taxing work ahead in trying to set up scientifically valid and politically useful criteria for laboratory studies of these elusive but all-important hazards. This line of protective research should surely be the mandate of many more institutions than are now involved in looking for trouble in the human condition. I would not, however, want to rely too heavily on institutionalized answers to these kinds of problems—they are likely to become mere counterestablishments. After a flurry of resounding successes, they will have their own dogmas to defend. Instead, the responsibility must be diffused through the entire scientific–

academic community to provide innovative and unrelenting criticism, from every possible source of expertise and insight.

The project orientation of research support is fatal to this kind of vigilance, for it buys a scientist's time in order to accomplish a prespecified and negotiated task. So long as such projects are not too closely supervised, much critical and creative work is still possible with their indispensable support. The universities have, however, reached a state of such abject dependence on project funding that their academic freedom is in serious jeopardy. A reasonable answer would be a demand on the part of the university faculties and administrations that a modicum of *undirected* research is an essential adjunct of a system of project support. This could even be regarded as an indispensable "overhead" item, to sustain the environment of a free university that, it is generally agreed, is most conducive to effective basic research. Without some room for a maneuver of this kind, the very abundance of centralized support for university research may stifle the scientists from the full exercise of their obligation of vigilant criticism. And a period of recession after vigorous growth is even more perilous.

John W. Gofman

is Professor of Medical Physics at the University of California at Berkeley, and Research Associate at the Lawrence Radiation Laboratory at Livermore. He received his B.A. in chemistry from Oberlin College in 1939, and a Ph.D. in nuclear and physical chemistry from Berkeley in 1943. He also earned an M.D. from the University of California Medical Center, San Francisco, in 1946.

Doctor Gofman's research career has spanned a wide range of scientific endeavors, including the discovery of isotopes of heavy elements, the invention of processes for plutonium separation, the investigation of the physiology of blood serum fats, and research on the effects of low-dose radiation on chromosomes and on cancer induction. He is the author of some 130 scientific publications and three technical books, and since 1963 has served as coeditor of *Advances in Biological and Medical Physics*.

Arthur R. Tamplin

is a Group Leader in the Biomedical Division of the Lawrence Radiation Laboratory, where he has worked since 1963. He was awarded his B.A. in biochemistry in 1953, and his Ph.D. in biophysics in 1959, both from the University of California at Berkeley. Between 1959 and 1963, Dr. Tamplin served as Research Associate with the RAND Corporation.

In this article, Drs. Gofman and Tamplin discuss radiation hazards posed by nuclear reactors and other sources of nuclear energy, and the failure of the Atomic Energy Commission to understand the magnitude of the hazard and to deal with it in a manner which would ensure the health and safety of the American people.

Nuclear Radiation

The threat of radiation poisoning looms large on the American horizon. We estimate that many thousands of our countrymen are contracting radiation-induced leukemia and other forms of cancer, and that the number will increase in the near future. This public health disaster is a manifestation of the ultimate retribution and irony that face a society of which it can be said, at best, that it is possessed of a grossly inverted set of values centering around greed and lust for power, and, at worst, that it functions as though it were devoid of any system of human values. The irony aspect arises because it appears that eventually nobody—the perpetrators included—will be able to find a place to hide from the consequences of our having so deeply involved ourselves with products and pastimes totally unrelated to worthwhile human needs and goals. A prime example of this kind of worthless and destructive activity is the production and application of nuclear explosives.

A HISTORY OF THE ATOMIC ENERGY COMMISSION

To understand the present threat we face from the radioactive contamination of the environment it is helpful to know the circumstances surrounding the founding and development of the Atomic Energy Commission. The Atomic Era was ushered in during World War II with the development and use of atomic bombs. The newly-found ability to destroy life in a wholesale, efficient, inexpensive manner was indeed awesome. The Congress of the United States recognized this potential and, in what appeared a sound move, decided that the further development of atomic energy must be kept out of the hands of the military establishment. Thus, the Atomic Energy Act created a civilian Atomic Energy Commission and charged it with the dual responsibility of meeting the national security needs in atomic weapons and at the same time of bringing to society all the benefits which nuclear energy must surely have in store. A last proviso was duly added: that all this should be accomplished with careful attention to the safety and health of the public. No doubt the motivation of the Congress was of the highest. The result, however, has been a fiasco of mammoth proportions.

Several hopeless ingredients are now evident in the mix which has led to the present danger to life provided by the technology of atomic energy as developed under the aegis of the Atomic Energy Commission:

1. The same cast of characters held the responsibility for the military and "peaceful" aspects of the development of atomic energy. Indeed, throughout the structure, people with their points of view, philosophy, and goals shuttled daily between the tasks of developing nuclear explosives for military purposes, testing such explosives, seeking out beneficial by-products of atomic technology, and protecting the health and welfare of the public.

2. The military aspects provided a wondrous cloak of cover for any stupidity, rashness, and lack of concern for human health and safety that could occur in this overall activity. Criticism of direction, of goals, of errors was easily silenced through the use of security classification and secrecy, and it is still so silenced.

3. A conflict of interest was inevitable for an agency, in this case the Atomic Energy Commission, charged with the dual responsibility for gung-ho development of a most treacherous technology and for simultaneous protection of health and safety of the public.

4. The stage was set for the creation of a bureaucratic

super-agency of government, virtually free of many of the check-and-balance restraints that are requisite in a democracy.

As a consequence of these factors there has been, over the last 25 years, an unbridled promotion of atomic energy by the AEC, with scant regard to public health and safety. This has brought us, we will show, to a potentially disastrous situation.

ATOMIC ENERGY PROGRAMS

The atomic energy commodity has been promoted by the AEC in two forms. The nuclear reactor, which utilizes controlled nuclear fission for the production of electrical energy, was groomed as the answer to America's growing use of electric power, the output of which has been doubling every eight years. Quietly put aside is the question of disposing of the radioactive waste products of the reactors. The topic of "thermal pollution" is also inadequately treated. Reactors require huge amounts of water, for cooling. This requirement for coolant water is such that the projected development of power reactors would lead to the raising of the temperature of our waterways. Through adverse effects in the interaction of aquatic organisms and their environment, this thermal pollution could trigger an ecological catastrophe.

The AEC has never asked the fundamental question: Why should our power requirements double every eight years, when the population is only growing at 1 percent per year? All the evidence indicates that the additional electrical power might be for the production of additional consumer garbage which only adds to our pollution problems.

The nuclear bomb, hydrogen or atom type, also releases copious quantities of energy, albeit a bit rapidly. Obviously, thought the atomic-energy developers, such bombs have to be good for something, especially since no one was particularly enthusiastic about firing them off all over the landscape à la Hiroshima–Nagasaki. And so was born the wondrous child known as Plowshare—the "peaceful" nuclear explosive which would move mountains, divert rivers, create harbors, carve canals, loosen underground natural gas so it could become available, and do many other marvelous tasks for man. Unfortunately, when you move a mountain with a nuclear bomb you also release tremendous amounts of radioactivity into the atmosphere. And after you release natural gas with underground nuclear explosions, as proposed in the "Gas Buggy" program, you then are left with the prospect of pumping radioactive gas into the kitchens of millions of unsuspecting housewives.

The by-product radioactive substances were promoted with a vigor equal to that for the energy commodity. Industry could use strong radiation sources for many tasks, and medicine surely could use radiation sources and radioactive substances for the treatment, diagnosis, and study of disease. The curve of shipment of such radioactive by-products has risen steadily over the years, to the great satisfaction of atomic-energy promoters, for this meant obvious success of the endeavor. That some of the radioactive materials get lost in shipment, and irradiate unknown numbers of people in unknown places, was a minor nuisance. That the utilization of these radioactive substances meant the radiation of workers, of bystanders, and of medical subjects obviously could not be of concern, for the handling would, of course, be with great care.

AEC MYTHOLOGY

Obviously there are grave dangers associated with all uses of atomic energy. Instead of attempting to cope with these difficulties in a reasonable and scientific manner, the AEC has developed a set of myths calculated to obscure the scientific facts. One can properly regard these myths as an invention, conscious or subconscious, that always serves the purposes of the atomic-energy promoters.

Myth No. 1: "Maybe there exists some amount of radiation that is a 'safe *threshold*.' " By this is meant that possibly cancer or leukemia or genetic injury won't occur provided the total radiation dose is kept below some magic number. We now know that this is a convenient hope—especially of atomic-energy promoters—but it is a hope unsupported by any scientific evidence. Indeed, what *supposed* evidence was said to exist for so-called "safe" thresholds has repeatedly been discredited by numerous reputable scientists. But the promoters keep hoping that somehow, somewhere, evidence will be developed that a safe amount of radiation exists. Indeed, even now, the present leadership of the Bio-Medical Division of the Lawrence Laboratory (AEC supported) has a program labeled "The Search for a Safe Threshold of Radiation." At the same time, stronger and stronger direct evidence in man and in experimental animals points clearly to the law that *no safe* amount of radiation exists. Harm, in the form of extra cancers, extra leukemias, will occur down to the lowest doses. We even know from the remarkable work of Dr. Alice Stewart in England, confirmed in the United States by Dr. Brian MacMahon, that just a diagnostic x-ray examination in late pregnancy provokes a *50 percent* increase in childhood cancer *and* leukemia! So, as you can see, the idea of a "safe" amount of radiation has been rather hopelessly shattered.

Myth No. 2: "Maybe slow delivery of radiation, as in atomic energy applications, won't produce as much cancer and leukemia as delivery all at once." Some *apparent* evidence in experimental animals seemed to support this idea. Many scientists did question this—notably E. B. Lewis and Linus Pauling. Indeed, the International Commission on Radiological Protection had repeatedly stated clearly that it was *unsound* to *count* on any protection against cancer and leukemia from *slow* delivery of radiation. They refused to count on such protection. Strangely enough, even the U.S. Federal Radiation Council claimed it didn't count on such protection by slow delivery of radiation. The real point concerning the FRC is that they didn't use their own statement in practice.

THE FACTS OF THE RADIATION HAZARD

On the basis of these myths, the Federal Radiation Council has set a "tolerance level" for radiation at 0.17 Rads per whole body weight per year. (A Rad is a unit of measure for radiation absorbed per body weight.) It is now clear, from scientific evidence that has been accumulating over the past 20 years, that there is *no* evidence for a tolerance level for radiation. *Any* amount of radiation, delivered at *any* rate, can be expected to cause damage. Unless the FRC guidelines are reduced *now* by at least tenfold, down to 0.017 Rads, the consequences to the public's health will be disastrous. This statement is based on estimates of radiation-induced cancer cases from several important sources of information, including:

a. Study of survivors of Hiroshima–Nagasaki by the Atomic Bomb Casualty Commission.

b. Study of patients *treated* with radiation for nonmalignant diseases earlier in life and then developing cancer or leukemia.

c. Study of children who commonly received irradiation to the neck area in one unfortunate era of American medicine.

d. Study of the occurrence of lung cancer in uranium miners in the United States.

The data from these studies is summarized in Table 1. The doubling dose is the amount of radiation exposure it takes to double the rate of cancer over the spontaneous rate of occur-

Table 1
Best Estimates of Doubling Dose of Radiation for Human Cancers and the Increase in Incidence Rate per Rad of Exposure

Organ Site	Doubling Dose	% Increase in Incidence Rate per Rad
Leukemia	30–60 Rads	1.6–3.3%
Thyroid Cancer		
Adults	100 Rads	1%
Young persons	5–10 Rads	10–20%
Lung cancer	~ 175 Rads	0.6%
Breast cancer	~ 100 Rads	1%
Stomach cancer	~ 230 Rads	0.4%
Pancreas cancer	~ 125 Rads	0.8%
Bone cancer	~ 40 Rads	2.5%
Lymphatic plus other hematopoetic organs	~ 70 Rads	1.4%
Carcinomatosis of miscellaneous origin	~ 60 Rads	1.7%

rence. Also given is the percentage increase of cancer occurrence for an increase of 1 Rad of radiation exposure.

For such an array of widely divergent organ systems, *already including* hard data for nearly all the major forms of human cancers, it is amazing indeed that there is such a small range for the estimated doubling dose. Correspondingly, there is a very small range in the estimated increase in incidence rate per Rad for these widely differing organ sites in which cancers arise.

Studies have recently been presented on the incidence of cancer in the first ten years of life of children who for diagnostic purposes were irradiated while still in the womb. The general estimate of the amount of radiation received by the developing fetus in such procedures is 2 to 3 Rads. The studies show a 50 percent increase in the incidence rate, for all forms of cancer plus leukemia, associated with diagnostic irradiation of the infant *in utero*. So, for 2 to 3 Rads to the infant *in utero,* a 50 percent increase in incidence rate of various cancers leads to an estimate of 4 to 6 Rads as the doubling dose for childhood leukemia plus cancer due to diagnostic irradiation *in utero*. Let us underestimate the risk, and use the higher number, 6 Rads, as the doubling dose for *in utero* induction of subsequent leukemia plus other childhood cancers. This means a 17 percent increase in the incidence rate of such leukemias plus cancers per Rad of *in utero* exposure of the infant.

It is not at all surprising that infants *in utero* should appear *most* sensitive to irradiation, children *next* in sensitivity, and adults *third* (but *by no means* low). This is precisely the order in which these groups stand in terms of the fraction of their cells undergoing cell division at any time—and much evidence suggests these are the cells most susceptible to cancer induction.

GENERAL LAWS OF CANCER INDUCTION BY RADIATION

In view of the widely diverse forms of human cancers plus leukemias showing such striking similarity in their risk of radiation induction, it does not appear at all rash to propose some fundamental laws of cancer induction by radiation in humans:

Law I: All forms of cancer, in all probability, can be increased by ionizing radiation, and the *correct* way to describe the phenomenon is either in terms of the dose required to double the spontaneous incidence rate of each cancer or, alternatively, as the increase in incidence rate of such cancers per Rad of exposure.

Law II: All forms of cancer show closely similar doubling doses and closely similar increases in incidence rate per Rad.

Law III: Youthful subjects require less radiation to increase the incidence rate by a specified fraction than do adults.

Based upon these laws and the extensive data already in hand and described above, the following assignments appear reasonable for all forms of cancer:

For Adults* ⎰ ~ 100 Rads as the doubling dose
⎱ ~ 1 percent increase in incidence rate per year per Rad of exposure

For Youthful Subjects
(< 20 years of age) ⎰ Between 5 and 100 Rads as the doubling dose
⎱ Between 1 and 20 percent increase in incidence rate per year per Rad of exposure

For Infants *in* Utero ⎰ ~ 6 Rads as the doubling dose
⎱ ~ 17 percent increase in incidence rate per year per Rad of exposure

The Implications of these Laws for the Population Exposure Associated with Atoms-for-Peace Programs

What do these laws mean in terms of additional cancer cases in the United States? The *statutory allowable dose* to the

* Our more recent estimates indicate that the true situation is even much worse. The doubling dose for cancer production in adults is approximately 50 Rads, and there is a 2 percent increase in incidence rate per year per Rad of exposure.

John W. Gofman and Arthur R. Tamplin

population-at-large in the United States is 0.17 Rads per year from peaceful uses of atomic energy in all forms. If everyone in the population were to receive 0.17 Rads per year from birth to age 30 years, the integrated exposure (above background) would be 5 Rads per person. If the risk for all forms of cancer plus leukemia is an increase of 1 percent in incidence rate per Rad, we have $5 \times 1 = 5$ *percent* increase in incidence rate for all forms of cancer plus leukemia per year.

For a population of 200,000,000 persons in the U.S., roughly half can be estimated to be over 30 years of age. In this group, irradiated from birth, the latency period might, on the average, be expected to be over by ∼35 years of age.

The *spontaneous* cancer incidence is ∼280/100,000 persons per year.

Five percent $\times$ 280 = 14.0—and therefore, 14 additional cancer cases per 100,000 persons per year due to irradiation.

Thus, *14,000 additional cancer cases per year* in the U.S., considering *only* those over 30 years of age.

If we estimate that latency plus lower accumulated dosage provides a smaller number of additional cases in the under-30 age group, it would by no means be an overestimate to add 2,000 cases to that group. (This is especially true when we see the data above concerning the greater sensitivity of this group to radiation-induced cancer.)

There should be added some contribution of additional cases each year to take into account the fact that 0.13 Rads will have been received by each infant *in utero* (0.17 Rads/year $\times$ 40/52 years). It is hard to know whether this *in utero* radiation carries an increased cancer risk for the whole lifetime or not. The additional contribution for the *in utero* radiation (at a period when the effectiveness per Rad is very high) could be between a few hundred and several thousand additional cancer cases per year. We shall not attempt to guess the additional contribution due to *in utero* irradiation.

Therefore, 14,000 + 2,000 = *16,000 additional cancer plus leukemia cases* per year in the U.S. if everyone received the Federal Radiation Council statutory allowable does of radiation. This would, for the several reasons outlined, appear to be a *minimum* value. Sixteen thousand cases is equivalent to the mortality rate from one recent high year of the Vietnam war! It would appear that this is rather a high price to consider as being compatible with the benefits to be derived from the orderly development of atomic energy.* And we must add to these estimates the comment that we have used only the *hard data* in hand based upon cancer and leukemia induced in humans by radiation. We have said *nothing* of the additional possible burden of loss of life and misery from genetic disorders in future generations, fetal deaths, and neonatal deaths. Furthermore, we have not used the vast array of experimental animal data which indicate that not only does cancer mortality increase from irradiation, but that many, if not all, causes of death increase— and in about the same proportion as does cancer mortality.

Clearly, Myth No. 1—that there is a safe threshold for radiation exposure—is just a myth. Myth No. 2—that a slow delivery of radiation may not prove harmful—is refuted by the experience of the uranium miners. They were irradiated slowly over a period of years, and the high incidence of radiation-induced lung cancer among them hardly is any basis for comfort concerning slow delivery of radiation.

In the *absence of any direct evidence* in man that factors will operate to reduce these estimated cases of cancer plus leukemia, it would appear that the only sensible thing to do right now is to reduce *drastically* the Federal Radiation Council dose allowable to the population-at-large by at *least* a factor of 10. The new figure should be below 0.017 Rads for peaceful uses of atomic energy.

THE AEC RESPONSE

The response of the Atomic Energy Commission to the scientific facts of the radiation hazard is to mouth platitudes and reassure us that they will not even reach (no less exceed) the FRC guidelines. In other words, the AEC will spew no more

---

* The revised doubling dose would indicate 32,000 cancer plus leukemia deaths per year rather than 16,000 per year.

radiation into the air and water than the amount that we have shown will produce tens of thousands of unnecessary deaths each year! Not all officials are this cautious. The Executive Director of the Federal Radiation Council, Dr. Paul Tompkins, has frequently pointed out in Congressional testimony that he thinks the guidelines are not too high; indeed, he thinks they could be raised threefold or so. He usually adds that "operational requirements" are as important as risks in deciding guidelines. So, if AEC Programs burgeon forth and release radioactivity to the point where the current guidelines are in danger of being exceeded, his approach would be that "operational requirements" dictate giving people *more* radiation. A threefold increase in guidelines would mean 96,000 extra cancers plus leukemias instead of 32,000 per year!

The *reasonable* idea that maybe the wrong programs are being sponsored by AEC and lead to high exposure of humans simply doesn't seem to occur to some people.

Benefits versus Risks

In defending the current guidelines for radiation exposure, the AEC suggests that they have done a risk-versus-benefit calculation and have found that the benefit outweighs the risk. But, they never present a benefit value, and they detest people who dare to present a risk value. Consider the statement by Dr. Glenn Werth, Associate Director for Plowshare at LRL, commenting on a question posed by Senator Gravel (D., Alaska):

> It is difficult to balance a risk of radioactivity against benefit. There is a need for natural gas. One of the most thorough studies is that by the Federal Power Commission entitled "A Staff Report on National Gas Supply and Demand," Bureau of Natural Gas, Federal Power Commission, Washington, D.C., September 1969. If more gas were available, it could be burned in more cities and significantly reduce the smog and health hazard associated with the presence of smog. Balancing the health hazard due to smog against a possible health hazard due to background levels of radioactivity has not been done to my knowledge.

Why don't we do this study before spending millions of dollars on the gas stimulation program? Would this study show that piping radioactive gas into homes is a reasonable solution to the smog problem? Even the benefits seem dubious in this case when one realizes that 50 billion cubic feet of natural gas is shipped by the U.S. to Japan every year.

In fact, the AEC does not do benefit-versus-risk studies; it does cost-analysis studies which take into account only the profits of special-interest groups, not the health and safety of the American people. In the case of "Gas Buggy," the Plowshare project mentioned above, the benefits will go to El Paso Natural Gas Company (assets: $1,826,445,297), which is the joint partner with the AEC in the project. El Paso's eagerness to use the technology it has derived from the AEC for the production of contaminated products is apparent in the company's 1968 annual report:

> Geonuclear Nobel Paso [of which El Paso has 50 percent ownership] will offer a wide range of services in the application of nuclear explosives for the stimulation of hydrocarbon production and recovery, mining, earth moving techniques in the fields of public works and civil engineering, and in the underground storage of gas, water and polluted effluents.

So the spewing of radioactivity into the environment is now becoming big private business, courtesy of the AEC.

POLLUTION IS A PRIVILEGE

If we are to survive, we must realize that there is no such thing as a safe tolerance level of pollution. To properly protect the public health and safety, the laws should read that the acceptable limit of pollution is *zero* and that the *privilege* of releasing a pollutant to the environment must be negotiated. The prospective pollutor should be required to demonstrate in a meaningful manner that his activity will produce, for those affected, benefits that outweigh the risk. This weighing of benefit versus necessary risk should occur in public hearings before pollution control boards. It is important to emphasize the word "necessary"—the benefits must be weighed against the *necessary* risks. The right to overrule a decision of the control boards should be reserved for the public through the courts or by referendum.

Environmental pollution is a matter of extreme moment. Decisions concerning pollution should not be made in secret by so-called experts. The burden of proof should be shifted from the public and/or the government regulatory agency to the pollutor. The pollutor must be made responsible for convincing the public that he has done *everything possible* to reduce the level of pollution, and that the benefits to be derived from his activity outweigh the risk of the *remaining* pollution.

Thomas H. Brewer

is a clinical physician with the Contra Costa County Health Services in Martinez, California. An M.D. graduate of the Tulane University School of Medicine, New Orleans, he interned at Jefferson Davis Hospital in Houston, and spent a year working as a general-practice resident at the Lallie Kemp Charity Hospital, Independence, Louisiana. After several years of general practice of private medicine in Fulton, Missouri, Dr. Brewer returned to complete a residency in obstetrics–gynecology at Jackson Memorial Hospital, University of Miami School of Medicine, Miami, Florida, under Professor James H. Ferguson. He spent one year as a Fellow in Biochemistry at the Howard Hughes Medical Research Institute, Miami, Florida, and another year as an academic trainee and instructor in the Department of Obstetrics–Gynecology, University of California Medical Center, San Francisco. Since 1963, Dr. Brewer has been working as a county physician in general medicine, and carrying on prenatal nutrition research in the county clinics in Richmond and Martinez, California.

Thomas Brewer is the author of a number of scientific articles in national journals in the fields of pregnancy nutrition, "toxemia of pregnancy," clinical gynecology, and connective-tissue research. He is author of the book *Metabolic Toxemia of Late Pregnancy: A Disease of Malnutrition* (Springfield, Ill.: Charles C Thomas, 1966).

147

Medicine has long been one of the first fields to benefit from advances in science and technology. This is especially true of recent years, what with the tremendous progress in cell biology and molecular biology. But how much effect have these developments had on the state of health of the average man? Here, Dr. Brewer discusses the failure of the present health care system of the United States to deal with the most widespread and chronic health problems—especially those diseases which may be caused by social and economic conditions. The real cause of much of America's health problem, Brewer holds, is the inability and unwillingness of the medical profession to recognize the social causes of diseases (social change) and to take the appropriate corrective measures (public health education). Only when the profession does take these steps, he says, will technological advances in medicine benefit mankind.

Disease and Social Class

The United States is the richest country in the world when its wealth is measured in terms of per capita Gross National Product. Yet, in terms of health care, the U. S. can hardly be proud of its performance: It ranks 22nd in the world in dealing with infant mortality; the average life expectancy has been *decreasing* in recent years; and many of its people have no access to decent medical care.

In this report I will summarize the health problems that are attributable to social conditions, and take one disease—the widespread condition of "toxemia of pregnancy"—as an illustrative example of a disease of social class. I will also discuss the role of the AMA and of the medical profession in general in perpetuating disease of social origin, and will zero in on the social responsibility of the physician to restructure medical practice in the United States.

DISEASE AND SOCIAL CLASS
IN THE UNITED STATES

It is widely known by public health officials in all modern nations that preventable diseases, and especially those which occur in women and children, are much more common among people who are poorly educated, poorly nourished, and poorly housed, than among the comfortable middle and upper classes. This is especially true in the U.S., where proper health care has become a privilege available only to the relatively wealthy. In a statement to the 1968 AMA convention, the Medical Committee for Human Rights, itself a physicians' organization, stated:

> For the technically most advanced nation in the world, a most striking feature of the American health system is its backwardness. There is an amazing failure to introduce a universal insurance system [and] coordinated community and regional planning, and, perhaps most important, there has been a tenacious retention of a fee system which has, indeed, resulted in health care becoming a privilege rather than a human right.

Consequently, according to Dr. John H. Knowles, the man whom AMA pressure helped veto as President Nixon's top health advisor, "Any practical, reasonable man would agree that the costs of medical care are prohibitive today for 99 percent of the American people."

Let's examine the diseases which hit the poor the hardest.

Diseases Caused Directly by Poor Nutrition

In 1968 the Citizens' Board of Inquiry into Hunger and Malnutrition in the United States classified 280 counties throughout the country as having emergency nutrition problems. According to Dr. Jean Mayer, President Nixon's advisor on nutrition, "[from] ten to twenty million Americans are too poor to properly feed themselves. . . ."

Diseases caused by vitamin deficiency due to malnutrition include rickets, scurvy, pellegra, and certain anemias.

Iron deficiency anemia (lack of iron) is a disease common in women and children among the poor.

Protein deficiency, common among the malnourished poor, results in the stunting of physical and mental growth of infants and children.

Complications of pregnancy, such as metabolic toxemia of late pregnancy, are responsible for the high percentage of "premature" or low-birth-weight infants, abruptions (breakage) of the normally placed placenta, nutritional anemias, and lowered resistance to infections of the liver, lungs, and kidneys.

They make pregnancy a curse rather than a blessing for many poor and malnourished women.

Diseases Indirectly Related to Poor Nutrition

Diseases which many Americans believe have been eradicated are widespread among the poor and result from their poor nutrition and consequent poor ability to defend against infection. These diseases include tuberculosis, pneumonia, and liver and kidney infections. Malnutrition also results in the delay of healing of wounds and of broken bones.

Diseases and "Accidents" Resulting from
Poor Health Education

The poor and malnourished are generally the most badly educated in basic health rules and in the principles of modern medicine. For a number of economic and social reasons, poor people have the least access to a good education and to advice concerning matters of sex hygiene and birth control. This results in their relatively high rates of venereal diseases with severe complications, of cancer of the cervix, and of severe infections and bleeding associated with abortions.

The comparatively great lack of education among the poor concerning the dangers of smoking results in a relatively higher incidence of emphysema, a disease which suffocates more people today than died from tuberculosis in 1900.

"Accidents" of burnings and poisonings are more common among the children of the poor than among "better off" children.

Diseases Related to Poor Housing,
Overcrowding, Poor Sanitation

Housing is a national disgrace in the United States. One out of every ten American families lives in irreversibly dilapidated housing. An even higher number of dwellings lack common sanitary facilities. Poor housing and overcrowded and unsanitary conditions contribute to rheumatic fever and rheumatic heart disease, to common respiratory diseases like influenza and the common cold, and to complications such as middle-ear infections and meningitis. These conditions increase the occurrence of diarrhea, dysentery, and other intestinal infections, including worms and other parasites.

Diseases Related to Poor or Inadequate Medical Care

In a society like ours, which has a "fee for service" medical system, where it costs a lot of money to see a doctor and to get complicated, modern medical care, the poor man or woman will often put off a visit to a doctor for too many months or years. When this happens, diseases which could be cured early in their courses are allowed to advance to an incurable state. This is particularly true in many types of cancer, eye diseases, chronic infections, and mental and emotional diseases.

Diseases Directly Related to Racial Discrimination

Minority peoples have additional burdens imposed upon their health because of the pervasive racism in this society. For instance, in our southern states, high blood pressure and death therefrom occur four times more commonly among blacks than among whites. High blood pressure has many severe complications, such as brain stroke, and kidney and heart failure. Too, in many states the maternal mortality rates are five times higher in blacks and chicanos and other minority groups than in whites. Severe complications of gonorrhea are much more common among nonwhites, and so are the resulting complications: abscesses of the uterine tubes and ovaries. (In Southern hospitals I have heard gynecologists refer to operations on diseased tubes and ovaries as "nigger surgery.")

The state of health of the American Indian is a particularly shocking public disgrace. In some areas one-third of the Indian children suffer from trachoma, a preventable and treatable virus disease which causes blindness. Almost one-fourth of all American Indians are judged mentally ill by health authorities working with them. The life expectancy of an American Indian is only 43 years. About 90 percent of all American Indians live in houses virtually unfit for human occupancy. Sixty-six percent of them haul water from unsanitary sources in unsanitary vessels, many from a distance of over a mile from their homes. The death rate from tuberculosis among the 400,000 original Americans surviving is five times higher than that of the general population.

METABOLIC TOXEMIA OF LATE PREGNANCY (MTLP): A CASE STUDY OF A DISEASE OF SOCIAL ORIGIN, AND THE INADEQUATE RESPONSE OF THE HEALTH PROFESSION

The Problem

> In 1966, about 3,629,000 babies were born in the United States and 84,800 died in their first year of life, according to provisional data. These figures translate into a rate of 23.4 infant deaths per 1,000 live births, which is an all-time low for the nation. However, an examination of the variations among states and between racial groups, the slowed pace of improvement in recent years, and the substantially lower infant death rates reported by other countries, make it abundantly clear that much can still be done to improve our records.
> —Metropolitan Life Insurance Co.
> *Statistical Bulletin,* May 1967

United Nations statistics for 1968 show that the United States lags behind at least 17 other countries, including Japan and most of Europe, in dealing with the problem of infant deaths. In these countries the infant mortality rate averages under 20 per 1,000 live births, while in the United States the rate is 25 per 1,000 for the entire population and 41.3 for the nonwhite population. (I realize that these figures would be even more indicative if they were available in terms of income and not just in terms of the white and the nonwhite.)

In 1950 among nonwhites there were some 47,000 registered births of infants weighing less than 2,500 grams (about 5½ pounds)—or 9.7 percent of the total of nonwhite births. By 1964 this number had risen to over 91,000—or 13.8 percent of the nonwhite births. This shocking rise in infants' low birth-weight occurred (and continues to occur) among the poorest people in all states; it did not spread throughout the socioeconomic scale (as would be expected if, for instance, radioactive fallout were the basic cause). During the same period there was only a very slight rise in incidence of white low-birth-weight infants.

Many cases of abortive births are caused by a disease known as toxemia of late pregnancy. This disease, which affects women in the last half of their pregnancy, is characterized by high blood pressure, swelling of the limbs and joints, protein in the urine, convulsions, shock, heart failure, and coma. It is responsible for about 30,000 infant deaths per year, as in 1963 when it also killed 1,466 mothers along with a high percent of their newborn.

What is the reason for this tragically high rate of infant and maternal mortality and what has been done to remedy the problem? The evidence which follows suggests that poverty and malnutrition are contributory factors to toxemia of late pregnancy.

As early as 1933, M. B. Strauss, Associate Dean of Tufts Medical School in Boston, suggested that toxemia of late pregnancy is caused by malnutrition. His clinical histories detected a very low intake of high-biological-quality proteins in patients suffering from toxemia. He also observed beneficial effects from feeding them before delivery a high-protein, high-vitamin diet. Bertha Burke, of the Harvard School of Public Health, in a careful clinical study of the nutritional status of pregnant women, reported in 1943 that toxemia of pregnancy did not occur in a single woman she considered well-nourished during pregnancy.

The following account (courtesy of Dr. James Ferguson) of a midwife meeting in Mississippi indicates the toll taken by toxemia in terms of human life and misery. The person speaking is a Dr. O'Neil; the italicized replies are those of the midwives.

"I would like to show you a map that I think you all will be interested in. [A map of Mississippi is projected on a portable screen. The map is divided into counties and on it appear colored dots—yellow, red, green, and blue.] Now this here is a map of Mississippi. Here's Hattiesburg and here's Jackson. Away down below here someplace is New Orleans. Do you see where we are?"

"*Yassah.*"

"Now each one of these dots means that a woman died having a baby in 1947. Now that's a lot of dots, isn't it?"

"*It shore is.*"

"That's too many. A lot of these women did not have to die."

"*That's right.*"

"There are 176 dots. That means that 176 women died in 1947 in Mississippi from having babies. Now, do you see the yellow dots?"

"*Yassah.*"

"There are 76 of them. These women had what you hear the public health nurse calling toxemia—when the woman had high blood and swelling of the legs and the urine test is bad, and you know that's bad."

"*It shore is.*"

"Each one of these women probably had convulsions or fits and then died. How many of you have seen a pregnant woman with fits? Raise your hands. [About half of the midwives raise their hands.] You know that when a woman in your district has that trouble she has to pay particular attention to what the doctor says or she's going to be in a bad way."

"*She shore is.*"

"And these red dots mean that these women bled to death. . . ."

Ferguson also studied the nutrition of pregnant women in Mississippi and published two valuable reports which clearly establish the widespread malnutrition of the lowest class in Mississippi. Examples of some of the worst menus he encountered among pregnant women were:

Breakfast	3 tablespoons grits
	1 tablespoon butter
	2 pieces toast
	1 cup coffee
Dinner	1 candy bar
	1 apple
	1 soft drink
No Supper	

No Breakfast

Dinner   1 root beer
2 plates field peas
4 biscuits (large)

Supper   ½ plate water gravy
1½ plates fried okra
2 biscuits (large)

Only 6 percent of 402 pregnant women interviewed in 1950 in rural Mississippi were receiving the National Research Council's recommended allowance of specific nutrients for pregnancy. These diets were deficient in proteins, iron, vitamin C, and calcium. Eighty-nine percent were not receiving a quart of milk a day, and 57 percent ate no eggs. These same conditions exist today in many parts of this country (especially in the rural South). A 1967 report to Senator Joseph Clark's Subcommittee on Manpower stated: "The boys and girls we saw were hungry, weak, in pain, sick; they are suffering from hunger and disease and directly or indirectly they are dying from them. Health conditions in the South among the poor are as bad as or worse than those among primitive tribal Africans."

The deep contrast between the nutritional conditions in the U. S. and other modern nations is dramatized by the following ironic editorial note which was attached to an article on toxemia I published in the Swiss journal *Gynaecologia:* "The present paper shows a fairly rare aspect of gestosis of late pregnancy, since undernourishment is rather rare in Central Europe. . . . We hardly ever see a 'metabolic toxemia of late pregnancy'."

What is the response of the health establishment to the social and economic conditions that cause such diseases as toxemia of late pregnancy?

Despite the evidence cited indicating that toxemia of late pregnancy is a nutritional disease, the latest official definition of it by the American Committee on Maternal Welfare (Eastman, *et al.*) gives no indication of nutritional factors. Toxemia is defined by the Committee as "acute toxemia," a disease of unknown cause; or as acute glomerulonephritis, a renal disease; or as a chronic hypertensive vascular disease; or as unclassified toxemia. Though acute glomerulonephritis does of course occur, I (after the work of Strauss and Hamlin) have classified the several *causes* of the *syndrome* known as toxemia of late pregnancy. I have identified acute toxemia of late pregnancy as a specific nutritional disease—*metabolic toxemia of late pregnancy*—and I have developed a scientific differential diagnosis of this disease entity. Because the official definition of "toxemias of pregnancy" is so confusing and does not recognize the role of malnutrition in etiology, I have offered the following classification. (Note that in my classification the term "toxemia of pregnancy" as a *syndrome* has been discarded.)

1. Disorders which occur only in pregnant patients

  a. Metabolic toxemia of late pregnancy: mild, severe
  b. Physiological edema of pregnancy
  c. Molar pregnancy with toxemia syndrome

2. Disorders which occur in pregnant or in nonpregnant patients

  a. "Essential" hypertension
  b. Other medical causes of hypertension (including renal and adrenal diseases)
  c. Urinary tract diseases
  d. Central nervous system diseases
  e. Malnutrition with hypoalbuminemia and edema as the only manifestation
  f. Hepatic diseases
  g. Congestive heart failure from other causes
  h. Diabetes mellitus

3. Combinations of disorders 1 and 2 occurring in the same patient

See RIPPMANN E. T.: Prä-eklampsie oder Schwangerschafts-Spätgestose? Gynaecologia (Basel) *167*, 478–490 (1969).

It is necessary to consider here the important concept of the "physiological edema of pregnancy." The majority of otherwise normal, healthy, adequately nourished pregnant women will show some swelling, or "edema," of their feet, ankles, fingers, hands, and face during the last weeks of pregnancy. This is not metabolic toxemia but rather a useful adaptation of the body to the stress of pregnancy. Extra water and salt in the mother's tissues make lactation easier and prevent shock in case of excessive blood loss during or after delivery of the baby. Thomson, Hytten, and Billewicz have shown from a study of 24,000 pregnancies in Aberdeen that this edema or swelling is common and normal. (See: Thomson, A. M., Hytten, F. E., and Billewicz, W. Z.: "The epidemiology of oedema during pregnancy," *J. Obstet. Gynaec. Brit. Cwlth.*, 74:1, 1967). In their study edema appeared to be associated with an enhanced reproductive performance. The weight of babies born to edematous mothers was greater than that of babies born to mothers who had no edema. The "prematurity rate," or incidence of low-birth-weight infants, was lower for edematous mothers, and infant mortality was lower.

Thanks to the promotions of the private drug industry, U. S. physicians have been blindly "treating" this normal physiological phenomenon with inadequate low-salt diets and salt diuretics in the futile attempt to prevent "toxemia of pregnancy." This has created a vast amount of iatrogenic (physician-induced) malnutrition both for the pregnant woman and for the unborn fetus; it has in many cases created iatrogenic metabolic toxemia of late pregnancy!

Since classical teachings have ignored the social and economic aspects of malnutrition in human reproduction, the official methods of treatment of "toxemia of pregnancy" are aimed at the symptoms of the disorder. This treatment involves the prescription of salt diuretics (which cause the kidneys of both mother and fetus to excrete extra amounts of salt and water) and low-calorie, low-salt diets which are usually low in high-quality proteins. Also, diet pills (amphetamines) are often prescribed to "control weight gain" by suppressing the pregnant woman's normally healthy appetite. Little or no account is taken of the quality of the pregnant woman's diet, of her need for adequate quantities of all known essential nutrients, and of adequate calories from carbohydrate and fats to spare proteins for tissue synthesis in the uterus and to maintain normal liver function. This method of management is not only useless, but often it is harmful because nothing is done to correct the dietary deficiencies which lie at the root of the problem. In fact, the prescription of low-salt, low-calorie diets, salt diuretics, and diet pills tends to decrease the intake of high-quality proteins even further and makes the toxemia disorder more severe.

I have abandoned this conventional method of treatment (as has Margaret Robinson of London) and have substituted nutritional education and improved diets for my patients.

In July, 1963, I began a nutrition education project in our county prenatal clinic serving the medically indigent women and girls of Richmond, California. I decided to deemphasize sodium intake and "weight control" and to make every effort to insure optimal, well-balanced nutrition for each patient, with primary emphasis focused on high-biological-quality proteins, vegetables, and fruits. Since then, by means of a special lecture given to new prenatal patients in a group during their first visit to the clinic, and by constant subsequent reminders about the importance of good nutrition, I have observed a most excellent reproductive performance among these "women in poverty." In over 1,500 pregnancies there has been no convulsive MTLP, and the incidence of low-birth-weight infants (birth weight less than 5½ pounds) is only 2.2 percent. Among 318 primiparous patients in the Richmond Nutrition Project whose records I have reviewed in detail, only one developed severe MTLP. While I have decreased the incidence of toxemia and related difficulties associated with pregnancy dramatically, the national incidence has *increased* in recent years. And in a clinical study where women were treated with low-sodium diets and diuretics, the incidence of toxemia and low birth weights *increased* (as in the Tuskegee Institute in Alabama, where in 1968 toxemia complicated *31 percent* of all pregnancies delivered!).

Despite all the compelling evidence that MTLP is caused by malnutrition and can be prevented by providing a decent diet to the patient, this idea will not be found in any publication of the U. S. Public Health Service, or in the *Journal* of the

AMA, and it is not taught in medical schools in the United States. The U. S. Public Health Service has done almost nothing to deal with the public health problem of malnutrition. What little has been done, has been done by the Department of Agriculture. The only sign we have that the federal government recognizes malnutrition as a health problem is its grotesque arrangement with Medicare which allows some physicians in small Southern towns to prescribe food as a medicine to starving people.

Even more basic is the unwillingness or inability of organized medicine—specifically, of the AMA—to recognize and deal with the social and economic causes of disease. The medical profession refuses to admit to the existence of unconscionable poverty, and therefore of malnutrition, in the U. S. Since the major cause of metabolic toxemia is ignored out of existence, the disease becomes inexplicable, an "anomalous syndrome." It is treated only on the symptomatic level, with diuretics and low-salt diets, while the true cause, malnutrition, persists.

In the final analysis, the high incidence of MTLP reflects not only the avarice of the medical monopoly but also the failure of the present economic system to provide the simple necessities of a decent life to millions of citizens and their children. Why has the official medical establishment ignored the work of myself and others? I believe that the AMA and the interests it represents are unwilling to recognize and deal with the social and economic causes of disease because to do so would be to expose the privileged position of the medical profession in this society.

In a way, there is good reason for the medical monopoly to steer clear of social issues. Doctors are the highest-paid professionals by far, making an average $30,000 a year reported income (scientists and engineers average $12,000). There is a lucrative relationship between the medical profession and the pharmaceutical industry, too, where profits, at 19 percent, run double the average for American business. The drug industry spends over three-fourths of a billion dollars each year on advertising to doctors—$4,000 per doctor—to make sure that physicians prescribe such drugs as diuretics and diet pills in the form of the overpriced brand-name instead of as a generic drug. According to the Los Angeles Better Business Bureau, 70 percent of that county's physicians accept financial rebates from drugstores, medical supply houses, and laboratories. This unreported income is added on to their reported (average) $30,000.

The AMA has been a consistently reactionary force in American politics, opposing virtually all social welfare programs including social security, the minimum wage, the 40-hour week, *and* Medicare. Why the AMA finally accepted Medicare is made obvious from the fact that 25 physicians who collected $25,000 apiece in unreported income in 1969 from Medicare were members of the AMA executive committee at the time it opposed Medicare. Add this on to the $30,000 average.

The attitude of the AMA on universal health care was well stated by Dr. Milford O. Rouse, in his presidential address to the AMA in 1967:

> We are faced with many problems and challenges. We are faced with the concept of health care as a right rather than a privilege.
> Several major steps have already been taken by the federal government in providing health and medical care for large segments of the population. Other steps have been proposed—these we must continue to oppose. What is our philosophy? It is faith in private enterprise. We can, therefore, concentrate our attention on the single obligation to protect the American way of life. That way of life can be described in one word: Capitalism.

CONCLUSIONS

In order to really improve the health and well-being of a large number of our people who are trapped by poverty and discrimination, we will have to radically alter our entire socioeconomic system, and particularly our medical system. This has been done successfully in many modern nations. We must put people and their children *first,* before profits, prestige, and property. This difficult task can be accomplished only when the health of the American people is given the proper political emphasis. The chief end of American medicine must be changed from profit and financial security for a small number of doctors and paramedical people (those who make large profits on the manufacture and distribution of drugs and medical supplies) to service to our people's health needs. We must create a strong federal government program of support to medical education, public health and preventive medicine, and public clinics, laboratories, and hospitals. *The drug industry must be nationalized and run for the health of the people, not for profits.*

The present U. S. socioeconomic system is denying millions of our people in poverty their basic Constitutional and human rights of "life, liberty and the pursuit of happiness," for these are but empty phrases without good health, a satisfactory education, and a decent job. Conditions will never change until we, the common people, organize to change them—until we abolish the present class society and establish a truly democratic and classless society.

There is no more glaring contradiction in our modern "free, democratic, open" U. S. society than our medical system, organized and run by representatives of our wealthy business class for its own interests, prestige, and profits. It is only through a correct and scientific understanding of the class structure of our society—including its injustices, cruelties, and contradictions—that we can proceed to lay the foundations for a really modern, efficient, and scientific medical system dedicated to all our people and all their children.

Robert C. Stebbins

is Professor of Zoology and Curator in Herpetology at the Museum of Vertebrate Zoology, University of California, Berkeley. While his research interests span the broad fields of vertebrate population dynamics, ecology, and evolution, his special interest is in human population problems.

Professor Stebbins received the B.A., M.A., and Ph.D. degrees from the University of California, Los Angeles. A Guggenheim Fellow in 1949, and a National Science Senior Post-Doctoral Fellow during the 1958–59 academic year, he is a past chairman (1960–61) of the University of California Elementary School Science Committee, and continues to participate in the experimental development of science topics for the elementary grades.

The list of books authored by Professor Stebbins includes: *Amphibians of Western North America; Reptiles and Amphibians of Western North America; Birds of Yosemite* (coauthored by his father); *Reptiles and Amphibians of the San Francisco Bay Region; The Lives of Desert Animals in Joshua Tree National Monument* (coauthored by Alden H. Miller); and, most recently, *A Field Guide to Western Reptiles and Amphibians.* For the Sierra Club he has produced two motion pictures: *Nature Next Door* (film demonstrating the importance of nature areas), and *No Room for Wilderness?* (a conservation film).

Professor Stebbins has traveled widely throughout the United States, and to Mexico, South America, Europe, Africa, Asia, and Australia. While at the University of Witwatersrand, Johannesburg, South Africa, he devoted eight months to a study of vertebrate ecology; and in Asia he engaged in a cross-cultural exchange program devoted to the upgrading of science teaching in the secondary schools. During January and February of 1964, he was a member of the University of California Scientific Expedition to the Galapagos Islands. This expedition was sponsored by the Extension Division in cooperation with the Darwin Foundation and the International Union for the Conservation of Nature. Fifty-eight scientists, representing a variety of fields of science, participated; eighteen institutions and nine countries were represented. The objectives of the expedition were to study the climate, geology, and animal and plant life of the archipelago. Special attention was given to factors important to the evolution of organisms on these remote oceanic islands.

In the following pages, Professor Stebbins provides a thought-provoking essay on ecology which is at once a plea for understanding and a call for action.

The
Loss
of
Biological
Diversity

Animals, including man, and all plant life form a gossamer-thin layer on this planet, containing over 2,000,000 species—thinning out on the polar caps, on high mountain tops, on deserts, and in the ocean depths; becoming luxuriously thick in the tropics, where it is colorful and varied like the folds of an oriental rug. Woven in it are life forms ranging in size from bacteria to giant redwoods and protozoa to great whales. It is a layer over two billion years old that has changed and repaired itself throughout time without ever deteriorating. With the atmosphere it helped produce and the earth elements upon which it draws, it is the system upon which we completely depend—and upon which we must continue to rely to the end of our days as a species. Few if any of us or our descendants will ever reach another inhabitable planet.

I sensed as never before the precarious nature of our existence when through the eyes of our first lunar astronauts I saw our beautiful and lonely planet hanging in the void. They spoke with feeling of the royal blue of the oceans and the colors of the continents, while below in stark contrast spread the dead surface of the moon—barren, lifeless, resembling dirty sand.

But now, unless there is prompt action, life's two-billion-year success story may soon end. Man is bringing such rapid and far-reaching changes that the entire biosphere is threatened. We are a clever animal, adept at changing the environment to suit our needs. But we have usually acted with expediency rather than with understanding. The science of ecology—the study of organisms in relation to their environment—has only recently emerged. At this crucial time in earth's history, when ecological problems beset us at every hand, we find ourselves in the Stone Age of ecological awareness, seemingly bent on destroying our earth as rapidly as possible. We justify what we are doing with vague terms such as "growth," "development," and "progress." The protection of nature and of ourselves demands the immediate lessening of population growth, a rapid spread of ecological knowledge, and widespread concern for the protection of life.

Why is the study of ecology so important? It provides a breadth of understanding of man and his environment that cannot be achieved in any other way. It concerns itself with how and where plants and animals live, with how they interact with one another and the physical world; and it concerns itself with evolution—the dynamics of physical and organic change. Man is viewed as a part of the living whole, subject to the same laws of nature as are all other creatures, and not as a superior being set apart from the rest. An ecological point of view brings a sense of humility—an awareness of human limitations as well as of the complexities and interdependence in the living world. The interactions among organisms and their environment are so extensive, and the integration is so great, that a change in one part of the system, through a chain reaction, may have widespread and sometimes unpredictable effects. Destruction of a species of ant may cause a forest to decline; pesticides used in the fields of Kansas may end up in Antarctic penguins. Man is severely disturbing the system nearly everywhere and chain reactions, many of them deleterious, are moving in many directions. Few people are aware of what is happening and even scientists cannot predict the outcome of many of man's effects.

Why do we find ourselves so ecologically naive in an age of spectacular scientific advances? The trouble lies in our anthropocentric view of the world. We are in a phase of cultural adolescence from which by now we should have emerged. It has been over 100 years since Darwin's *Origin of Species* appeared, yet most people still look upon man as completely set apart from the rest of creation, as a different order of being. He is regarded as having the God-given right to extract from nature every last drop of sustenance, regardless of the cost to other organisms, to keep alive an ever-growing human population. Modern man, like Narcissus, has caught as it were a glimpse of his reflection and, fascinated by his own image and proud of his artifacts and prowess in shaping his environment, has lost sight of natural beauty and has disregarded the most elementary workings of nature.

Biologists must accept some part of the responsibility for this excessively man-centered view of the world, for it was incumbent upon them, regardless of field of specialization, to set forth the facts of evolution and ecology. These broad aspects of the workings of nature should by now have become common knowledge, as widely accepted as the concept of the atom—but, unfortunately, the hard facts of these disciplines impinge upon sensitive areas in human affairs.

Ecology has been called the subversive science, for it challenges long-cherished traditions. It has unsettling things to say about motherhood, death control, the expanding economy, and man's place in nature. Small wonder that biologists, being human and products of their culture, have had difficulty guiding their students into ecological and evolutionary lines of inquiry. Nature study, a rudimentary form of ecology popular when our country was young and commendable in its attention to nature outdoors, was permeated with sentimentality, anthropomorphism, and teleology. Before it could mature into a scientific approach, it was swept aside by a technologically oriented society flushed with the success of the great discoveries in the physical sciences that ushered in the mechanization and gadgetry of the modern world. Emphasis in our schools was on the practical applications of science. Biology was caught up in this trend, as can be seen by any brief examination of elementary and high-school textbooks of science written just after the turn of the century.

Long ago a few biologists, particularly those working closely with plant and animal populations in their natural environments, sensed the deleterious effects on the biosphere of an expanding human population; but they allowed themselves to be outvoiced by biologists committed to paramedical, agricultural, and other "practical" aspects of the science. Many fought feebly or not at all as cellular and molecular disciplines became popular and in some university departments overshadowed all other aspects of biology. Now there is a growing realization of the urgent need for the general public to become ecologically well informed. It is ironical that many schools are not prepared to meet the need, and unfortunate that a shift in emphasis cannot be made suddenly.

However, we must not now dwell on the past, but must take steps to avert catastrophe. The nuclear triggers are increasingly more likely to be pulled as population pressures increase. And as competition for water, food, space, and energy sources increases, social stresses mount and strife becomes more acute.

I think it is clear now that there are no technological solutions to the population problem and accompanying deterioration of the environment. Improvement of extractive techniques to supply sustenance, and measures to ameliorate damage to the environment, cannot go on indefinitely. The solution lies rather in changing social attitudes, which is far more difficult than developing new scientific techniques. It seems clear that until we can achieve a widespread change in our attitude toward nature, the degradation of the biosphere will continue. Farming the seas, the "green revolution" in agriculture, fresh water from salt water, even the perfect contraceptive will not be enough. The first three are palliative measures which, in the absence of adequate birth control, will only delay and ensure an even greater disaster. Adequate birth control depends on the willingness of people to limit their families—a question of attitude.

The most important thing to do now is to move on all fronts in the field of public education to bring about widespread ecological awareness and a view of the world that accords other parts of the biosphere, whether deemed helpful to us or not, a right to exist. It must be made clear that the preservation of the other organisms that share the earth with us cannot be achieved without stabilizing human population growth. It is thus particularly important for those of us who cherish the earth's wild creatures to see to it that there is instilled a concern for the preservation of untrammeled nature. Imagine a world in which

all nature is organized for human ends—a completely domesticated planet, all continents reduced to sameness and all human
cultures merged into a monotonous whole with mankind spending his remaining days occupied with nothing but his own antics
and artifacts, unrelieved by the freshness and variety of nature.
If such a world is unappealing to you, you must work to turn
man's attention outward, away from his reflected image. People
must come to love the works of nature as well as those of man.

I think we face the greatest challenge of our time. We must
find ways to change the most important thing in man's world:
his view of himself. There is no more important work. Fortunately, there are hopeful signs of a growing interest in ecological matters. Grass-roots groups are forming to help spread
ecological understanding. Conservation is becoming a popular
topic in our schools. Government at all levels is showing increasing concern over problems of pollution and population
growth, and is taking steps to protect threatened animal
species. But we still have a long way to go, and time is short.

There is much discussion of the population problem, but
little positive action. The United Nations Charter still carries
the statement, "any choice and decision with regard to the size
of the family must irrevocably rest with the family itself, and
cannot be made by anyone else." This seems an unfortunately
rigid position at a time when over half the world is faced with
malnutrition or outright starvation. In another generation, if
the present rate of population growth continues, the number of
people on earth will double. If values don't change, most will
aspire to live like us. The bonfire we are now making of the
fossil fuels, in itself, may make this impossible. But we need not
accept the idea of continual increase. Indeed, we must resolve
that population growth will stop. I believe that it would bring
hell on earth. Families forming now and in the future must be
persuaded to limit their children to two or less. The restriction must apply to all, regardless of eugenics or economic status.
Stopping the population juggernaut is of greatest immediate
concern; we can worry about quality later. Social pressure must
be exerted to ensure that people will cooperate.

All means, including voluntary abortion, must be sought to

achieve effective birth control. Let us divert a portion of our massive military budget into contraceptive research to obtain more effective and widely applicable methods. We should set an example for other countries by promptly instituting a program for population stabilization in the United States. We are in a weak position to urge population control on other countries when our own expanding numbers and overgrown technology are drawing heavily on the vital resources of other nations.

To solve our environmental problems, we must make sure that every citizen is exposed to the concepts of ecology and evolution (the teaching of which is either banned, resisted, or neglected in many of our schools). Only a few people have entered the world of knowledge into which Darwin led the way, and unless many more do so, our chances of survival are slim. Training in ecology and evolution must become an integral part of public education, as basic as the three R's. And to be most effective, such studies should include field work, conducted if possible in natural environments where primordial interactions still exist little disturbed by man. An intellectual grasp based on textbook knowledge is seldom enough. People must develop a fondness for the natural world—an emotional commitment. It is too easy to rationalize away intellectual restraints placed upon an environment-disrupting act.

I have many times witnessed nature itself as the teacher. In my course in vertebrate natural history, the students spend three hours in the field each week studying free-living wild animals in their natural habitats. I have seen disinterested students grow in enthusiasm as their field experience deepened. Recently a student who had approached bird-watching with disdain, and was slow to respond to the outdoor experiences, said to me: "Dr. Stebbins, this course has finally hooked me. I can't go anywhere now without noticing the birds."

Particularly needed are guidelines on how to use outdoor areas in teaching. Research will be required to develop new approaches and techniques that will appeal to the beginning student and encourage his interests. A technical treatment is not what is needed, but rather an approach resembling that of the old nature-study program—divested, however, of its moralizing and anthropomorphism, and enriched with an abundance of new scientific information. The program should develop the student's powers of observation, encourage personal discovery, and introduce him to simple procedures in quantification and measurement. But above all it is a fondness for nature that we wish to instill.

I regard inquiry as the greatest pursuit of man. It has the potential of providing him with some of his moments of greatest enjoyment. It carries with it a strong esthetic component, for through it the remarkable architecture of nature is revealed. One of the richest sources of subject matter is to be found in undisturbed portions of the biosphere. Wild plants and animals, with all their interesting adaptations and inter-relationships, can provide mankind with an almost endless supply of intellectual and esthetic pleasure for millenniums to come. People of all ages and stages of life can benefit. As wild animals disappear, our own lives are endangered, for their well-being is intimately tied to our own. They resemble the canaries that miners carried into the deep recesses of mines to warn of noxious gases. Their plight warns us of imminent ecological danger to man himself. It is the nature of the web of life that this should be so. We must not allow this priceless heritage to be degraded.

ACKNOWLEDGMENT

Many of the ideas I have presented and discussed have grown out of frequent discussions over the years with my dear friend and former major professor, Dr. Raymond Cowles, Emeritus Professor of Zoology, University of California, Los Angeles. I wish to express my gratitude for his constant stimulation and encouragement and to credit him for having contributed in great measure to whatever merit may exist in this presentation. I wish also to acknowledge suggestions offered by my colleagues, professors Richard M. Eakin and Richard C. Strohman of the Department of Zoology, University of California, Berkeley.

Barry
Commoner

is Professor of Plant Physiology at Washington University, St. Louis. He also is director of Washington University's Center for the Biology of Natural Systems, and a member of the Committee for Environmental Information, which publishes the excellent periodical *Environment*.

In this essay, Professor Commoner discusses the failure of modern technology to deal with environmental problems. He illustrates how scientists, by taking an atomistic approach to problems, have contributed to many of the ecological disasters we face today. For example, he points out the inadequacy of our present sewage disposal technology. (At a meeting of the American Chemical Society, Commoner challenged Presidential Science Advisor Dr. Lee Dubridge on the advisability of spending billions of dollars on "modern" sewage plants, illuminating the facts that such plants pass large amounts of phosphates and nitrates into lakes and rivers, and regenerate organic matter in the form of algae. Instead, said Commoner, a whole new approach is needed which takes cognizance of ecological principles.)

Environmental problems, says this expert, will be solved only when an integrated approach is taken which utilizes the collective wisdom of all the citizenry. The special role of the scientist, then, is to inform the public on the technical aspects of environmental problems so that the average citizen is armed with the knowledge necessary to favorably influence ecologically oriented political decisions.

The
Ecological
Crisis

For a long time the issue of the scientist's social responsibility was discussed only in occasional seminars, but now it has become an important, frequently discussed issue for many scientists. The consequences of scientific development have dominated the political life of this country and of the world. For example, when the public complains about the enormous burden of the military budget, we should remember that the costly armament is largely an achievement of modern science and technology. Every scientist now knows that almost anything he learns may quickly be converted to a military or commercial use. The gap between scientific discoveries and their application has become very narrow. Scientists can no longer evade the social, political, economic, and moral consequences of what they do in the laboratory.

What is required, then, is that we understand why the progress of science has led to the grave social issues which plague society, and to determine what role the scientist should play in resolving these issues.

I believe that the system of science and technology, as practiced in the United States and in all other developed countries, is in many ways unsound and unfit as a guide to the nature of man and the world in which he lives. We live in nature; society operates in nature, and our ability to exist in the natural world depends on our knowledge of it. Science should provide that knowledge and technology guide our application of it. But we are failing in these aims. In New York harbor the sewage bacterial count has risen a hundredfold in the last decade, even though marked improvements in the extent of sewage treatment have been made. Apparently there is something wrong with the technology of sewage treatment, which after all was designed to get *rid* of bacteria. This is an example of a very general problem; increasing environmental pollution is evidence that our technology is, in important ways, incompetent. Behind this incompetence is an intrinsic weakness in science. Let us consider the sewage disposal problem as an example.

SEWAGE TREATMENT AND THE ECOLOGICAL CONSEQUENCES

Sewage consists of waste materials, including bacteria (which can spread disease) and organic matter. Organic matter plays a role in a biological cycle which occurs in water and in soil. In surface water, organic matter is broken down by bacteria; the products are nitrate, phosphate, and carbon dioxide, inorganic materials. In the process, the microorganisms consume oxygen. These are nutrients for another group of organisms, the algae. These organisms take up the inorganic materials and reconvert them to organic matter. Algae are eaten by fish, which convert the algal organic matter into their own organic substance. As the fish produce wastes, or when they die, organic matter is released to the water and the cycle is complete. This cycle once offered what seemed like a good way to dispose of organic wastes: Let it flow through pipes into a lake or a river. Microorganisms decay the waste and the resulting inorganic matter (nitrate, for example) goes down the river, into the sea, and away.

This system of sewage disposal works fine as long as human population density around lakes and rivers remains relatively small. But when large amounts of organic material are poured into the waterways, the natural cycle breaks down. The oxygen content of water is limited by the low solubility of oxygen in water. If enough organic matter is added to the water, the bacteria working on it become so active that they consume all the available oxygen, and the bacteria asphyxiate themselves and die. The whole system breaks down; the water becomes foul. This problem was solved by sanitary engineers when they domesticated the bacteria. Domestication is a very interesting process. In domestication an organism doesn't change its biological functions, but it performs those functions in a place convenient for man. When sewage treatment plants were developed, the bacteria of decay were allowed to function in a convenient place—a sewage treatment pond. The pond was aerated to provide enough oxygen for the bacteria to function. Such a treatment plant is able to convert the organic matter to inorganic materials, which can then be released into surface waters without imposing a burden on their oxygen content. Most of the biological oxygen demand of the sewage is removed.

But this technological achievement, which is fundamental to the process of urbanization in the U.S., has already proven to be a disastrous failure. Why? Since such sewage treatment plants are capable of handling large amounts of sewage, they release inordinate amounts of inorganic materials into the surface water. But this excess of nutrients causes the algae to grow intensively, forming thick layers. The top layer absorbs the sunlight and the algae on the bottom are deprived of the wavelengths they require. The overall result is that large overgrowths of algae, called "algal blooms," grow up quickly, then die. And when the algae die they release organic matter to the water, again stressing its oxygen content. The end result is, again, the disruption of the natural cycle.

Lake Erie has become, in a sense, a huge underwater cesspool. Some 40 feet of organic matter, originating partly in raw sewage and partly in organic matter regenerated by the algae, has been deposited on the bottom of the lake in some places. The reason why this organic matter hasn't caused catastrophic trouble is that there is a thin layer of iron oxide which binds the muck on the bottom and doesn't let it get into the lake. But the iron oxide is in an oxidized form, and every summer when the oxygen content of the water tends to go to zero in the water, the iron oxide changes its chemical composition to a reduced form which is no longer capable of sealing off the bottom deposit. This Pandora's Box of accumulated biological oxygen demand opens to some degree every summer. There is a danger that at some point huge masses of accumulated organic matter may suddenly be released in the lake. If this happens all of the oxygen-using organisms of the lake will die.

A balance sheet has been drawn up for Lake Erie, for the amount of nitrogen and phosphorus entering and leaving the lake. It has been found that much of the nitrate and phosphate —inorganic products of sewage treatment—entering the lake remains in it. This means that the technology of sewage disposal around Lake Erie is a failure.

OTHER TECHNOLOGICAL FAILURES

There have been many other such failures in modern technology. A good example is DDT. In the Cañete Valley in Peru, when DDT and similar insecticides were introduced to check insect pests, the insect predators of these pests were also killed, while the pests themselves became resistant to DDT. Outbreaks of insect pests have thus been *caused* by DDT.

The huge electrical blackout in New England in November 1965 was a similar technological failure. The northeastern power system was designed to compensate for local power failures. It provided a network all across New England which could transfer power to an area where it was needed. In the blackout the network operated in reverse. A failure took place in a small power station in Canada; power surging into the area tripped safety relays throughout the network, blacking out the entire New England area.

THE ATOMISM OF MODERN SCIENCE

If modern technology has failed, there must be something wrong as well with our science, which generates technology. Modern science operates well as long as the system of interest is not complex. We can understand the physical relationship between two particles, but add a third particle and the problem becomes extraordinarily difficult. Modern science has only poor methods for dealing with systems that are characterized by complex interactions. A living thing, or a single living cell, is such a system. Modern biology is dominated by the view that the most successful way to understand a biological system is to reduce it to molecular ones. Molecular biology is regarded as the cutting edge of modern biological research. But there is no way of achieving a "molecular biology" of a complex, circular process such as that operating in a sewage treatment pond, or in natural waters. What is decisive is the interaction among the separate parts—whether organisms in an ecosystem or molecules within a single cell. As a result, such studies are not regarded as part of advanced science, and become instead "applied science"—supposedly beneath the dignity of a "pure scientist" to consider. But sewage is relevant to the human condition—which depends on real, complex things. Nature is composed of living things, not enzymes. In nature, enzymes exist only as parts or products of living things. The tendency to atomize reality is a fundamental fault of modern science. It generates technology which fails to accommodate to the complex reality of nature.

This atomistic approach is characteristic of our technology. For example, John Kenneth Galbraith explains in *The New Industrial State* that the large corporations, the large manufacturers, have perfected the techniques of mass production and management to such an extent that they appear to run the society. But, Galbraith points out, there is no science or technology for producing a whole car; there is only a science and technology for engine blocks, paint, glass, or rubber. This kind of atomized technology is certainly a successful way to produce automobiles. But the approach fails as soon as the automobile leaves the factory and comes into contact with the environment. The automobile then becomes an instrument for producing lung cancer through the asbestos flaked off the brake linings, and emphysema from the noxious gases and particles it releases into the air. It contributes to algal overgrowths because it puts out nitrogen oxides which in the air may be converted to nitrates. (In New Jersey, 25 pounds of nitrogen fertilizer per acre is deposited, in rain, from the cars and trucks on the turnpikes.) All this came about because the automobile was regarded as a compilation of parts, rather than as an agent in environmental processes.

DIFFERING VIEWS ON THE SOCIAL ROLE OF THE SCIENTIST

If there are serious signs that science and technology are incompetent in understanding and reacting with natural systems, how are we in the scientific community to deal with this problem? One position is that our social system must be bent to accommodate the inherent competence of science. For example, Professor Immanuel Mesthene of Harvard proposes that in order to deal with modern technology we need a new political ethos.

To be able to vote intelligently and participate in democcracy, the citizen must understand various relationships between nature and science. To talk about superhighways versus rapid transit, he must know about smog. To talk about the Nuclear Test Ban Treaty, he must know about strontium 90 and iodine 131. To talk about bond issues for sewage, he must know about the nitrogen cycle. But most citizens lack this understanding. Therefore, Mesthene suggests that we need to take the control of policies from the public and turn it over to specialists, experts who do understand the technical background of such modern problems.

I reject this view. One reason is that it is antidemocratic. A second reason is that there is a better alternative. If the public is uninformed on technical matters it is only because scientists have not fulfilled their obligation to inform the public. When armed with technical information, the public is perfectly competent to make political decisions.

Some scientists take the position that there is no relationship between science and society. They believe that science exists in and of itself, as a kind of religion; that it has its own self-justification, as a personal, intellectual pursuit. However, scientists are, after all, people born into a society and educated by it. As they grow up they become (some more, some less) subject to effects of social forces.

Scientists have violated the precepts of science because of such social pressures. Secrecy is the enemy of scientific proof. Yet, the scientific community in the United States has for 20 or 30 years tolerated secrecy about important scientific and technological questions. For example, the simplest facts about fall-out were not declassified until 1956, more than 12 years after nuclear weapons were developed. Such secrecy is inimical to science, yet it is tolerated. We cannot claim that science is independent of society if the scientific community still tolerates secrecy.

The acceptance of secrecy has become so common that open sharing of information is the exception. I sometimes show foreign biochemists through my laboratory in St. Louis. I show them everything we are doing and then, before leaving, nine times out of ten they say to me, "Do you mind if we tell other people what we've seen here?" They *assume* that I am unwilling to let my colleagues know what I am doing, because they have been to other laboratories, where the scientists *do* mind. The only explanation I can offer for such self-imposed secrecy is that scientists value the social rewards of scientific priority—again, a social effect upon science. To a large extent science is a creature of social forces and cannot be—is not—independent of society.

THE UNIQUE SOCIAL ROLE OF THE SCIENTIST

Many physicists are concerned about the ABM and nuclear war. They are impatient to do something about this problem. Like everyone else, they can participate in anti-ABM demonstrations. But the physicist can play a *special* role in this problem. His unique contribution is his specific understanding about how the ABM may conflict with other social values. For example, if the ABM system is built, it is possible that we may run into a serious air traffic control crisis—because the construction of the vast radar systems needed to make sense out of the air traffic mess cannot be accomplished if the necessary resources and personnel are tied up in work on the ABM system. If this is true, physicists are needed to explain it to people; after all, they know about solid-state components and how they are involved in radar. In the same way, scientists can explain that using an automobile results in smog and emphysema; that the application of some insecticides to preserve a young tree from insects will also kill the robins; that every nuclear weapons test, each "peaceful" nuclear explosion, to some degree increases the incidence of birth defects.

The issues of nuclear war, insecticides, public transportation, and sewage disposal are not just scientific issues; they are moral, social, and economic issues. They should be decided by the public as a whole. But the public cannot exercise its conscience on these matters unless it knows the scientific facts. In the old days, morality worked on the basis of simple Newtonian mechanics. That is, hitting somebody with a rock would hurt him so much that the moral issue of throwing rocks at your neighbor was clear. The hurt that rock-throwing can cause is obvious; no scientist is needed to explain it. But scientists who understand the subtle laws of ecology are needed to tell people how using insecticides on Mississippi Valley farms will kill the catfish and wipe out the Cajun fishing industry in Louisiana. The issues resulting from the failures of science and technology are social, political, and moral ones; the scientist's job is to get the relevant information before the public, so that a democratic decision can be made.

There *is* a relation between science and society. The unique responsibility of a scientist is not to determine how his knowledge shall be used, because that determination does not involve his unique capabilities as a scientist. It involves only his moral position as a person. He ought to acknowledge that every person has the same right to a moral position as he does.

I believe that the scientist has a unique responsibility. He is the custodian of the knowledge that everyone needs to exercise his own conscience. If the scientist doesn't get the information to the public, the public is being cut off from the exercise of its morality.

Humanity is living under the shadow of a nuclear war. A nuclear holocaust would destroy our society. This is the gravest moral crisis in the history of the world. Yet we all live with it, tolerate it. If most people in the United States *understood* the facts of nuclear warfare, I am convinced that we would disarm. Unfortunately, the public has been protected from its own conscience by the failure of the scientific community to get the facts before the public.

When the public is informed, action comes quickly. When, much to everybody's surprise, 80 Senators voted to approve the Nuclear Test Ban Treaty, a careful analysis was made of the factors influencing the vote. The study found that the Senators had received a lot of mail from mothers who feared the dangers of fallout. What influenced the Senators most was that the mothers who wrote the letters knew how to spell "strontium 90." They knew the facts, and the Senators feared facing not simply enraged women, but informed enraged women. The force behind this informed public was education by the scientists of the community. After all, it was the scientists who first knew how to spell "strontium 90."

The unique role of the scientist, then, is to inform the public about the failures in science and technology, and to give the public a chance to let its conscience operate on the huge and potentially disastrous social problems that have been generated by the progress of modern science and technology.

Daniel
Luten

is Lecturer in Geography at the University of California, Berkeley. He holds a Ph.D. in chemistry from Berkeley. In 1962, after 25 years as a research chemist in the petroleum industry, he joined the Berkeley Geography Department in order to study the problems of population and natural resources. He has written widely on these subjects in the literature of the conservation movement.

The population explosion is often talked about in vague terms. In the following article Dr. Luten gives a quantitative description of population growth from earliest times to the present, and examines several patterns of population growth. Why is there a quarrel over the existence of a population problem? How can people disagree so completely? These are the questions Dr. Luten deals with.

Population
Growth

Everyone has been told repeatedly that we have a "population problem." It has gotten to be a bit like the weather. Let me offer, perhaps as a straw man, that this is not necessarily so; perhaps it is all in our minds. A population problem exists only for those individuals in whose minds certain necessary conditions are met. I think these necessary conditions can be reduced to three: First, such individuals must be concerned for the future. Second, they must have the perhaps quaint notion that men are masters of their own destiny. Third, possibly a corollary, they must agree that exercise of this mastery requires decisions aimed at promoting their purposes. So, as with any "problem" of this sort, it comes down to decisions, always decisions. The decisions are to promote our purposes, and our purposes reflect our concern for the future. However, our concern for the future may take many forms; the matter is not simple.

But, turning away for the moment from this direct confrontation of my topic, I want to give you, as tersely as possible, a history of human population—a curve of growth, no more. It is not necessary for me to go into even this much history. I *could* start simply by telling you that in 1960 the world's population was about 3 billion, and growing at 2 percent per year. But the curve of growth *is* dramatic, and it will help me to persuade you of my major premise. I could limit the curve to the era of good censuses (merely the past few decades), or to the era of good estimates (merely the past two millennia), but if it is to be informative, and I want it to be, I should try to cover all human history. Let us not fall into that trap of the unwary statistician, of rejecting all but the nicely tabulated and ordered information. Imprecise information may still be valuable. This is one warning. A second warning is: Don't take a foreshortened view of the past. Time passed just as slowly a hundred thousand years ago as it does today. Were we to discuss man's past, estimated at 600,000 years, in an hour, at the rate of 10,000 years per minute, the time would go like this: 30 minutes (300,000 years) on learning how to use and make tools; 15 minutes on the technology of using, maintaining, transporting, and initiating fire; 14 minutes on the exploration of the earth and the domestication of plants. In the sixtieth minute, the first 48 seconds would be spent on field agriculture, village life, and ancient empires. Finally, after the pause of a deep breath for the Dark Ages, we would have to cover the Renaissance, the Reformation, the Industrial Revolution, and the technological revolution in the last six seconds.

With these warnings, examine (Figure 1) the curve of human population growth. Over most of human history, this growth has been imperceptibly slow. Essentially all of it has occurred during the most recent 1 percent of human existence. You can draw it dramatically, with little error, on any blackboard by walking (left to right) the length of the board rubbing the chalk on the chalk ledge, then rounding slightly at the lower right-hand corner and going straight up the right-hand edge. Even when the time scale is expanded tenfold (lower curve), the transition from slow to rapid growth is abrupt. The shape of the curve almost inescapably brings the phrase "population explosion" to mind.

Table 1 gives the numbers on which the curves in Figure 1 are based. The earlier numbers (shown in parentheses) are estimates based on the supposition that the rate of growth has increased steadily throughout human existence. Some will disagree with this supposition, but I think it the most conservative of several alternate suppositions. In any event, the general form of the curve cannot be disputed. Note, in the third column, the low rates of growth in ancient times. They tell us that the rare man who lived to a great age perceived a world on the last day of

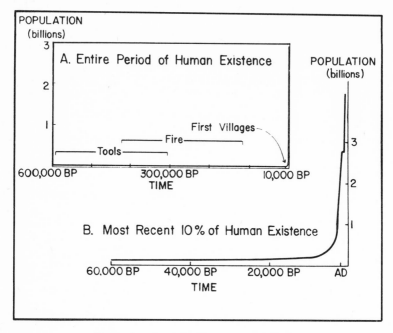

Figure 1　Growth of human population.

his conscious life which differed imperceptibly from the world of his earliest memories, both with regard to the numbers of people and, by implication, in all the patterns of living. Matters

Table 1
Estimates of Human Population

Year	Population (millions)	Increase (percent per year)	Doubling time (years)
600,000 BC	(1)		
300,000	(2)	0.00023	300,000
150,000	(4)	0.00047	150,000
50,000	(10)	0.00092	75,000
6,000	(25)	0.0021	33,000
0 AD	275	0.040	1,700
1000	275	0	—
1400	373	0.076	900
1650	470	0.093	750
1825	1,000	0.43	160
1930	2,000	0.67	100
1960	3,000	1.36	50
1968	3,500	1.8	38
		2.0	35

are different today, especially in California, where fields have turned into cities during a man's life, where a great bay has become fields, where even mountains seem about to disappear. Robinson Jeffers has used these words*:

Slowly the passenger pigeons increased, then suddenly their numbers
Became enormous, they would flatten ten miles of forest
When they flew down to roost, and the cloud of their rising
Eclipsed the dawns. They became too many, they are all dead,
Not one remains.
And the American bison: their hordes
Would hide a prairie from horizon to horizon, great heads and storm-cloud shoulders, a torrent of life—
How many are left? For a time, for a few years, their bones
Turned the dark prairies white. Now, Death, you watch for these things,
These explosions of life: they are your food,
They make your feasts.
But turn your great rolling eyes away from humanity, . . .
It is true we increase. . . .
In spite of wars, famines and pestilences we are quite suddenly
Three billion people: our bones, ours too, would make
Wide prairies white, a beautiful snow of unburied bones: . . .

PATTERNS OF POPULATION GROWTH

How should populations grow? How would you expect them to grow? Only a few patterns need to be mentioned.

1. If growth is *internally* generated and the environment

* This and the following poetry excerpt are from "Passenger Pigeons," copyright © 1963 by Garth Jeffers and Donnan Jeffers. Reprinted from *The Beginning and the End and Other Poems*, by Robinson Jeffers, by permission of Random House, Inc.

exercises no restraints, then growth should be proportional to the population and, barring other influences, the growth rate should be constant. This is the way a colony of bacteria in a stirred tank of nutrient will grow initially; this is the way money in the bank at compound interest will grow, provided inflation does not change the interest rate. You may call it "compound interest," or "geometric" or "exponential" growth. Its rules are simple, and the essence of them is easily abstracted: Such a population will double in a fixed interval, independent of how large the population is, or how often it has already doubled. The doubling time is dependent on the growth rate and is $\frac{69}{A}$, where A is the percent growth per year. The trebling time is $\frac{110}{A}$, the tenfolding time is $\frac{230}{A}$.

If the growth rate is 2 percent per year, the doubling time is $\frac{69}{2}$ or 35 years. As long as it remains 2 percent per year, the population will double in 35 years. And so double, double, double, a population of 1,000 today will be 2,000 in 35 years, 4,000 in 70 years, 8,000 in 105 years, and so on, to a million in 350 years, a billion in 700 years, a trillion in a millennium.

2. In contrast, if a population's growth stems from *outside* influences, the growth will reflect those influences. If the population is of men only (no women!) brought in from the outside at a constant rate, then, barring deaths, their numbers will grow in a linear or arithmetic fashion. The doubling pattern becomes proportional to the population, not independent of it; the curve of growth is quite different. If the capacity of the environment to support people were to grow in this fashion—say 25,000 this year, 26,000 the next year, 27,000 in the third, and so on— it would double in 25 years, but with the growth still going on at 1,000 per year, the second doubling would take 50 years, the third 100 years.

Thomas Malthus, in 1799, thought people tended to increase geometrically but food arithmetically, and that it was unlikely that food supplies could stay ahead of demand.

3. If, as a third alternative, population growth is (again)

internally generated with no initial environmental constraint, then it should begin to grow exponentially. If now the idea of a ceiling—of a limit to growth—is imposed, then as the population approaches that ceiling its growth is constrained and dwindles, perhaps approaching the ceiling asymptotically. Such growth curves have commonly been observed with experimental animals, and one form of them has been called the "logistic" growth pattern.

4. A fourth interesting possibility may be mentioned. A few years ago it was suggested that communication may be the real limit to human population growth and that population may in fact grow in proportion to the average proximity of people, the average density of population. The growth rate of such a population will increase as it becomes more dense and, when the population approaches infinity, the growth rate will approach infinity. The article postulating this, published in *Science* in 1960, was titled "Doomsday: Friday, 13 November, A.D. 2026." The moment of the infinite population was about 4 P.M. on that day. The authors of the paper had used 2,000 years of data and had extrapolated for only 66 years. Was this unreasonable? Their graphical presentation is given in the emphasized lower right-hand corner of Figure 2.

While everyone scoffed at this thesis no one rejoined, as any good scientist should, that from data covering little more than one order of magnitude they had extrapolated over an infinite number of orders of magnitude. I mention this, however, mostly for another reason. I am not competent at the mathematics of infinity, but let me examine for a moment the projection to 2 P.M. on "Doomsday." The population reached at that moment is 10^{15}, and I will come back to this shortly. If the population of 1960 (3 billion, or $10^{9.5}$) were to grow to 10^{15} in 66 years, average family size over that interval would be 200 children per woman. In fact, a physiological limit to human growth does exist and we are, today, quite close to that limit. Doomsday will not come, *in this fashion,* in the year 2026.

Now let us ask: What *has* been the pattern of human population growth? Recalling Table 1, the population of 1650 A.D. was double that of 1000 A.D.; 650 years to double. The

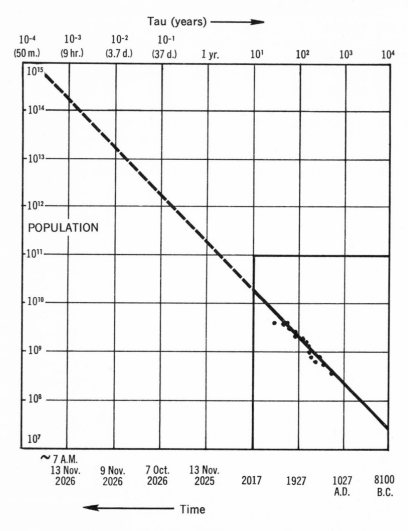

Figure 2 World population growth: "Doomsday" forecast.

population of 1825 was double that of 1650; 175 years to double. The doubling time today appears to be about 35 years. The best one can say of such growth is that it seems to be "more than exponential."

Doubling time cannot become much less. What if it continues at this rate; what if the growth remains exponential at 2 percent per year? In Figure 3 we have taken advantage of a simple rule—namely, that the logarithm of an exponentially growing population appears graphically as a straight line when plotted against time. We have put world population on a logarithmic scale; the diagonal dashed line is for exponential growth at 2 percent per year. At the year 2600 A.D. I have indicated "SRO Day." This, the Standing Room Only population, I have taken as 10^{15} (a number already mentioned on the

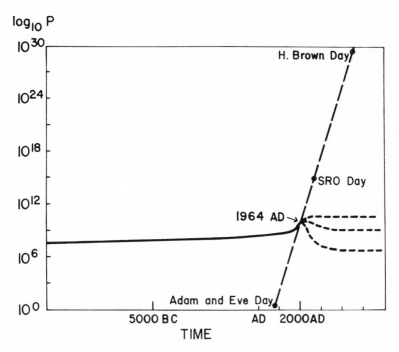

Figure 3 Semi-logarithmic plot of most recent 1 percent of world population changes.

Doomsday plot), because the earth's area, land and sea, is 5×10^{15} square feet. A population beginning at 3 billion in 1960 and growing at 2 percent per year would have 5 square feet per person in A.D. 2600. You can imagine them agrarian, spread over the state of Texas, each holding his sweet potato flat over his head; or you can imagine them urbanized, with 300,000 people living where each single one of you now lives. The next point on the curve is "HB Day" because Harrison Brown once calculated that, some time later, if such growth continued, the earth would be a mass of humanity expanding outward at the speed of light. The lowest point on the curve, "Adam and Eve Day," at about 900 A.D., is the time at which a population of two individuals growing at 2 percent per year would have begun, if it were to increase to 3 billion in 1960.

You are probably saying to yourself now that this is all a lot of nonsense; that this sort of thing cannot come to pass. I agree. So you must never say that I forecast such events. My reason for going through this exercise is simple. It is to persuade you of one thing alone: *The growth which is so familiar to you*, which is so much a part of your lives, *was unknown to all but the most recent of your ancestors and must be unknown to all but the most immediate of your descendants.* You live at a unique moment. It has never happened before in human history; it can hardly happen again. We must, in fact, be very close to the great inflection point, close to the moment when the growth rate, which has been increasing for a million years, begins, enduringly, to decline. It is an implicit corollary that the earth has limits, and that regardless of where those limits are, an exponentially growing population will run into them— and surprisingly quickly.

Some people have thought superficially about unending 2 percent growth and have suggested migration to the planets as a solution. Let me destroy this idea as quickly as possible. I will grant you that the planets are so accessible that it will cost you nothing to get there, that each of them will support exactly as many people as the earth, if you will let me ignore Pluto and will assent that one day we will have to agree: "Yes, the earth is now full. All additional growth must go to Venus." How long to fill Venus? Thirty-five years. And in the next 35 years? Mercury and Mars; The doubling time is 35 years. Two planets full; four will be full 35 years later. And in a third 35 years, Jupiter to Neptune. A century will see the planets overrun. So much for those who cannot accommodate their minds to the idea of exponential growth.

But why exponential growth, anyway? While, almost inescapably, we have to think about growth in exponential terms, it is not this habit of mind which makes growth exponential. Rather, exponential growth stems from a constant life-expectancy and a family size larger than that just needed to maintain a static population. It is *not* a consequence of increasing life-expectancy or increasing birth rates. Constant life-expectancy plus constant family size gives exponential growth. If you insist that neither of these is possible, then you must concede that either family size or life-expectancy must decline.

This is where the population problem begins. Which will you choose: long life or a large family? It is a substantial problem because all of our experience says that the world of short life-expectancy is the primitive world we have just escaped. Certainly it is not our purpose to slide back into it. But the large family has a long cultural tradition and, perhaps, even a genetic tradition; it may be instinctive.

So, the harsh decision to be faced is, on the one hand, to let things go their way until our descendants, such few as make it, find themselves again in the hazardous world of an Eskimo hunter, the grinding world of the Bolivian Altiplano, the deprived world of India in the famine year of 1943. On the other hand, some chance of a society of the sort we dream of might come to pass if family size came down close to two children. But this is *all* families, not merely families of the poor, of the ignorant; not merely the families of Asians, but also the families of the wealthy, of the educated, of the Americans. Who, in all humanity, can obtain human agreement to such a humane crusade?

This is where the matters of concern for the future, of purpose, and of making decisions all come in. If I am overwhelmed with personal problems, as most of us are in this society, if I am willing to let the future take care of itself, it is easy to pass the buck on to our children. They will, after all, be better informed on it and on what to do than we—of this we can be quite sure—and will know better how to proceed. And as for our grandchildren, what have they ever done for us? We ignore the proposition that this is one problem not to be solved overnight, nor even over a generation. But this, itself, is of course a terribly difficult, a compounding complication. Why exercise restraint when a later generation may find an easier way? Why exercise restraint when a later generation may be too ill-disciplined to hold ground gained? What *have* our grandchildren done for us?

Another approach is virtually sleight-of-hand. My efforts, such as those evidenced earlier in this essay, to demonstrate the presence of limits are categorized by opponents as "ridiculous forecasts" even though I have carefully said they are *not* forecasts. And an audience is persuaded to focus on a detailed examination of the adequacy of resources for the short run, and to study the question of how many people the world can support. This turns out to be a silly operation because it hangs on "other things being equal," on a "ceteris paribus" so elusive that nothing constructive comes out of the argument except agreement that, yes, things will be all right in this country until the end of the century. But during the argument the existence of a limit is forgotten. Again, by asking insistently how many people the world can support, we quite forget that it is certainly not our purpose to see how many people the world can support. Why ask, why go through the calculation if we do not wish an experimental confirmation or rejection of the calculation?

A corollary of this approach is the proposition that science and technology have shown an increasing capability for meeting human wants and that no reason exists to believe that this trend will end. But, equally, no reason exists to believe it will persist. Perhaps this falls in the same class as the statement, "Since I have never died, I never will."

The noted scientist Edward Teller once expressed the belief that this is not yet a major problem. Only in another century, he said, would the world face a major problem. I suspect he foresaw a day when peaceful nuclear explosives would become

utterly necessary to meet desperate resource needs. His purpose, as I see it, is not the promotion of human welfare, but
rather promotion of the use of nuclear explosives—peacefully,
that is. Thus, in contrast to his adamant opposition to political
compromise to secure "peace in our time," he did advocate social compromise. Surely, he could not have wished to be known
as the Neville Chamberlain of the population movement!

Economists have said that "natural trends" will resolve the
problem. This is "gut thinking" which quite outdoes any "gut
conservation." One manifestation of this mode of thought is
the preliminary paragraph commonly found in lectures on the
"food problem." In this paragraph, the speaker pays deference
to a population problem which, however, he suggests, will be
easily resolved if the really difficult food problem of the next
generation can be managed. But this "natural trend" must be
either smaller families or shorter life—and how natural are
they? In truth, the problems of another field always seem
simpler than those immediately before one.

In fact, the food problem *is* a population problem. Provision
of more food will only alleviate, only postpone, only magnify
the population problem. And yet, in a monstrous misallocation
of effort, we spend a thousand dollars on food research for each
dollar we spend on population study. It is the more "humane,"
if the more witless approach. I can hear Henry Thoreau in the
wings now, with his "There are a thousand hacking at the
branches of evil to one who is striking at the root."

Again, we support the proposition of family planning. But
here we can easily fall into an old trap: "If only we had a plan;
any plan is better than no plan." And so on, until we agree that
anything that is planned will turn out all right. But Kingsley
Davis has shown that Americans would plan for families which
are too large, and that family planning in America with present
notions of "ideal family size" will lead to continued exponential
population growth.

All of this controversy has become formalized in an argument, now at least 25 years old and peculiarly American, between two schools of thought. These may as well be called "op-
timism" and "pessimism." The optimists speak confidently of a

cornucopian world of enough and to spare; the pessimists of a plundered planet. The optimists focus on the United States for the short run and on economic commodities; the pessimists are concerned for a longer run—they look at the predicament of the world, and are concerned with aesthetic as well as economic attributes. The optimists are dominantly economists with a host of camp followers including a smattering of other social scientists, engineers, and developers. They allege that Thomas Malthus, bellwether of the pessimists, is discredited, disproven. The pessimists are biologists, perhaps ecologists. They still have a strong Malthusian tinge, inherited through Charles Darwin; they are not aware that Malthus has been discredited and disproved, and in fact they believe that disproof is impossible.

The entire matter can be boiled down to the two components on which population control depends: incentive and technique: Perhaps we can envision that the product of the two components must exceed a minimum. Ancient societies with enormous incentive but poor technique managed to control their populations, whether by abortion, infanticide, human sacrifice, religious celibacy, or whatnot. Modern societies with refined techniques but with no incentive have failed.

A hypothesis of a basic law of conservation says, "Any society which can see the limits of its environment will control its conduct, including its numbers, so as to stay within those limits." Curiously, it seems that traditional primitive societies have had a clearer view of the limits of their environments, of the capacities of their lands to support them in whatever manner they judged appropriate. In contrast, we do not. We are too resourceful, too fluid, too revolutionary. We have been trying for 25 years to locate the capacity of our environment, to decide whether our planet is cornucopian or plundered, and we are not succeeding very well. If we could agree that the limits are close at hand, that our populations are in excess of what is optimum for our purposes, this would give us the incentive to limit our numbers. We have the techniques. But if we cannot agree, let Robinson Jeffers find the conclusion: *

* Also from "Passenger Pigeons," by permission of Random House, Inc.

Respect humanity, Death, these shameless black eyes
of yours,
It is not necessary to take all at once—besides that,
you cannot do it, we are too powerful,
We are men, not pigeons; you may take the old, the
useless and helpless, the cancer-bitten and the
tender young,
But the human race has still history to make. For look
—look now. . . .
We can explode atoms and annul the fragments, noth-
ing left but pure energy, we shall use it
In peace and war—"Very clever," he answered, in his
thin piping voice,
Cruel and a eunuch.
Roll those idiot black eyes of yours
On the field-beasts, not on intelligent man,
We are not in your order. You watched the dinosaurs
Grow into horror: they had been little efts in the
ditches and presently became enormous, with
leaping flanks
And tearing teeth, plated with armor, nothing could
stand against them, nothing but you,
Death, and they died. You watched the sabre-toothed
tigers
Develop those huge fangs, unnecessary as our sci-
ences, and presently they died. You have their
bones
In the oil-pits and layer-rock, you will not have ours.
With pain and wonder and labor we have bought intelligence.
We have minds like the tusks of those forgotten tigers,
hypertrophied and terrible, . . .
We have invented the jet-plane and the death-bomb
and the cross of Christ—"Oh," he said, "surely
You'll live forever"—grinning like a skull, covering his
mouth with his hand—"What could exterminate
you?"

Donald
Dahlsten

is Associate Professor of Entomology at the University of California, Berkeley. He received his B.S. from the University of California, Davis, in 1956, and his Ph.D. from the University of California, Berkeley, in 1963. Professor of Zoology at California State College, Los Angeles, from 1962 to 1963, he has been at Berkeley since, where he teaches forest entomology and insect ecology. His special interest is the biological and integrated control of forest insects.

Synthetic organic pesticides have been used to an increasing extent, since their advent in the 1940's, to control insect pests which attack agricultural and forest crops. Only recently have scientists and the public become aware of and alarmed by the ecological consequences of pouring massive quantities of toxic chemicals into the environment. Professor Dahlsten holds that much of the application of chemical pesticides is unnecessary and is the result of ignorance on behalf of the users, coupled with high-pressure promotion by the chemical companies involved. He believes that in many cases the application of pesticides does nothing to control the pest and may even favor it by killing its natural enemies. More often than not, he says, pests can be dealt with by the kind of integrated control program that he is attempting to develop for combating forest insect pests. The armoratorium of this includes specialized hormones (pheromones), vertebrate predators, native and introduced insects as predators and parasites, and various cultural techniques. Only when other methods fail, says Dahlsten, is it justifiable to use even minimal effective dosages of mild chemical pesticides—and then, if at all possible, in combination with other techniques.

Pesticides

Many of the things that man does—often innocently enough—to protect his food and fiber, and to assure his health and comfort, unfortunately do little more than pollute his environment. There are many facets, however, to the solution of the complex pollution problems confronting man today. Many concerned people are finding that pollution is much more than a biological and ecological problem, for human attitudes and values are a part of these issues in one form or another. There are important legal and political aspects, education and communication difficulties, and sociological and psychological issues involved in solving pollution problems. Communicating the scientific facts on the causes of environmental deterioration to the layman is perhaps one of the most difficult tasks. The public must be educated about pollution so that the problems are clearly defined and so that alternatives are presented in such a way that the voter can make intelligent decisions regarding the solution of these complex situations. Environmental information committees have been formed across the country for the purpose of presenting scientific information in a meaningful form to the layman, and the movement is supported in print by such publications as *Environment* magazine.

There is no question that synthetic organic insecticides have a harsh effect on a broad spectrum of organisms, and that these chemicals can cause serious environmental problems. However, the severity depends not only on the chemical used, but on the attitude of the individual evaluating its pollutive effects, and on the values of society. Some persons feel that the only solution to (for example) our insect problems lies in the use of chemicals, while others feel that under current use practices, the adverse ecological effects of insecticides are too great a price to pay for the benefit gained. Yet another group feels that any use of insecticides cannot be justified. Quite apparently man must face up to a hard reevaluation of his pest control techniques and practices, and almost surely sacrifice certain goals and comforts in the interest of environmental integrity.

BASIC ECOLOGICAL CONSIDERATIONS

The many forms of pollution have a number of adverse biological and ecological effects on the environment. Among the pollutants, the chemical insecticides are somewhat unique in that not only are they designed to kill, but their toxicity covers a wide range of species within and outside the world of insects. Perhaps "biocide" would be a better term to describe many of the poisons used commercially for insect control. Other chemicals, such as fertilizers and some industrial wastes, though not directly toxic, add to the pollution problem by inducing algal bloom, which hastens eutrophication in lakes and ponds. A classic example of eutrophication is Lake Erie, a giant fresh-water body which is now essentially a huge cesspool.

A basic concern of many persons involved in controlling insects is that nonspecific chemicals cause severe disruption to the environment. Homeostasis (the balance of nature) exists in all natural environments, and any simplification of an environment has the potential to cause serious side-effects. One of the ecological precepts accepted by most biologists is that a complex environment (such as the tropics) is more stable than a simplified environment (the arctic, for instance). Fluctuations of animal populations in the Arctic attain greater amplitudes than do those in the tropics—a fact exemplified by the well-known "population explosions" of the lemmings in the Arctic. The conclusion that we can draw from this is that man was asking for trouble when he began to domesticate plants and animals. Certainly as man developed agriculture, trouble is exactly what he got. The single crop (monoculture) was a drastic simplification of the environment, and thus was vulnerable to insect "population explosions." To cope with these "explosions," man has resorted primarily to chemicals which, unfortunately, further simplify the ecosystem.

Entomologists studying agroecosystems have found them to be rather more complex than originally suspected. As a result, they have come to realize that this complexity can be utilized in the control of insect pests. Forest entomologists are also attempting to assure that our forests retain their complexity and do not become plantations of trees of the same species and the same age.

In a word, diversity in the environment is desirable—not only because of the balance of nature, but because diversity gives the environment a degree of plasticity. Any reduction in genetic diversity can be viewed as detrimental. From the viewpoint of educators, particularly those who take field trips in natural areas, a variety of plants and animals is desirable in order to teach various ecological and biological principles (food chains, competition, etc.). Another aspect of genetic diversity relates to man. Man has used many plants and animals, and their byproducts, to advantage for many years. Any simplification of the environment, or loss of species due to extinction, may be a loss of a potential means of survival. And man's survival as a species is a topic of increasing concern these days.

Organisms do not increase in numbers indefinitely. They are subject to a variety of both favorable and inimical biological agents and physical factors which, in their respective ways, either encourage or dampen population growth and thus afford what is commonly referred to as "natural control." Insects are attacked by many natural enemies that restrain insect population increase. Included among the insect's enemies are pathogens, parasitoids, and invertebrate and vertebrate predators. An insect such as the spotted alfalfa aphid, when introduced into the United States from another country, flourished and spread rapidly because of the absence of its natural enemies in the newly invaded environment. Insecticides can cause a similar effect with native pests by killing natural enemies and thus creating an environment conducive to a rapid increase of the pests.

It is obvious that the decision to control an insect pest with chemicals is no simple matter, although more often than not it has been treated as such during the past two decades. Many times there are large numbers of pest insects present but they are not causing any economic damage. It is critical in pest control that economic levels of pest insect density be established so that control will only be considered when the pest insect constitutes a problem. When this critical level is reached, then the adverse side-effects of using insect poisons must be weighed carefully. The (monetary and ecological) cost–benefit ratio must be evaluated critically in the control decision-making process.

CREATION OF INSECT PESTS

Although no insect is a pest until we call it one, insects can be pests for many reasons. They cause costly damage to crops and forests, transmit diseases to animals and plants, irritate us and domesticated animals alike. Man's degree of irritation with the insect world no doubt will increase as he becomes more civilized, more affluent, and less tolerant of the cohabitants of his natural environment. In actuality only a very tiny fraction (i.e., 6,000± of 1,000,000±) of the earth's insect species are as yet considered pests, but the number is increasing. This increase is due to the simplification of the environment, to destruction of the natural enemies of target species, as well as nontarget species, and to man's changing definition of what constitutes a pest. In a sense, the creation of insect pests is good business for the pesticide salesman!

The housewife and the homeowner have also done their share in the creation of insect pests. The "perfect fruit, vegetable, and flower" concept is not a reasonable one, to say the least. What is wrong with having an apple with a worm in it?

The larva could even be thought of as an additional protein source. The Indians used insects as a food source; perhaps our values need reevaluating. Of course, the larva could be removed from the apple and the nutritional value of the apple *per se* would not be affected. A common practice in Chile with the corn earworm is to cut the infested tassel-end of the corn ear off. Good thinking. Thus the corn earworm is considered a minor pest, at most, in Chile.

The average American homeowner practices "chemical overkill" around his home and grounds—a custom related perhaps to his thoughtless habit of "pill popping." (The good American doctor is of course the one who prescribes pills each time a patient visits him!) He has been so thoroughly convinced that his body chemistry benefits from all the myriad chemical doses that he swallows in pill form that his first rule of thumb when in the garden or among the greenery is: "The more chemicals, the better the results." His dosages approach ridiculous proportions. For example, he has been known to apply DDT, as a control for lawn moth, at the rate of 40 pounds per acre. The dosage used for control of agricultural and forest insect pests seldom exceeds two or three pounds per acre and is usually one pound per acre.

The companies that sell insecticides must also share the blame. The profit motive is certainly an important factor, and the creation of pests through advertising and salesmanship is good business. A salesman almost always will suggest a chemical means to control a pest in agriculture, because he usually receives a commission on the sale and, after all, he makes his living this way. This is good business, but it is not good pest control, and it is disastrous for the environment. The salesman treats pest control as a marketing situation rather than as a biological and ecological issue.

However, the problem is not just biological and ecological; it is one of communication. The public as well as government officials must be educated concerning what constitutes scientific or ecological pest control. Chemical companies will have to produce specific chemical insecticides, or maybe even biotic insecticides (insect diseases and beneficial insects). The margin of profit may have to be reduced. Salesmen will have to be examined and licensed by a federal or state government bureau. New legislation will have to be enacted to control the abuse of insecticides, and the existing laws will have to be enforced by impartial agencies. Most difficult of all, the public will have to be made to examine its attitudes and values, and see the need for a new way of thinking about solutions to environmental problems. The new era may well be one in which many of our present insect "pests" will be of entomological interest only.

MODERN INSECT CONTROL

Since the advent of DDT in 1946, the arsenal of insect-control weaponry has been overstocked with chemical insecticides. The industry associated with this has become a multi-million-dollar business. There has been considerable benefit to man in the areas of disease control and crop production increase. Chemical insecticides usually act quickly as compared to other types of control measures (e.g., biological, cultural, genetical), and isolated treatments are relatively inexpensive. There are a number of problems, however, which arise from the use of chemicals in pest control.

The argument over the benefits and hazards of insecticides continues, but often the real problems in pest management are not even touched upon. Economic entomologists with an ecological bent think in terms of natural control, environmental diversity, and pest population dynamics, and are more concerned with adverse effects of chemicals on the ecosystem than are those myopic entomologists who view control as the use of chemical insecticides alone.

One of the great misconceptions about insecticides is that they are invariably effective. This just is not so—although in most cases of commercial use there is never any check on effectiveness. (This is particularly true with some forest insect-control projects, though there are examples from agriculture, too.) Not only are the chemicals ineffective in some cases, but effectiveness may be enhanced by natural agents in other situations. The Douglas fir–tussock moth project in northeastern California in 1965 is a good example of an apparently successful chemical-control project. Approximately 60,000 acres of forest land were sprayed with DDT at a rate of three-fourths of a pound per acre. However, at the time of treatment, tussock moth populations were afflicted with a nucleopolyhedrosis virus disease and these populations were declining naturally. The project was hailed as a success, but tussock moth populations disappeared from the untreated areas as well as from those areas that were sprayed. To most scientists this would mean that the chemical spray was totally ineffective. The authorities responsible claimed that there would be less damage in the sprayed areas because of the time it would take for the disease to kill all of the larvae. This was not well documented and is a weak argument for broad-scale application of a persistent chemical like DDT.

Continuous evaluation is a necessary part of any spray operation, commercial or not, because natural controls can become predominant over a period of time. In agriculture where crops are harvested annually, decisions can be made rapidly, but in forestry there is some flexibility because the harvest interval may be 30 to 60 years. Contracts for forest chemical-control projects are often bid on six to eight months prior to actual application. Continuous monitoring is therefore a necessity. Many times, infestation areas are spotted "after-the-fact" in forestry, usually by airplane. It is common knowledge that when insect populations reach such proportions that damage is noticeable from the air, the population has reached its zenith and will decline from natural causes. This was the situation with the Douglas fir–tussock moth affair: The spray application was one year late. In other regions, blocks of land have been sprayed after insect populations had already disappeared due to natural causes. A "no insect–no spray" clause should be part of every forest insect-control contract as a protection to the environment. A 10 percent penalty fee should also be included to protect the company bidding on the project.

In this way, the company would receive 10 percent of the cost of the control should the insect populations decline naturally and the need to spray no longer exist.

Some problems are common to all pest-control practices. One serious problem is that of insect resistance to insecticides. Some 200 pest species of insects and mites have developed resistance to one insecticide or another, and the number is increasing annually. This is a simple natural selection process whereby those insects unaffected by the insecticide remain after the application. These organisms breed, and soon a resistant population results. Sometimes cross-resistant forms develop and these organisms develop resistance to a group of insecticides—for example, to the chlorinated hydrocarbons (DDT, dieldrin, aldrin, etc.).

Residues of insecticides pose different problems. ("Residues" pertains to those insecticides that have a long residual action—in other words, those that remain in the environment for a long time.) The persistent pesticide and its metabolites move along food chains and concentrate in the animals at the end of the food chain. But there are residue problems with some of the short-lived materials (such as parathion), too. A sequence of events may go as follows: An acreage of forested land suffering from unwanted defoliation is sprayed with DDT. Eventually the DDT breaks down into the metabolites DDE and DDD. These materials eventually are washed into the soil, then gradually are picked up along with soil particles and carried to the sea or to a lake. Transfer of these toxic materials also occurs through air currents. All of this may explain why penguins in the remote Antarctic have been found to have DDT residues. The residues become incorporated in plant tissues or organic debris which are fed upon by other organisms (fish, for this example). The herbivorous fish are of course fed on by other fish, and so on. In the end the fish-eating bird (penguin, pelican, grebe, etc.) that feeds on the bigger fish gulps down fairly concentrated doses of DDT and its metabolites.

What is the explanation for the abnormally thin-shelled eggs of pelicans living along the coast of California? Some say the condition may be due to enzyme induction. In some birds DDT induces the synthesis of hepatic microsomal enzymes which have a broad spectrum of activity in the liver. One activity includes the ability to hydroxylate the steroid sex hormones testosterone, progesterone, and estrogen. Estrogens affect calcium metabolism and eggshell formation in birds. An increase in estrogen metabolism because of these enzymes could depress the estrogen level and result in thin-shelled eggs. The concentration of insecticide residues along food chains has been documented at Clear Lake, California, where reproduction of a fish-eating bird, the Western grebe, was drastically affected.

Pesticide residues are of concern to us due to their movement along food chains (as discussed above), but we are also concerned about those residues occurring on our food. Pesticide control over residues on foods is regulated by the Federal Food, Drug and Cosmetic Act of 1938 and an amendment to it, Public Law 518 (the Miller Amendment). In the United States approximately 400 chemicals are added to or sprayed onto food as preservatives, mold inhibitors, antioxidants, tints, bleaches, thickeners, thinners, emulsifiers, and moisteners. At least the more questionable of these agents should quickly come under much closer scrutiny, if only because they are so very widely and heavily used: An estimated 100 billion pounds of these synthetic organic chemicals is sold annually in the United States.

It took twenty years to find out the truth about DDT. Can we afford *not* waiting to discover all the latent hazards within chemicals before approving them for wide usage? What amount of residue really *is* safe—and *how* safe—for human consumption? What dosages of insecticide really *are* needed to do a specific job—and *exactly* what side-effects can be expected? How many more mistakes can we make in an environment that is already under considerable strain?

There is a need for new laws to replace the 1947 Federal Insecticide, Fungicide and Rodenticide Act. This law governs the marketing of pesticides and of other poisons marketed in interstate commerce. New laws are needed to enforce the registration of, and to improve the labelling of, these toxicants. Labels in the future might read "Caution, pesticide usage may be hazardous to the environment," and then list some of the consequences of side-effects (resistance, resurgence, creation of new pests, destruction of wild life, and so on).

Some feel that a compromise solution can be reached by applying Paracelsus' Law: "Poison is in everything, and no thing is without poison. The dosage makes it either a poison or a remedy." However, insecticide damage occurs at recommended dosages, so this is surely no solution to the problem. Further, if an insect problem can be solved by other means, then why insist on using chemicals? Once again we are confronted by the profit motive. A reevaluation of our value system is a must— and the entomologist must realize that he, too, has a social responsibility.

THE CHEMICAL TREADMILL

Resurgence of the target species, and the actual creation of new pests, are common phenomena in modern insect control following a spray application. To explain this we can return to a consideration of some basic ecological precepts—the balance of nature, diversity, and simplification of the environment. Resurgence of pest species occurs when the natural enemies and the target insect are killed but the pest reinvades or rebounds explosively because it is free of its natural enemies. The balance between the pest and its natural enemies has tipped in favor of the pest. There has been a loss of diversity and a simplification of the environment. New pests are created in much the same way. In this situation an insect that had not been a pest suddenly warrants pest status because it has been freed of its natural enemies or because interspecific competition with other phytophagous (plant-eating) insects has lessened. Use of a disruptive force (insecticides) in this case is a demonstration of how changes in the local environment can favor one species over another. In both of these situations the farmer or the forest manager is forced into the regular use of chemicals. Obviously, then, chemicals should be used as a last resort, right from the start.

THE ALTERNATIVES

There are many alternatives to chemical insecticides for insect control. Many are quite simple. If the money expended on the development and use of insecticides were used to develop these alternate means of control, the pesticide pollution picture might be very different. But how much profit is there in a pound of ecology?

The first alternative is to do nothing. Let nature take its course, so to speak. In forestry this is a particularly good alternative because, as we have said, most detection is done on the basis of damage surveys. In other words, by the time injury appears it is usually too late to do anything but spray and disrupt the natural controls that have started to operate. This concept would be functional in agriculture and in home gardens, too, with just a slight adjustment in value systems. Depending on the economic values involved, however, it may be necessary to treat before damage reaches a certain threshold.

Any number of nonchemical control techniques have been tried—the use of insect-resistant plant varieties, for example. Various cultural techniques have also been tried, such as changing planting dates and plowing stubble fields. The sterile-male technique developed by the U. S. Department of Agriculture for the screw worm fly may also have potential for control of other insects. Huge numbers of flies were raised, irradiated so that the male sperm would be sterile, and then released into screw worm-infested areas. The female mates only once in her lifetime, so if mated with a sterile male she will not produce any offspring. This sterilization method has worked particularly well on Curaçao, the well-known island off the coast of Venezuela, as well as in the southeastern United States.

Biological control has also been shown to be effective on both insect pests and weed pests alike. The cottony cushion scale on oranges was controlled by the importation of the Vedalia ladybird beetle. This was the beginning of a formalized science of biological control. Klamath weed was controlled in California by introducing a phytophagous beetle. There have been many successful programs, despite a number of partial successes and outright failures, in agriculture and forestry. Biological control traditionally has been thought of as only the importation of natural enemies of exotic (introduced) insect pests. However, the definition has been broadened to include the augmentation and conservation of naturally occurring parasites and predators.

Probably the most sound and innovative approach to pest control has been developed at the University of California. Called "integrated control," it incorporates three general principles: (1) Consider the ecosystem; (2) Utilize economic levels; and (3) Avoid disruptive actions. This is a scientific and ecological approach to pest management. A control program is devised for each species of insect pest on the basis of "weak points" in its life cycle. The program may involve only one type of control technique, or possibly the use of chemicals in combination with other approaches. For example, the spotted alfalfa aphid program in California involved the selective use of a chemical insecticide, native predators, resistant strains of alfalfa, a naturally occurring fungus disease, and imported parasites. The approach to the problem is the critical issue.

COMPLEXITY OF THE PROBLEM

The pesticide problem, extremely complex, is worldwide in scope. What with the increased concern over DDT in the United States, one would think that production of this insecticide would have decreased. This is not the case: Use has decreased in the United States, but *exportation* has increased. This will certainly not solve the problem, not even for the United States. Examples of the worldwide movement of persistent chlorinated hydrocarbons (discussed above) should attest to this. The public should be made aware of this and not be tricked into thinking a problem has been solved when in reality it has not.

Other issues involved in insect control can best be illustrated by several pest-control programs. In both South and Central America, insect problems on cotton have increased as production and pest control have increased. In Guatemala the average number of treatments per season has reached 30. A program which so outrageously ignores ecology and relies solely on insecticides is surely headed for disaster. On the other hand, the growing of cotton in the Cañete Valley of Peru can be cited as an example of how pest problems can be solved. There, prior to the appearance of DDT, chemical control of cotton pests was based primarily on arsenicals and nicotine sulfate. In the late 1940's some chlorinated hydrocarbons were used. In 1949 there was a severe outbreak of one pest, *Heliothis virescens,* along with heavy aphid infestations. These outbreaks were attributed to the introduction of chlorinated hydrocarbon insecticides and the use of ratoon cotton (second and third-year cotton). From 1943 to 1948 the average yield of cotton in the Cañete Valley varied from 415 to 526 pounds per acre. In 1949 the average yield dropped to 326 pounds per acre.

Between 1949 and 1956 some cultural practices were modified to increase yields. New strains of cotton were introduced, more efficient irrigation practices were initiated, and heavy reliance was placed on the new organic insecticides. Watching the cotton yields increase from 440 pounds per acre in 1950 to 648 pounds per acre in 1954, the farmers became convinced that the more insecticide they used, the better. They even cut down trees in order to facilitate the spraying of the fields by airplane.

A sequence of events then began to take place which was to spell disaster for the farmers. Birds that had nested in the trees disappeared. Other beneficial organisms, such as parasitoids and predators, disappeared. The number of treatments was increased. Several of the insecticides became ineffective as pests developed resistance. Organophosphorous compounds were used to replace the chlorinated hydrocarbons. The interval between treatments grew progressively shorter, from 15 days to eight days to three days. A whole complex of insects which were never pests suddenly reached pest status. During the 1955–56 season, insects ran amok in the cotton fields. The ecological nightmare inevitably became an economic disaster for the growers as yields dropped to 296 pounds per acre. It had become

painfully obvious that insecticides alone were not the answer—
that the large amounts used did nothing but line the pockets of
the chemical salesmen.

In 1957 an integrated control program was initiated. A
number of changes were made in the pest control practices, and
certain cultural practices were adopted. Ratoon cotton, and cotton
production on marginal land were prohibited. Natural enemies
from neighboring valleys were introduced. Such salutary practices
as uniform planting dates and cotton-free fallow periods were
established. The use of synthetic organic insecticides was prohibited in specific fields except by approval of a special commission. Arsenicals and nicotine sulfate were put into use again.

Because of the new integrated control program, the severity
of the cotton pest problem subsided. There was an overall reduction in direct pest-control costs. By the next year, yields were
up to 468 pounds per acre, and since have varied between 644
and 922 pounds per acre.

This project demonstrates that sound pest management is
possible and that chemicals can safely be used but not safely
overused. Herein lies a conflict that is neither biological nor
ecological in nature: How can an individual whose livelihood
depends on sales and commissions think in ecological terms or
recommend that the amounts of chemicals used be reduced? No
doubt there is an "education gap," too. Most salesmen are not
trained biologists.

FOREST INSECT CONTROL

Among the several ways in which forest insect control
differs from agricultural pest control is that insecticide salesmen
do not usually abound because of the relatively low volume of
sales. But this makes for a most distressing situation, for although the officials who make the pest-control decisions are
under no particular pressure from salesmen, they nevertheless
rely heavily on chemicals. Forest landowners may be expected
to exert some pressure to control insects on their property because the U. S. Forest Service absorbs one-half of the cost, and
in California the State Division of Forestry one-fourth of the

cost, of control projects on private property. This arrangement was created by Public Law 110, the Forest Pest Control Act, in 1947, and by the California Forest Insect Control Law, Public Resources Code 4451–4459. Again, we are confronted with values and attitudes: "If I can get three-fourths of the control project paid for, then I am really getting a good deal; and besides, if there are no insects there, I'll be protecting my forest from them." Again, this is fallacious thinking, since prophylaxis can itself create many problems.

The 1965 Douglas fir–tussock moth project in California obviously involved misguided attitudes and values. Why was control enacted at a time when natural agents were gaining the upper hand? Why was the area sprayed four to five times larger than the high-density population areas that could have been treated? Any biologist knows that this decision could have created more problems than it solved; that insect control must have a sound ecological basis.

Chemical control of bark beetles is another practice that is questionable. No one seems to know if lindane, a chlorinated hydrocarbon, controls populations of bark beetles, or if there are any side effects—though indications are that this procedure does little, if any, good. And the situation in general has not been helped by the fact that some sound biological recommendations from early forest entomologists have been ignored. It was suggested 30 years ago that bark beetle-infested trees that were to be treated be cut high on the stump in order to preserve predators (it had been found that they go to the base of the tree). The remainder of the tree was to be treated. This practice was not observed until recently. It was also suggested that samples be taken of trees prior to treatment, to check for the incidence of bark beetle parasitization. Those trees with high numbers of parasitoids should not be treated but should be left as a source of parasitoids. This has never been practiced. It is encouraging that a cultural technique, salvage logging, is now being recommended in California for bark beetle control. However, it took 30 years of introducing chemicals into the environment before salvage logging was put into practice. Beetle-infested trees are now logged and sold; the insects are hauled out of the forest.

In time this practice is certain to replace chemical control of bark beetles everywhere.

One final insect-control situation illustrates how an insect pest is created. The 1968 outbreak of pine needle scale (a tiny white scale insect) in the area of the California city of South Lake Tahoe is an indicator of what forest entomologists can expect in the future as more of the state's montane regions are subdivided and urbanized. Hopefully, the integrated control approach at Lake Tahoe will serve as a prototype for the solution of other insect problems.

The pine needle scale is rarely thought of as a pest. The only time this insect reaches high densities is in ecologically disturbed situations, such as on conifers along dirt roads (and, in the days of the steam locomotive, along railroad grades). Apparently the dust and the soot protect the scale insects in some way from their natural enemies. When the massive outbreak on the pines in Tahoe was discovered, it was found that the areas where the scale was heavy had been fogged with malathion at weekly intervals for mosquito control. Although it has not yet been proven, it appears that the natural controls of the scale were disrupted by the spray program for mosquitoes. It was recommended to the city that the fogging operation to control adult mosquitoes cease at once. The city fathers tried to cooperate, but some officials were reluctant to give it up completely. (Fogging cost the city and the taxpayers approximately $35,000 in 1968.) Apparently some officials were worried that the public would think that nothing was being done with their money. During the summer of 1969, when the city fogged on a limited basis, residents came out of their homes and cheered when the fogging truck arrived. It is unfortunate that they were not made to realize that water or any other placebo would have been much better for their insect problem than spraying with the organophosphate malathion.

Fogging with chemical insecticides for adult mosquitoes has long been thought of as an inefficient means of control. In most areas of California the practice has been discontinued in favor of source abatement—controlling the insects at the source (larvae in brooks, ponds, and the like). The control program being studied for Lake Tahoe has an ecological basis; the mosquito control problem is being studied along with the pine needle scale problem. Mosquitoes are always troublesome in the Sierras, as any back-packer will tell you, and they well may always be. However, as soon as people begin to live in the area and talk to their neighbors, they begin to agitate for action to get rid of the bothersome little pests. Such was the case at South Lake Tahoe. A mosquito control operation was initiated in 1963 and, despite the negative recommendation of entomologists at one of the state agencies, fogging was decided upon as the means of control.

The control program being developed at South Lake Tahoe is a complicated one. First of all, there are two types of mosquitoes, both troublesome: the *Aedes* snow mosquitoes in the early spring, and *Culex tarsalis* in the summer. In order to handle the snow mosquitoes trout fingerlings will be released in the snow pools—small pools formed by melting snow. The trout feed voraciously at the cool temperatures and can eat many larvae per day. As the season progresses, the trout will be removed from the pools and transferred to the local streams to the delight of sport fishermen. These trout will have been raised on natural food rather than on liver and cheese—a boon to the fisherman as well as to persons annoyed by mosquitoes. A different fish, the mosquito fish (*Gambusia*), will be used in ponds during the summer against the *Culex* mosquitoes. Chemical larvicide will also be used in some smaller pools as needed.

The pine needle scale's natural enemies are just now beginning to reestablish themselves since the cessation of fogging. An attempt will be made to augment natural establishment with insectary-reared parasitoids, or to move parasitoids from area to area, in the near future in order to hasten the return to balance.

CONCLUSION

The pesticide problem is a complicated one in many respects. Not only are complex biological and ecological issues involved, but there are also such things as the profit motive, and apathy toward the environment, confronting the entomologist.

The scientists working in this area must treat each insect problem separately, and an ecological approach must be followed so as to put as little pressure as possible on an already strained ecosystem. The scientist also has a social responsibility. He must speak out and help to educate the community about sound ecological approaches to insect control such as integrated control techniques. He must also be willing to confront those with no concern for the environment, and those with a myopic approach to pest control, and show the land manager, farmer, and homeowner that there are alternatives which will maintain insects at tolerable levels while maintaining the integrity of the environment.

Rodney
Arkley

is Lecturer in the Department of
Soils and Plant Nutrition at the University of California,
Berkeley. Raised on a citrus farm in California, he earned
his B.A. in chemistry from the University of California,
Berkeley (1940), and a Ph.D. in soil science from the same
school (1961). Professor Arkley has been a soil surveyor for
the U. S. Department of Agriculture and for the University of
California, where he has taught since 1957. His research
interests include soil genesis, morphology and classification,
land classification, climatology, and geomorphology.

Although advances in agricultural technology have by
themselves made it possible for American agriculture to
feed a growing urban population, Arkley warns, social and
economic factors will also have to be considered in the
future performance of that task. In particular, as urban
populations increase, land best suited for agricultural purposes must not be urbanized. Professor Arkley maintains
that the urbanization of present or potential farmland is not
inevitable but is a result of ecological ignorance and of the
unwillingness to put long-term ecological well-being before
real-estate profits. And, says he, this is not just a problem
for his home state, California: The whole of the continental
United States is scheduled to run out of excess prime agricultural land in the not-too-distant future.

Land
Misuse

For several million years man survived and increased in numbers essentially because he was able to adapt to changing environmental conditions. Then about 10,000 years ago, a significant change in this pattern took place. Man learned to manipulate his environment. He began to plant crops and cultivate the soil. The development of cultivated agriculture initiated a chain of processes which have modified the face of the earth: clearing the forests, plowing up the great prairies, damming or diverting rivers. Agriculture provided the basis upon which civilization has developed, and for the exponential growth of population during the past few millennia.

With this tremendously rapid increase in population, the demand for food has led to a similarly rapid expansion in cultivated agriculture and in the area which has been modified for this purpose. It is evident that these processes will continue even more rapidly for some time in the future. However, it has also become clear that each modification of the environment causes interactive changes in the relationships among soil, plants, and animals. These changes may or may not be desirable in the long-run ecological balance between man and nature.

In order to increase the food supply for the growing population, man must develop a sustained agriculture which is in equilibrium with the forces of nature. He cannot continue to use exploitive methods which are ultimately destructive of the resources upon which he depends for his food supply. I view the agricultural scientist as having a key role in the survival of mankind. He must develop and disseminate the knowledge which will make it possible for the world community to carry on a permanent, sustained agriculture, and must help guide the policy decisions of society that will make this possible.

SOIL RESOURCES OF CALIFORNIA IN RELATION TO POPULATION GROWTH AND URBANIZATION PRESSURE

Almost everyone in California has seen the expansion of cities onto areas of good agricultural land. It is particularly evident in Southern California, where vast areas of citrus orchards and other farmland have been replaced by housing developments, shopping centers, and industrial plants at the rate of 90,000 acres per year. But the conversion of cropland to urban use is not confined to the Los Angeles area; it is proceeding rapidly around every major city in the state. The process is evident in the Bay Area, where orchards and vegetable cropland are being urbanized rapidly in Santa Clara, Alameda, and Sonoma Counties. It is equally rapid around such cities as Fresno, Bakersfield, Modesto, and Sacramento, and almost every other fairly large city. The urbanization of California farmland is, in reality, a national problem. California produces 25 percent of all table food for the United States, including 42 per cent of tree fruits and nuts, 43 percent of all vegetables, and 75 percent of all wine.

Up to the present time, the effect upon the total agricultural economy of the state has not been particularly evident. The reason for this is that farmers who sell out to urban developers at a high price per acre often use the proceeds to develop new or more intensive farms elsewhere. However, the soil resources of California are limited. Of the total area of the state (100,000,000 acres), only about 21,000,000 are suitable for cultivated crops, of which 12,250,000 already are under cultivation. Only about 5,000,000 acres can be considered really first-rate soils, and unfortunately the centers of most rapid urbanization are located in the midst of areas of these better soils. As the population of California continues to grow, more and more of our better soils will become urbanized. The question is: What are the implications of the present trend toward urbanization? Are they desirable? What will happen to agriculture when urbanized cropland can no longer be replaced by developing new cropland?

Population Growth

WORLD POPULATION   The great expansion of our cities is mainly due to population increase and to the fact that, with mechanization, a steadily declining percentage of the population is needed on our farms. Let us examine first the population growth-rate for the world as a whole. An article in *Science* magazine (Foerster, Mora, and Amiot, November 1960) stated that the world population has doubled and redoubled almost five times in the past 1,960 years. The amazing thing about this rate of growth is not that population tends to double and redouble, but that the doubling rate keeps accelerating. In other words, during the past 1,960 years, each time-period required for the population to double itself is shorter by almost half than the previous doubling time. This is illustrated by Table 1.

Table 1
World Population Growth and Doubling Times

World population (billions)	Date (A.D. 1–1965)	Doubling time (years)
0.1	A.D. 1	—
0.2	1000	1,000
0.4	1500	500
0.8	1750	250
1.6	1900	150
3.2	1965	65

If this acceleration is continued, the world population will reach 10 billion by about 2006, and 100 billion by 2024. These figures are so vast and so frightening that few scientists will concede that such a growth rate can continue unabated. However, with the life span steadily increasing due to improved health and sanitation, it appears that at least the current doubling rate of 65 years will be maintained until starvation or some other factor curtails the rate of population growth. UNITED STATES POPULATION From 1800 to 1900, the U. S. doubling rate was much more rapid than that of world population in general, due largely to immigration. Doubling times averaged approximately 25 years. Since 1900 (when the population reached 76,000,000 and the nation became quota conscious), immigration has contributed only insignificantly to U. S. population growth. However, the doubling rate is still more rapid than that of the world as a whole. By 1950, the U. S. population stood at 151,000,000 and indications are that by 1990 it will reach 300,000,000.

CALIFORNIA POPULATION Census data show that the population of California has doubled every 20 years or less since 1850. If this rate continues, the state's population will be 30,000,-000 by 1980, 60,000,000 by 2000, and 120,000,000 by 2020. This very high growth rate may well diminish, but unless it falls to zero this will only extend the time required to attain these high populations.

Urbanization Pressure

THE URBAN MIGRATION There are now less than 7,000,000 people employed on farms in the United States. This great change from a primarily agricultural population began about 1937. (It was probably delayed somewhat by the Depression; the number of tractors on farms was increasing during the 1920's.) Since 1937 the output per hour of farm labor has increased over 400 percent. The great shift of population from rural to urban areas has resulted mainly from mechanization, but also from increased production per acre due in part to the efforts of the soil-, plant-, and animal scientists. The great migration to cities has thus been due in part to the activities of agricultural scientists. But the mechanization process was probably an inevitable result of the general industrial revolution. Also, the lag between the prices received by the farmer and his costs of production has forced the farmer to seek ever-increasing efficiency. Therefore we conclude that agricultural science merely accelerated an otherwise inevitable process. If one stands in front of Hilgard Hall on the Berkeley campus one reads: "To rescue for human society the native values of rural life." This statement implies that rural life was going down for the third time in 1917 and needed to be rescued. If this was a responsibility of agricultural science it clearly has failed in its mission.

What are the prospects for California agriculture? California is a large state (again, 100,000,000 acres) and still has a great deal of open space. By 1955, 2,760,000 acres of the state's cropland was occupied by urban areas, roads, railroads, and airports. This appears to be a small percentage—until we recall that of the state's total area, only about 21,000,000 acres are suitable for cultivated crops. How much of this potential cropland has been urbanized, and how fast will the urbanization process continue?

Comparing the total population and the cropland urbanized by 1955, we find that 220 acres have been urbanized per 1,000 residents. Nationwide estimates of the rate of urbanization of cropland vary from 238 acres per 1,000 persons (in areas where mountainous terrain tends to concentrate urbanization on the valley lands) to 178 acres per 1,000 (in the Great Plains area). If we adopt a very conservative estimate of 200 acres of cropland urbanized per 1,000 population, we can predict the effect of future population growth on the cropland area of California.

Up to 1969 about 4,000,000 acres of cropland had been lost to other uses. With 21,000,000 acres suitable for cultivation, 12,250,000 presently under cultivation, and 3,760,000 already urbanized, only 5,000,000 acres of land suitable for cultivation remain undeveloped. The farmers displaced from urbanized land can be expected to bring this land under cultivation by about 1980, at the present rate. After that, all areas of cultivated land in the state can be expected to decline as urbanization continues. If our population continues to double every 20 years, and cropland continues to be urbanized at the rate of 200 acres per 1,000 population, there will be only 6.2 million acres under cultivation by the year 2000, and all of California's cropland will be lost before 2020. Thus, in less than 50 years we can expect almost the entire San Joaquin and Sacramento Valleys, as well as the coastal valleys and a good bit of the desert region, to be urbanized.

Not only does this trend threaten the agricultural production of California, but this very pattern of urbanization endangers the health and welfare of the people who will live in these newly urbanized areas. Agricultural valleys are the worst places for the placement of large populations because, like the Los Angeles basin, they would be natural traps of smog. Professor Kenneth Watt of the University of California, Davis, has predicted that the Los Angeles area will soon experience "killer smog" attacks which will lead to the deaths of at first tens of thousands, and later hundreds of thousands, of people. Within a 100,000-acre area around Los Angeles, 75 percent of the Ponderosa pine trees have been damaged by smog; and in the San Francisco Bay Area, where smog is relatively light, damage to flowers, lettuce, apricots, spinach, and grapes has been attributed to smog. The urbanization of California's agricultural valleys is threatening to make such smog attacks a way of life for future generations in California. These are the inevitable results if the present trends continue unchanged.

TOWARD A SANE LAND-USE POLICY

If we wish to retain cultivated agriculture in California and avoid the urbanization of all the valley land in the state, it is clear that the present trends must be changed. There appear to be two things that can be done:

(1) Urbanization can be diverted from the good agricultural lands in the valleys, and toward the hill lands, where soils are generally shallow and unsuitable for intensive cultivation. There is plenty of such land in California. This can only be accomplished if the people of the state recognize the problem and support the planning, zoning and taxation laws necessary to prevent the needless conversion of good arable land to other uses. Admittedly the cost of building on the hills is higher than on flat land, but not unduly so.

Such a land-use policy may prove detrimental to the short-term economic interests of real-estate developers. But when considering the allocation and usage of our most vital natural re-source, land, it seems advisable to consider the long-term eco-logical consequences for all the people.

(2) Reduce the rate of California's population increase. However, since migration to California cannot be prevented by law under the Constitution, it is evident that the control of population growth must be on a nationwide basis. Any attempt to do this on a local basis will be quickly nullified by immigra-tion.

The necessity for simultaneous action on both fronts seems clear, for zoning laws are very difficult to maintain against the demands for living space by an ever-increasing population.

The outlook for California agriculture is by no means hopeless. Many people are aware of the trends. Attempts are under way in many parts of the state to establish the necessary zoning and taxation policies to protect the better croplands for agricultural purposes. People are becoming more and more aware of the problems resulting from the rapid population growth and urban expansion. Surely, effective action can be taken in time to prevent California from becoming the "Anthill State" instead of the "Golden State."

It is obvious that Malthus was right, but not altogether for the right reasons. Starvation is not the first disaster resulting from explosive population growth; it is accompanied or preceded by the crowding of people onto precious fertile soils, so that the space for crop production declines. When there is no longer room to expand agricultural production, then the specter of starvation will become a reality. Mankind has the power of choice. It is hoped that he will choose the path of a good life for a limited number rather than starvation in a world of unlimited population, with its soil resources buried under concrete and asphalt.

Robert E. Feeney

is Professor of Food Science and
Technology at the University of California, Davis. He received his B.S. in chemistry from Northwestern University
in 1938, and his M.S. and Ph.D. from the University of
Wisconsin in biochemistry in 1938 and 1942, respectively.
A former researcher for Harvard Medical School and the
U.S. Department of Agriculture, he was Professor of Chemistry at the University of Nebraska from 1953 until 1960,
when he began teaching at the University of California. His
fields of interest include protein biochemistry, comparative
biochemistry, and molecular genetics.

Professor Feeney discusses the world food problem in
terms of famine due to problems of food distribution, and
surveys potential worldwide problems due to the pressure
of population on our agricultural resources. He emphasizes
that though technological approaches to this problem are
appealing because they fit comfortably with the atomistics
of modern science, the most basic problems involved in feeding mankind are social, economic, philosophical, and political in nature. It is very unlikely, he says, that the food problem will be solved until all of us learn to take all factors
into account.

The World Food Supply

Population experts calculate that by the year 2000 there will be over twice as many people as there are now, and that we will need over three times as much food as we presently have in order to provide adequate nutrition worldwide. The problems facing us in our efforts to provide sustenance for all people everywhere are so great and so varied that we must literally do what is supposed to be virtually impossible: move vigorously in many directions at one and the same time. The temptation, of course, is to follow the easiest route, which is the physical one: produce the food. The social, political, economic, and philosophical routes are much harder to travel along, and there is grave danger that these will receive much less traffic than is necessary.

Secretary of Agriculture Clifford Hardin has made the following three suggestions for action:

1. Family, national, and international policies for effective population control *now,* i.e., reducing the propensity to reproduce.
2. Agricultural development to increase food production in hungry nations, with interim food aid from advanced countries.
3. Economic, political, and social changes in developing countries, designed to promote total economic development.

The President's Panel on the World Food Supply reached four basic conclusions:

Robert E. Feeney

1. The scale, severity, and duration of the world food problem are so great that a massive, long-range, innovative effort unprecedented in human history will be required to master it.
2. The solution of the problem that will exist after about 1985 demands that programs of population control be initiated now. For the immediate future, the food supply is critical.
3. Food supply is directly related to agricultural development and, in turn, agricultural development and overall economic development are critically interdependent in the hungry countries.
4. A strategy for attacking the world food problems will, of necessity, encompass the entire foreign economic assistance effort of the United States in concert with other developed countries, voluntary institutions, and international organizations.

We in the United States are not accustomed to thinking of production scarcities. Even our food shortages almost always are based on problems of economics or distribution rather than on availability. But the world picture is very different.

THE WORLD FOOD SUPPLY NOW AND IN THE FUTURE

The entire population of the world probably could be fed in a very satisfactory manner (for the next several years, at least), merely through a more widespread application of modern methods of food production and distribution. The question is: Who will initiate and follow through on this application, and who will pay for it all? The people who need the most help are the least capable of helping themselves.

The billion people of the developed countries consume half again as many calories and five times the amount of high-quality animal protein per person as do the two billion people living in the underdeveloped countries. Table 1 contains estimates of the calorie and protein consumptions of these peoples. (The figures are at least ten years old but are not outdated.)

Table 1
Calorie and Protein Consumptions of Developed
and Undeveloped Countries

	Developed countries	Underdeveloped countries
Calories per person, daily	2,941	2,033
Total protein per person, daily grams	84.0	52.4
Animal protein only, per person, daily grams	38.8	7.2
Population in millions	1,089	1,923

SOURCE: *Food and Fiber for the Future,* Report of the National Advisory Commission on Food and Fiber (Washington, D.C.: Superintendent of Documents, U. S. Government Printing Office, 1967), p. 308.

Some of the differences in Table 1 are not as bad as they look because of the different physical sizes of the peoples in some of the less well-developed countries, but others are worse than they appear. One of the bad aspects is the fact that these are average figures—that there are many millions of individuals in the underdeveloped countries who are on less-than-subsistence diets. Thus, hunger and malnutrition is the rule rather than the exception in many areas. One bright side of the picture is that, food-wise, the world is a much better place to live in now than it was not too many years ago. In fact, according to Don Paarlberg: "Our age is unique in the rarity of famine. . . . Hunger is not new. The new thing is our awareness of it, our concern about it, and our intention to help alleviate it."

Estimates of the requirements for food in the year 2000 are given in Figure 1. The Group II countries are those developed countries that are engaged in modern agriculture and modern food distribution, and have the economic means to continue it. These include the United States and Canada, and most of northern and western European countries. It can be seen that the Group II countries will need an increase in production from 59 percent of the recent level to 92 percent of the recent level, or an increase of slightly over 50 percent, whereas the Far East and the Near East will need to increase production to approximately 400 percent of the current level. The Far East and Near East are where the experts say the pinch will be felt the most. But, even given the applications of all the methods that we conceive during the next 30-year period, will it be pos-

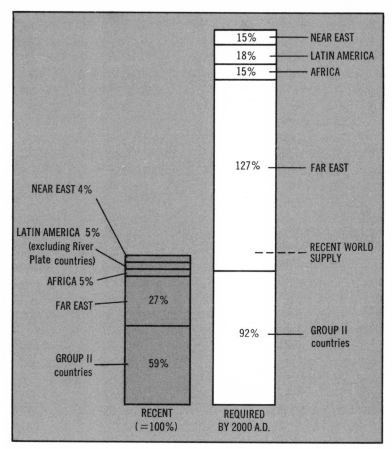

Figure 1 Estimated recent and required (2000 A.D.) total food supplies.

ADAPTED from Pawley, W. M., "Possibilities of Increasing World Food Production," FFMC Study, No. 10. Rome, 1963.

sible to increase the production to the level needed for that part of the world? I would like to take the optimistic viewpoint and say yes—*but* that this by no means should be interpreted as signifying that between 2000 and 2030 we could feed the world's entire population if during that period it increased as rapidly as it will between now and 2000. Perhaps we should consider that as another problem and solve first the frightening one that will be facing us over the next three decades!

Gale Young of the Oak Ridge National Laboratory in Tennessee emphasizes the great importance of water in food production. A large part of the world which is suited to practical approaches to agriculture (that is, land not in extremely cold areas or in mountainous and rocky areas) has nevertheless not been good production land, or even has been useless for production because of lack of water. According to Young, one of the big engineering advances in the next few years will be the supplying of water to the arid zones and to other areas facing water problems (See Figure 2). Much more land will be brought into production when this occurs. Only a fraction of the arid zones is in reasonable production at this time, and this fraction is primarily in certain areas of the United States where water is transported long distances for irrigation. Young predicts that man will tap large reservoirs of water deep below the earth's surface, and that ocean water will be made suitable for agricultural use. The desalination of ocean water, and its transportation mechanically to inland areas, seems only around the corner.

The diet-deficient subregions estimated for 1970 are shown in Figure 3. Comparison of these with the arid regions in Figure 2 reveals some relationships, but, by and large, the two maps are quite different. This is easily understandable when we remember that man has overwhelmingly favored with his presence those parts of the world where both water and climate are favorable features. Large areas which receive abundant amounts of water are still considered diet-deficient, for good reason. Much of the land with abundant rainfall is in tropical areas of Africa, South America, and the islands of the Southwest Pacific, and agriculturally goes to waste in the form of wild tropical plants.

The arid land probably constitutes the largest area wherein future agriculture development can occur. This is seen in Table 2. The arid area greatly exceeds the total area now used for crops. Gale Young offers a quotation from Charles Lowe of the University of Arizona:

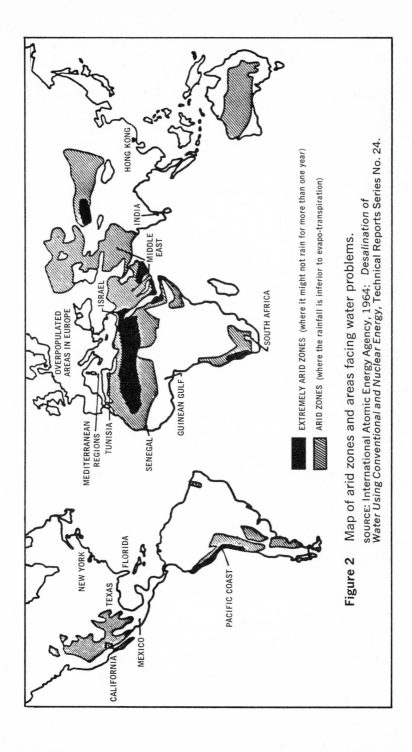

Figure 2 Map of arid zones and areas facing water problems.

SOURCE: International Atomic Energy Agency, 1964: *Desalination of Water Using Conventional and Nuclear Energy*, Technical Reports Series No. 24.

EXTREMELY ARID ZONES (where it might not rain for more than one year)

ARID ZONES (where the rainfall is inferior to evapo-transpiration)

OVERPOPULATED AREAS IN EUROPE

MEDITERRANEAN REGIONS

TUNISIA

ISRAEL

MIDDLE EAST

INDIA

HONG KONG

SENEGAL

GUINEAN GULF

SOUTH AFRICA

NEW YORK

FLORIDA

TEXAS

CALIFORNIA

MEXICO

PACIFIC COAST

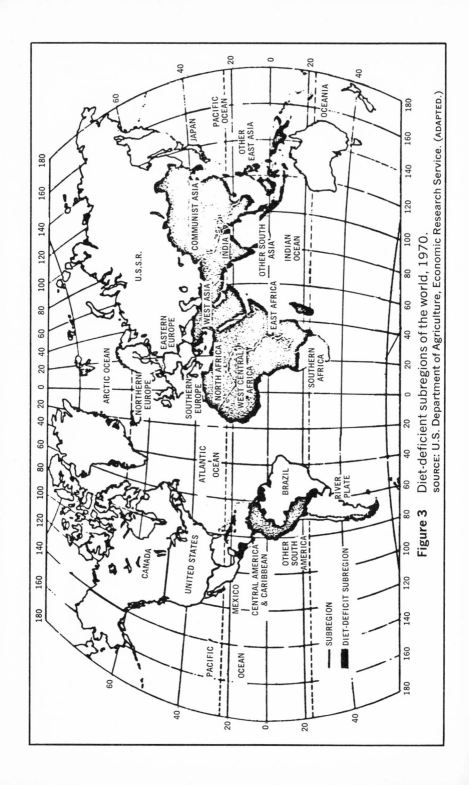

Figure 3 Diet-deficient subregions of the world, 1970.
SOURCE: U.S. Department of Agriculture, Economic Research Service. (ADAPTED.)

Table 2
Agricultural Use of Land (10⁹ Acres)

Grain		1.6
Other major crops		0.7
Minor crop use		1.1
Permanent pastures and meadows		6.4
Irrigated		0.3
Arid		12.1
within 500 miles of sea		8.0
within 300 miles of sea		5.2
Africa	1.8	
Asia	1.5	
Australia	0.9	
South America	0.6	
North America	0.4	

Adapted from Gale Young, *Dry Land and a Hungry World*, Trans. N.Y. Academy of Science, Series II, Vol. 31, No. 2, 1969.

The desert is man's future land bank. Fortunately it is a large one, offering 8,000,000 square miles of space for human occupation. It is also fortunate that it is a wonderously rich bank which may turn green when man someday taps distilled sea water for irrigation. Bridging the gap from the sea to the desert will be greatly facilitated by the geographical nearness of most of the world's deserts to the oceans. When this occurs, it will surely be one of the greatest transformations made by man in his persistent and successful role in changing the face of the planet.

In Table 2 it can be seen that over three times as much arid land is within 300 miles of the sea as is currently used for the production of grain. This distance, 300 miles, has been selected as a currently practical distance to transport purified (deionized or distilled) water from the ocean.

One of the obvious requirements for the purification and transportation of large amounts of water is energy. (Large requirements for energy will also be needed for the production of fertilizer.) Most scientists now expect atomic reactors to provide the tremendous amounts of energy that these efforts will require. Some of these high-energy operations can be performed as a unified process. Young has presented an artist's conception of a nuclear-powered agro–industrial complex in a desert area (Figure 4). Here we see a site for the production of ammonia, salt,

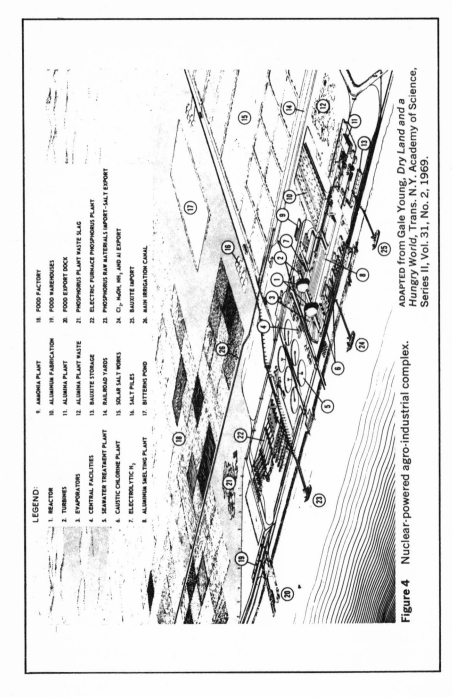

LEGEND:

1. REACTOR
2. TURBINES
3. EVAPORATORS
4. CENTRAL FACILITIES
5. SEAWATER TREATMENT PLANT
6. CAUSTIC CHLORINE PLANT
7. ELECTROLYTIC H$_2$
8. ALUMINUM SMELTING PLANT
9. AMMONIA PLANT
10. ALUMINUM FABRICATION
11. ALUMINA PLANT
12. BAUXITE STORAGE
13. RAILROAD YARDS
14. SOLAR SALT WORKS
15. SALT PILES
16. BITTERNS POND
18. FOOD FACTORY
19. FOOD WAREHOUSES
20. FOOD EXPORT DOCK
21. PHOSPHORUS PLANT WASTE SLAG
22. ELECTRIC FURNACE PHOSPHORUS PLANT
23. PHOSPHORUS RAW MATERIALS IMPORT–SALT EXPORT
24. Cl$_2$, NaOH, NH$_3$, AND Al EXPORT
25. BAUXITE IMPORT
26. MAIN IRRIGATION CANAL.

Figure 4 Nuclear-powered agro-industrial complex.

ADAPTED from Gale Young, *Dry Land and a Hungry World*, Trans. N.Y. Academy of Science, Series II, Vol. 31, No. 2, 1969.

minerals, food, and usable water—all as part of one big power complex on the ocean's edge.

MORE FOOD AND BETTER NUTRITION

The following is a mixed list of some things that are being done (but can be greatly improved on or accelerated) to increase the world's food supply, and some which one hopes will be accomplished before 1980:

1. Addition to (fortification of) cereal grains of those dietary constituents in which the grains are deficient. These additions should include essential amino acids and vitamins. Sometimes such fortifications can be accomplished by the proper mixtures of foodstuffs or by use of concentrates.

2. Development of new foods based on materials which are now either consumed in low amount or which are not consumed by man. The leaves and grasses of the world's meadows and forests may someday be an important supply of food for man's direct use rather than through the inefficient intermediacy of other animals. A much higher consumption of proteins from oil seeds appears probable, and the conversion of cellulose to the sugar glucose should increase.

3. Development of marine resources and protein concentrates therefrom. Fish protein concentrate is now included in dietary supplements in various parts of the world. The idea of farming the sea is an old idea, indeed, but it is only practiced to a limited extent, and then primarily in areas where highly sophisticated approaches are used. Very little is known about the ecological aspects of removing large tonnages of marine life from certain areas of the ocean. Indeed, there is uncertainty as to how much tonnage of krill (the small crustacean in Antarctic waters formerly consumed by the large blue whale) can be taken without upsetting the ecology. Each large blue whale probably consumes thousands of pounds of krill each day, but these species of whale now exist in only very small numbers because of former uncontrolled whaling operations. Perhaps extensive tonnages of the krill population can be removed and

it will be replenished at a rapid rate, but this is not known as of this time. Large ships specifically constructed to serve as experimental commercial "krill catching and processing factories" have recently been operated by the Russians in Antarctic waters. The Japanese have developed marine biology industries in which eggs of small marine species are fertilized, hatched, and raised until they are large enough to be released in huge self-contained salt-water enclosures, where they are fed until they are of commercial size. Although it may be unwise to say that the oceans can provide the tremendous amounts of food that will be necessary in the future, we must admit that they have the potential to provide vast supplies of food.

4. Development of new genetic lines of crops which are high-yielding and high in protein content. This area is presently under intensive investigation and is discussed further below.

5. Development of high-protein foods from microorganism (single-cell) cultures. The possibilities of using algae as a source of food have long been recognized, and yeasts have been used for food supplementation for many years. The uses of microorganisms are presently tied closely to the possible direct biological conversion of petroleum to animal feed supplements.

6. Conversion of the animal industry to new feeds which are not in direct competition with the food of man. It appears more likely that major advancements will be on the feed-supplement basis, with feeds prepared or modified chemically or enzymatically. Probably of great importance here will be the development of processes to utilize the wastes of modern society efficiently. Such studies have already shown promises of success in the use of algae and microorganisms grown on sewage for the feeding of cattle and pigs. Many of the waste products of society which are now serious pollutants might be converted into animal and poultry feeds, and even into foods for humans. With proper supervision by public health authorities this should be a feasible and acceptable practice in the future.

7. The development of new foods and modified foods by application of chemical and biochemical processes. Here is an area the surface of which has only been scratched. In the future many new items will appear on the consumer's table. Some of

the things we now take for granted we challenged a few years ago. There is a tremendous amount of research necessary in this area in order to make new nontoxic and nutritionally sound foods which will have the palatability to make them acceptable for human consumption. The toxicity and nutritional aspects are approachable by straightforward pharmacological and nutritional studies. The palatability aspects require study of all those factors that make for a material which gives satisfaction when eaten. These include the obvious quality of flavor; but the right texture, degree of solubility, and other physical factors also are very important. The protein chemist already changes the physical structure of proteins in many ways, and it seems to be only a matter of time before something can be made from an oil-seed protein which will have the right characteristics to be at least a good substitute for many meat products. One item is presently being marketed in the United States as a simulated canned bacon. This product apparently has a soybean base and, while it may be argued that it is inferior to cooked bacon when fresh, according to some people the reverse is true after the product is stored several months in the can.

8. The development of genetic strains of crops capable of withstanding freezing conditions or growing at lower temperatures than presently are optimal, or a combination of these characteristics. A forebearer of these is the extensively used winter-hardened wheat so prevalent in the northern states of the U.S.A. Lowering of the optimal growth temperature a few degrees centigrade could greatly increase the production of many crops by extending the growing season in the northern and southern latitudes. This is largely an unexplored area. Only recently has it been realized that there is extensive plant growth and animal (fish) activity at the $-1.8\,^{\circ}C$ temperatures of Antarctic waters. Enzymatic systems have also been found to function quite well below $0\,^{\circ}C$. But the commercial possibilities of growing materials in some of the colder areas of the world have not been explored with modern means now available.

9. Adequate and safe control of agricultural pests. These consume large quantities of food, and this occurs by direct consumption of the food by rats, mice, and other vertebrates, and

by infections or infestation which lower crop yields. This is an active area of research as of this time and must continue to be so. Two of the hopeful approaches are the use of biological control measures, and the use of chemicals which are short-lived, once they are applied, so that harmful residual amounts do not affect wildlife or man. The toxic-residue problem is currently a great hazard, and life on earth will not be worth living if food production is achieved at the expense of a healthy population!

10. Biochemical control of growth and development of agricultural materials. Some of this is already being done, such as the use of plant growth factors and animal hormones.

There are many more items that could be included in such a list, and no doubt new approaches unthought of today will appear before long.

One of the more active and successful endeavors, the development of new varieties and strains of crops, is presently being pursued in many places throughout the world. This serves as a fine example of international cooperation and assistance to undeveloped countries by the "haves." One of the most successful cooperative efforts has been that of the Rockefeller Foundation. An early commitment was in Mexico, where a fine cooperative venture was begun in the early 1940's between the Rockefeller Foundation and the government of Mexico. A principal program was the development of new strains of corn and wheat which would grow well under Mexican conditions. By 1955, Mexico was a food-producing country; and by 1968 the average wheat yield was 40 bushels an acre, or about four times the 11-bushel average of 1943. Corn yields doubled in the period. Gains were found in other foods as well.

South American nations have now become involved in these ventures, and there is under way a development of research networks. Today there is a true internationalization of efforts in agriculture. Among the various international agricultural centers developed are: (1) The International Corn and Wheat Improvement Center, which has its headquarters in Mexico; (2) The International Rice Research Institute, located in the Philippines; (3) The International Center for Tropical Agriculture, in Colombia, South America; and (4) The International Institute of Tropical Agriculture, in Nigeria, Africa. All these institutes are working hand-in-hand, and the applications of some of their efforts are most gratifying. Commercial wheat seed produced in Mexico has greatly increased the production of wheat in India and Pakistan. In some areas the yields are from 50 percent to 200 percent over previous yields. This type of cooperation gives one faith that man will be able to at least be intelligent about his food supply for the future!*

THE HUMAN ASPECT OF THE FOOD PROBLEM: SOCIAL, ECONOMIC, POLITICAL, AND PHILOSOPHICAL

Don Paarlberg says:

The concern about food in the less developed countries will not be satisfied if per capita food availability merely holds its own. Hunger and malnutrition are fact. These people are increasingly aware of their hunger and poverty. They are experiencing a revolution of rising expectations. They insist that life be better for them or, if not for them, then certainly for their children.

He then quotes Edwin Markham in asking: "How will the future reckon with this man? How answer his brute questions in that hour when whirlwinds of rebellion shake all shores?"

Frank Notestein of Princeton University speaks in this vein:

It is my own belief that the greatest risk of loss of life facing the less developed regions is not that of malnutrition, or slow starvation from food supply that just barely falls short of the traditional requirements. The greatest threat is that the loss of political coherence will bring a breakdown of a public order, tripping off both famine and epidemic, as in Biafra, for example.

* *Editor's note:* It has been observed, however, that the requirement of these hybrids for large amounts of artificial fertilizers may create environmental and socio-economic problems.

Clyde L. Rasmussen of the Western Regional Research Laboratory, U.S. Department of Agriculture, has suggested that the economic side is currently the main problem, and that malnutrition will be solved only when populations can pay the price of the food. I agree that malnutrition and poverty are certainly now closely related. However, with the possibilty of the earth's population increasing beyond reason, the crushing effects of a crowded environment may make economic and dietary factors secondary problems to those of the maintenance of moral sanity. We have "solved" many of our problems and desires by clubbing, spearing, burning, poisoning, shooting, exploding, and eating one another. The president of one Southeast Asian nation has reputedly said that the increasing starvation on earth may soon result in mass outbreaks of humans eating humans. Is this so remote a possibilty? We still do everything else.

Are we really ready to meet the challenges? Will our sophisticated food industry change its direction, as it does in wartime, to meet the challenge of helping to provide low-cost food? This would certainly seem to be necessary. Jacques M. May (Chief, International Unit, Nutrition Program, U.S. Public Health Service) offers this severe criticism of the food industry:

> The fourth component of a comprehensive program is the food industry. It is perfectly appropriate to help the food industry, if it cannot help itself, in creating a market when none exists or in protecting its investment when the returns are uncertain. What I object to is that, in the past, this has been made almost the sole approach to the fight against malnutrition. Certainly the sophisticated food industry has a place in the cities where a market exists amongst the "haves." But it does little, like I said before, to combat malnutrition on a sustained basis in the slums unless some captive market benefits from the government subsidy. Yet there is an important role for the food industry and its know-how in the developing countries, provided certain principles are respected.

What are these principles May talks about? Are they the principles expounded on television ads for (for example) new breakfast foods or party snacks? Many of the things we hear now from the food industry concern "convenience foods." How can "convenience foods" solve the world's food problems and keep man from starving? It may be unfair to single out the food industry as not contributing to the solution of world social problems, because the same thing can be said about the automobile industry, the television industry, or the pleasure-boat industry. But the food industry is that segment of society with the sophisticated know-how to make food, so there is no choice except to put the question to them: "Will you, the food industry, some day be economically working towards food for the world's millions?"

Roger Revelle may have had the right idea in suggesting that there needs to be a greater involvement of American industry in agricultural research and development, but using new marketing methods—perhaps like those the defense and space programs have with the government as the market.

The land-grant colleges of this country were originally subsidized by the federal government to aid agriculture and the individual farmer by research and education. During the last few decades there was a swing away from helping the farmer to helping and working directly with agri–business corporations and associations. The complexity of the handling and processing of agricultural commodities undoubtedly made this necessary, but today there appears to be occurring a return to considerations of the farmer, the farm worker, and the population at large. An example of this shift is the renaming of the College of Agriculture (at the University of California at Davis) to the College of Agricultural and Environmental Science. Another is the renaming of the Home Economics Division to Consumer Sciences. Both of these renamings reflect responses to current social pressures and needs. Let us hope that such renamings do not result only in the expenditure of energy in the pursuit of trivial objectives on the part of teams, but rather allow opportunities for individuals to work toward a better society by clearly and vigorously searching for and exposing problems and then seeking solutions to them. Much, much more than this is necessary—but every step forward will make the next one easier.

Paul
Goodman

is the author of many well-known
sociologically oriented works, including the popular *Grow-
ing Up Absurd*. After graduating from City College in New
York, he went on to receive his Ph.D. in humanities from the
University of Chicago. A former teacher at the University
of Chicago, New York University, and Black Mountain
College, he is now a Fellow of the New York and Cleveland
Institutes for Gestalt Therapy.

Goodman has written for many magazines, including
*Commentary, Politics, Kenyon Review, Resistance, Libera-
tion,* and *Partisan Review*. His fiction includes *The Facts
of Life, The Break-up of Our Camp, Parent's Day,* and *The
Empire City*. *Kafka's Prayer* and *The Structure of Literature*
are two of his books of criticism. In the area of social science
he has written *Art and Social Nature,* and is coauthor of
Communitas and of *Gestalt Therapy*. His recent works include *Like a Conquered Province, Five Years, Adam and
His Works, The Hawkweed* (a collection of poems), and
The New Reformation: Notes of a Neolithic Conservative.

The present essay, originally written for the Innovation Group for Technology Communications, first appeared
in print in *The New York Review of Books*. In it, Goodman
discusses the current dilemma in science, but in theological
terms. Science and technology have become the predominant religion and theology in modern industrial society. But

245

today, the clerics are distressed. They demand reforms so that the theology can be brought back into line with the religion. But little do they realize, according to Goodman, that they are precipitating a Reformation which will transform the entire society.

Can Technology Be Humane?

[1.] On March 4, 1969 there was a "work stoppage" and teach-in initiated by dissenting professors at the Massachusetts Institute of Technology, and followed at thirty other major universities and technical schools across the country, against misdirected scientific research and the abuse of scientific technology. Here I want to consider this event in a broader context than the professors did; indeed as part of a religious crisis. For an attack on the American scientific establishment is an attack on the worldwide system of belief. I think we are on the eve of a new Protestant Reformation, and no institution or status will go unaffected.

March 4 was, of course, only the latest of a series of protests in the twenty-five years since the Manhattan Project to build the atom bomb, during which time the central funding of research and innovation has grown so enormously and its purposes have become so unpalatable. In 1940 the federal budget for research and development was less than 100,000,000 dollars, in 1967 17 billion. Hitler's war was a watershed of modern times. We are accustomed, as H. R. Trevor-Roper has pointed out, to write Hitler off as an aberration, of little political significance. But, in fact, the military emergency that he and his Japanese allies created confirmed the worst tendencies of the giant states, till now they are probably irreversible by ordinary political means.

From Paul Goodman, "Can Technology Be Humane?" in *New York Review of Books,* November 20, 1969. Used by permission of *New York Review of Books.*

After Hiroshima, there was the conscience-stricken movement of the atomic scientists and the founding of their *Bulletin*. The American Association for the Advancement of Science pledged to keep the public informed about the dangerous bearings of new developments. There was the Oppenheimer incident. Ads of the East Coast scientists successfully stopped the bomb shelters, warned about the fallout, and helped produce the test ban. There was a scandal about the bombardment of the Van Allen belt. Scientists and technologists formed a powerful (and misguided) *ad hoc* group for Johnson in the 1964 election. In some universities, sometimes with bitter struggle, classified contracts have been excluded. There is a Society for Social Responsibility in Science. Rachel Carson's book on the pesticides caused a stir, until the Department of Agriculture rescued the manufacturers and plantation-owners. Ralph Nader has been on his rampage. Thanks to spectacular abuses like smog, strip-mining, asphalting, pesticides, and oil pollution, even ecologists and conservationists have been getting a hearing. Protest against the boom has slowed up the development of the supersonic transport. Most recent has been the concerted outcry against the antiballistic missiles.

The target of protest has become broader and the grounds of complaint deeper. The target is now not merely the military, but the universities, commercial corporations, and goverment. It is said that money is being given by the wrong sponsors to the wrong people for the wrong purposes. In some of the great schools, such funding is the main support, e.g., at MIT, 90 percent of the research budget is from the government, and 65 percent of that is military.

Inevitably, such funding channels the brainpower of most of the brightest science students, who go where the action is, and this predetermines the course of American science and technology for the foreseeable future. At present nearly 200,000 American engineers and scientists spend all their time making weapons, which is a comment on, and perhaps explanation for, the usual statement that more scientists are now alive than since Adam and Eve. And the style of such research and development is not good. It is dominated by producing hardware, figuring logistics, and devising salable novelties. Often there is secrecy, always nationalism. Since the grants go overwhelmingly through a very few corporations and universities, they favor a limited number of scientific attitudes and preconceptions, with incestuous staffing. There is a premium on "positive results"; surprising "failures" cannot be pursued, so that science ceases to be a wandering dialogue with the unknown.

The policy is economically wasteful. A vast amount of brains and money is spent on crash programs to solve often essentially petty problems, and the claim that there is a spinoff of useful discoveries is derisory, if we consider the sums involved. The claim that research is neutral, and it doesn't matter what one works on, is shabby, if we consider the heavy funding in certain directions. Social priorities are scandalous: Money is spent on overkill, supersonic planes, brand-name identical drugs, annual model changes of cars, new detergents, and color television, whereas water, air, space, food, health, and foreign aid are neglected. And much research is morally so repugnant, e.g., chemical and biological weapons, that one dares not humanly continue it.

The state of the behaviorial sciences is, if anything, worse. Their claim to moral and political neutrality becomes, in effect, a means of diverting attention from glaring social evils, and they are in fact—or would be if they worked—for warfare and social engineering, manipulation of people for the political and economic purposes of the powers that be. This is an especially sad betrayal since, in the not-too-distant past, the objective social sciences were developed largely to dissolve orthodoxy, irrational authority, and taboo. They were heretical and intellectually revolutionary, as the physical sciences had been in their own Heroic Age, and they weren't getting government grants.

This is a grim indictment. Even so, I do not think the dissenting scientists understand how deep their trouble is. They still take themselves too much for granted. Indeed, a repeated theme of the March 4 complaints was that the science budget was being cut back, especially in basic research. The assumption was that though the sciences are abused, Science would rightly maintain and increase its expensive preeminence among social institutions. Only Science could find the answers.

But underlying the growing dissent there is an historical crisis. There has been a profound change in popular feeling, more than among the professors. Put it this way: Modern societies have been operating as if religion were a minor and moribund part of the scheme of things. But this is unlikely. Men do not do without a system of "meanings" that everybody believes and puts his hope in even if, or especially if, he doesn't know anything about it; what Freud called a "shared psychosis," meaningful because shared, and with the power that resides in dream and longing. In fact, in advanced countries it is science and technology themselves that have gradually and finally triumphantly become the system of mass faith, not disputed by various political ideologies and nationalisms that have also been mass religions. Marxism called itself "scientific socialism" as against moral and utopian socialisms; and movements of national liberation have especially promised to open the benefits of industrialization and technological progress when once they have gotten rid of the imperialists.

For three hundred years, science and scientific technology had an unblemished and justified reputation as a wonderful adventure, pouring out practical benefits, and liberating the spirit from the errors of superstition and traditional faith. During this century they have finally been the only generally credited system of explanation and problem-solving. Yet in our generation they have come to seem to many, and to very many of the best of the young, as essentially inhuman, abstract, regimenting, hand-in-glove with Power, and even diabolical. Young people say that science is antilife, it is a Calvinist obsession, it has been a weapon of white Europe to subjugate colored races; and manifestly—in view of recent scientific technology—people who think "scientifically" become insane. With science, the other professions are discredited. The academic "disciplines" are discredited.

The immediate reasons for this shattering reversal of values are fairly obvious: Hitler's ovens and his other experiments in eugenics, the first atomic bombs and their frenzied subse-

quent developments, the deterioration of the physical environment and the destruction of the biosphere, the catastrophes
impending over the cities because of technological failures and
psychological stress, the prospect of a brainwashed and drugged
1984. Innovations yield diminishing returns in enhancing life.
And instead of rejoicing, there is now widespread conviction
that beautiful advances in genetics, surgery, computers, rock-
etry, or atomic energy will surely only increase human woe.

In such a crisis, in my opinion, it will not be sufficient to
ban the military from the universities; and it will not even be
sufficient, as liberal statesmen and many of the big corporations envisage, to beat the swords into ploughshares and turn
to solving problems of transportation, desalinization, urban
renewal, garbage disposal, and cleaning up the air and water.
If the present difficulty is religious and historical, it is necessary
to alter the entire relationship of science, technology, and social
needs both in men's minds and in fact. This involves changes
in the organization of science, in scientific education, and in
the kinds of men who make scientific decisions.

In spite of the fantasies of hippies, we are certainly going
to continue to live in a technological world. The question is a
different one: Is that workable?

2. PRUDENCE

Whether or not it draws on new scientific research, technology is a branch of moral philosophy, not of science. It aims
at prudent goods for the commonweal and to provide efficient
means for these goods. At present, however, "scientific technology" occupies a bastard position in the universities, in funding, and in the public mind. It is half tied to the theoretical
sciences and half treated as mere know-how for political and
commercial purposes. It has no principles of its own. To remedy
this—so Karl Jaspers in Europe and Robert Hutchins in America
have urged—technology must have its proper place on the faculty as a learned profession important in modern society, along
with medicine, law, the humanities, and natural philosophy,
learning from them and having something to teach them. As a

moral philosopher, a technician should be able to criticize the programs given him to implement. As a professional in a community of learned professionals, a technologist must have a different kind of training and develop a different character than we see at present among technicians and engineers. He should know something of the social sciences, law, the fine arts, and medicine, as well as relevant natural sciences.

Prudence is foresight, caution, utility. Thus it is up to the technologists, not to regulatory agencies of the government, to provide for safety and to think about remote effects. This is what Ralph Nader is saying and Rachel Carson used to ask. An important aspect of caution is flexibility, to avoid the pyramiding catastrophe that occurs when something goes wrong in interlocking technologies, as in urban power failures. Naturally, to take responsibility for such things often requires standing up to the front office and urban politicians, and technologists must organize themselves in order to have power to do it.

Often it is clear that a technology has been oversold, like the cars. Then even though the public, seduced by advertising, wants more, technologists must balk, as any professional does when his client wants what isn't good for him. We are now repeating the same self-defeating congestion with the planes and airports: The more the technology is oversold, the less immediate utility it provides, the greater the costs, and the more damaging the remote effects. As this becomes evident, it is time for technologists to confer with sociologists and economists and ask deeper questions. Is so much travel necessary? Are there ways to diminish it? Instead, the recent history of technology has consisted largely of a desperate effort to remedy situations caused by previous overapplication of technology.

Technologists should certainly have a say about simple waste, for even in an affluent society there are priorities—consider the supersonic transport, which has little to recommend it. But the moon shot has presented the more usual dilemma of authentic conflicting claims. I myself believe that space exploration is a great human adventure with immense aesthetic and moral benefits, whatever the scientific or utilitarian uses. Yet it is amazing to me that the scientists and technologists involved have not spoken more insistently for international co-operation instead of a puerile race. But I have heard some say that except for this chauvinist competition, Congress would not vote any money at all.

Currently, perhaps the chief moral criterion of a philo-sophic technology is modesty, having a sense of the whole and not obtruding more than a particular function warrants. Immodesty is always a danger of free enterprise, but when the same disposition is financed by big corporations, technologists rush into production with neat solutions that swamp the environment. This applies to packaging products and disposing of garbage, to freeways that bulldoze neighborhoods, high-rises that destroy landscape, wiping out a species for a passing fashion, strip mining, scrapping an expensive machine rather than making a minor repair, draining a watershed for irrigation because (as in Southern California) the cultivable land has been covered by asphalt. Given this disposition, it is not surpris-ing that we defoliate a forest in order to expose a guerrilla and spray teargas from a helicopter on a crowded campus.

Since we are technologically overcommitted, a good general maxim in advanced countries at present is to innovate in order to simplify the technical system, but otherwise to innovate as sparingly as possible. Every advanced country is over-technol-ogized; past a certain point, the quality of life diminishes with new "improvements." Yet no country is rightly technologized, making efficient use of available techniques. There are ingeni-ous devices for unimportant functions, stressful mazes for essential functions, and drastic dislocation when anything goes wrong, which happens with increasing frequency. To add to the complexity, the mass of people tend to become incompetent and dependent on repairmen—indeed, unrepairability except by experts has become a desideratum of industrial design.

When I speak of slowing down or cutting back, the issue is not whether research and making working models should be encouraged or not. They should be, in every direction, and given a blank check. The point is to resist the temptation to apply every new device without a second thought. But the big corporate organization of research and development makes pru-

dence and modesty very difficult; it is necessary to get big contracts and rush into production in order to pay the salaries of
the big team. Like other bureaucracies, technological organizations are run to maintain themselves but they are more dangerous because, in capitalist countries, they are in a competitive
arena.

I mean simplification quite strictly, to simplify the *technical*
system. I am unimpressed by the argument that what is technically more complicated is really economically or politically
simpler, e.g., by complicating the packaging we improve the
supermarkets; by throwing away the machine rather than re-
pairing it, we give cheaper and faster service all around; or
even by expanding the economy with trivial innovations, we
increase employment, allay discontent, save on welfare. Such
ideas may be profitable for private companies or political parties,
but for society they have proved to be an accelerating ratrace.
The technical structure of the environment is too important to
be a political or economic pawn; the effect on the quality of
life is too disastrous; and the hidden social costs are not calculated, the auto graveyards, the torn-up streets, the longer
miles of commuting, the advertising, the inflation, etc. As I
pointed out in *People or Personnel,* a country with a fourth of
our per capita income, like Ireland, is not necessarily less well
off; in some respects it is much richer, in some respects a little
poorer. If possible, it is better to solve political problems by
political means. For instance, if teaching-machines and audio-
visual aids are indeed educative, well and good; but if they are
used to save money on teachers, then not good at all—nor
do they save money.

Of course, the goals of right technology must come to terms
with other values of society. I am not a technocrat. But the
advantage of raising technology to be a responsible learned
profession with its own principles is that it can have a voice
in the debate and argue for *its* proper contribution to the community. Consider the important case of modular sizes in building, or prefabrication of a unit bathroom: These conflict with
the short-run interests of manufacturers and craft-unions, yet
to deny them is technically an abomination. The usual recourse

is for a government agency to set standards; such agencies accommodate to interests that have a strong voice, and at present technologists have no voice. The crucial need for technological simplification, however, is not in the advanced countries—which can afford their clutter and probably deserve it—but in underdeveloped countries which must rapidly innovate in order to diminish disease, drudgery, and deepening starvation. They cannot afford to make mistakes. It is now widely conceded that the technological aid we have given to such areas according to our own high style—a style usually demanded by the native ruling groups—has done more harm than good. Even when, as frequently if not usually, aid has been benevolent, without strings attached, not military, and not dumping, it has nevertheless disrupted ways of life, fomented tribal wars, accelerated urbanization, decreased the food supply, gone wasted for lack of skills to use it, developed a do-nothing élite.

By contrast, a group of international scientists called Intermediate Technology argue that what is needed is techniques that use only native labor, resources, traditional customs, and teachable know-how, with the simple aim of remedying drudgery, disease, and hunger, so that people can then develop further in their own style. This avoids cultural imperialism. Such intermediate techniques may be quite primitive, on a level unknown among us for a couple of centuries, and yet they may pose extremely subtle problems, requiring exquisite scientific research and political and human understanding, to devise a very simple technology. Here is a reported case (which I trust I remember accurately): In Botswana, a very poor country, pasture was overgrazed, but the economy could be salvaged if the land were fenced. There was no local material for fencing, and imported fencing was prohibitively expensive. The solution was to find the formula and technique to make posts out of mud, and a pedagogic method to teach people how to do it.

In *The Two Cultures,* C. P. Snow berated the humanists for their irrelevance when two-thirds of mankind are starving and what is needed is science and technology. They have perhaps been irrelevant; but unless technology is itself more humanistic and philosophical, it is of no use. There is only one culture. Finally, let me make a remark about amenity as a technical criterion. It is discouraging to see the concern about beautifying a highway and banning billboards, and about the cosmetic appearance of the cars, when there is no regard for the ugliness of bumper-to-bumper traffic and the suffering of the drivers. Or the concern for preserving an historical landmark while the neighborhood is torn up and the city has no shape. Without moral philosophy, people have nothing but sentiments.

3. ECOLOGY

The complement to prudent technology is the ecological approach to science. To simplify the technical system and modestly pinpoint our artificial intervention in the environment makes it possible for the environment to survive in its complexity evolved for a billion years, whereas the overwhelming instant intervention of tightly interlocked and bulldozing technology has already disrupted many of the delicate sequences and balances. The calculable consequences are already frightening, but of course we don't know enough, and won't in the foreseeable future, to predict the remote effects of much of what we have done. The only possible conclusion is to be prudent; when there is serious doubt, to do nothing.

Cyberneticists—I am thinking of Gregory Bateson—come to the same cautious conclusion. The use of computers has enabled us to carry out crashingly inept programs on the bases of willful analyses. But we have also become increasingly alert to the fact that things respond, systematically, continually, cumulatively; they cannot simply be manipulated or pushed around. Whether bacteria or weeds or bugs or the technologically unemployed or unpleasant thoughts, they cannot be eliminated and forgotten; repressed, the nuisances return in new forms. A complicated system works most efficiently if its parts readjust themselves decentrally, with a minimum of central intervention or control, except in cases of breakdown. Usually there is an advantage in a central clearing house of information about the gross total situation, but decision and execution require more minute local information. The fantastically simulated moon landing hung on a last split-second correction on the spot. In social organization, deciding in headquarters means relying on information that is cumulatively abstract and irrelevant, and chain-of-command execution applies standards that cumulatively do not fit the concrete situation. By and large it is better, given a sense of the whole picture, for those in the field to decide what to do and do it (cf. *People or Personnel*, Chapter III).

But with organisms too, this has long been the bias of psychosomatic medicine, the Wisdom of the Body, as Cannon called it. To cite a classical experiment of Ralph Hefferline of Columbia: A subject is wired to suffer an annoying regular buzz, which can be delayed and finally eliminated if he makes a precise but unlikely gesture, say by twisting his ankle in a certain way; then it is found that he adjusts quicker if he is *not* told the method and it is left to his spontaneous twitching than if he is told and tries deliberately to help himself. He adjusts better without conscious control, his own or the experimenters'.

Technological modesty, fittingness, is not negative. It is the ecological wisdom of cooperating with Nature rather than trying to master her. (The personification of "Nature" is linguistic wisdom.) A well-known example is the long-run superiority of partial pest-control in farming by using biological deterrents rather than chemical ones. The living defenders work harder, at the right moment, and with more pinpointed targets. But let me give another example because it is so lovely–though I have forgotten the name of my informant: A tribe in Yucatan educates its children to identify and pull up all weeds in the region; then what is left is a garden of useful plants that have chosen to be there and now thrive.

In the life sciences there is at present a suggestive bifurcation in methodology. The rule is still to increase experimental intervention, but there is also a considerable revival of old-fashioned naturalism, mainly watching and thinking, with very modest intervention. Thus, in medicine, there is a new diagnostic machinery, new drugs, spectacular surgery; but there is also a new respect for family practice with a psychosomatic background, and a strong push, among young doctors and students, for a social–psychological and sociological approach, aimed at preventing disease and building up resistance. In psychology, the operant conditioners multiply and refine their machinery to give maximum control of the organism and the environment (I have not heard of any dramatic discoveries, but perhaps they have escaped me). On the other hand, the most interesting psychology in recent years has certainly come from animal naturalists, e.g., pecking order, territoriality, learning to control aggression, language of the bees, overcrowding among rats, trying to talk to dolphins.

On a fair judgment, both contrasting approaches give positive results. The logical scientific problem that arises is: What is there in the nature of things that makes a certain method, or even moral attitude, work well or poorly in a given case? This question is not much studied. Every scientist seems to know what "the" scientific method is.

Another contrast of style, extremely relevant at present, is that between Big Science and old-fashioned shoestring science. There is plenty of research, with corresponding technology, that can be done only by Big Science; yet much, and perhaps most, of science will always be shoestring science, for which it is absurd to use the fancy and expensive equipment that has gotten to be the fashion.

Consider urban medicine. The problem, given a shortage of doctors and facilities, is how to improve the level of mass health, the vital statistics, and yet to practice medicine, which aims at the maximum possible health for each person. Perhaps the most efficient use of Big Science technology for the general health would be compulsory biennial checkups, as we inspect cars, for early diagnosis and to forestall chronic conditions with accumulating costs. Then an excellent machine would be a total diagnostic bus to visit the neighborhoods, as we do chest X-rays. On the other hand, for actual treatment and especially for convalescence, the evidence seems to be that small personalized hospitals are best. And to revive family practice, maybe the right idea is to offer a doctor a splendid suite in a public housing project.

Our contemporary practice makes little sense. We have ex-

pensive technology stored in specialists' offices and big hospitals, really unavailable for mass use in the neighborhoods; yet
every individual, even if he is quite rich, finds it almost impossible to get attention to himself as an individual whole organism in his setting. He is sent from specialist to specialist and
exists as a bag of symptoms and a file of test scores.

In automating there is an analogous dilemma of how to
cope with masses of people and get economies of scale, without
losing the individual at great consequent human and economic
cost. A question of immense importance for the immediate
future is: Which functions should be automated or organized
to use business machines, and which should not? This question
also is not getting asked, and the present disposition is that the
sky is the limit for extraction, refining, manufacturing, processing, packaging, transportation, clerical work, ticketing, transac-
tions, information retrieval, recruitment, middle management,
evaluation, diagnosis, instruction, and even research and invention. Whether the machines can do all these kinds of jobs and
more is partly an empirical question, but it also partly depends
on what is meant by "doing a job." Very often, e.g., in college
admissions, machines are acquired for putative economies
(which do not eventuate); but the true reason is that an overgrown and overcentralized organization cannot be administered
without them. The technology conceals the essential trouble,
e.g., that there is no community of scholars, and students are
treated like things. The function is badly performed, and finally
the system breaks down anyway. I doubt that enterprises in
which interpersonal relations are important are suited to much
programming.

But worse, what can happen is that the real function of the
enterprise is subtly altered so that it is suitable for the mechani-
cal system. (E.g., "information retrieval" is taken as an adequate
replacement for critical scholarship.) Incommensurable factors,
individual differences, the local context, the weighting of evidence are quietly overlooked though they may be of the essence.
The system, with its subtly transformed purposes, seems to run
very smoothly; it is productive, and it is more and more out of
line with the nature of things and the real problems. Meantime

it is geared in with other enterprises of society—e.g., major public policy may depend on welfare or unemployment statistics which, as they are tabulated, are blind to the actual lives of poor families. In such a case, the particular system may not break down, the whole society may explode.

I need hardly point out that American society is peculiarly liable to the corruption of inauthenticity, busily producing phony products. It lives by public relations, abstract ideals, front politics, show-business, communications, mandarin credentials. It is preeminently overtechnologized. And computer technologists especially suffer the euphoria of being in a new and rapidly expanding field. It is so astonishing that the robot can do the job at all or seem to do it, that it is easy to blink at the fact that he is doing it badly or isn't really doing quite that job.

4. DECENTRALIZATION

The current political assumption is that scientists and inventors, and even social scientists, are "value-neutral," but their discoveries are "applied" by those who make decisions for the nation. Counter to this, I have been insinuating a kind of Jeffersonian democracy or guild socialism, that scientists and inventors and other workmen are responsible for the uses of the work they do, and ought to be competent to judge these uses and have a say in deciding them. They usually are competent. To give a striking example, Ford assembly-line workers, according to Harvey Swados, who worked with them, are accurately critical of the glut of cars, but they have no way to vent their dissatisfactions with their useless occupation except to leave nuts and bolts to rattle in the body.

My bias is also pluralistic. Instead of the few national goals of a few decision-makers, I propose that there are many goods of many activities of life, and many professions and other interest-groups each with its own criteria and goals that must be taken into account. A society that distributes power widely is superficially conflictful but fundamentally stable.

Research and development ought to be widely decentralized,

the national fund for them being distributed through thousands of centers of initiative and decision. This would not be chaotic. We seem to have forgotten that for four hundred years Western science majestically progressed with no central direction whatever, yet with exquisite international coordination, little duplication, almost nothing getting lost, in constant communication despite slow facilities. The reason was simply that all scientists wanted to get on with the same enterprise of testing the boundaries of knowledge, and they relied on one another.

What is as noteworthy is that something similar holds also in invention and innovation, even in recent decades when there has been such a concentration of funding and apparent concentration of opportunity. The majority of big advances have still come from independents, partnerships, and tiny companies. (Evidence published by the Senate Sub-Committee on Antitrust and Monopoly, May 1965.) To name a few, jet engines, xerography, automatic transmission, cellophane, air-conditioning, quick freeze, antibiotics, and tranquilizers. The big technological teams must have disadvantages that outweigh their advantages, like lack of singlemindedness, poor communications, awkward scheduling. Naturally, big corporations have taken over the innovations, but the Senate evidence is that 90 percent of the government subsidy has gone for last-stage development for production, which they ought to have paid out of their own pockets.

We now have a theory that we have learned to learn, and that we can program technical progress, directed by a central planning board. But this doesn't make it so. The essence of the new still seems to be that nobody has thought of it, and the ones who get ideas are those in direct contact with the work. *Too precise* a preconception of what is wanted discourages creativity more than it channels it; and bureaucratic memoranda from distant directors don't help. This is especially true when, as at present, so much of the preconception of what is wanted comes from desperate political anxiety in emergencies. Solutions that emerge from such an attitude rarely strike out on new paths, but rather repeat traditional thinking with new gimmicks; they tend to compound the problem. A priceless advantage of widespread decentralization is that it engages more minds, and more mind, instead of a few panicky (or greedy) corporate minds.

A homespun advantage of small groups, according to the Senate testimony, is that co-workers can talk to one another, without schedules, reports, clock-watching, and face-saving.

An important hope from decentralizing science is to develop knowledgeable citizens, and provide not only a bigger pool of scientists and inventors but also a public better able to protect itself and know how to judge the enormous budgets asked for. The safety of the environment is too important to be left to scientists, even ecologists. During the last decades of the nineteenth century and the first decade of the twentieth, the heyday of public faith in the beneficent religion of science and invention, say from Pasteur and Huxley to Edison and the Wright brothers, philosophers of science had a vision of a "scientific way of life," one in which people would be objective, respectful of evidence, accurate, free of superstition and taboo, immune to irrational authority, experimental. All would be well, is the impression one gets from Thomas Huxley, if everybody knew the splendid Ninth Edition of the *Encyclopaedia Britannica* with its articles by Darwin and Clark Maxwell. Veblen put his faith in the modesty and matter-of-factness of engineers to govern. Sullivan and Frank Lloyd Wright spoke for an austere functionalism and respect for the nature of materials and industrial processes. Patrick Geddes thought that new technology would finally get us out of the horrors of the Industrial Revolution and produce good communities. John Dewey devised a system of education to rear pragmatic and experimental citizens to be at home in the new technological world rather than estranged from it. Now, 50 years later, we are in the swamp of a scientific and technological environment and there are more scientists alive, etc., etc. But the mention of the "scientific way of life" seems like black humor.

Many of those who have grown up since 1945 and have never seen any other state of science and technology assume that rationalism itself is totally evil and dehumanizing. It is probably more significant than we like to think that they go in for astrology and the *Book of Changes,* as well as inducing psychedelic dreams by technological means. Jacques Ellul, a more philosophic critic, tries to show that technology is necessarily overcontrolling, standardizing, and voraciously inclusive, so that there is no place for freedom. But I doubt that any of this is intrinsic to science and technology. The crude history has been, rather, that they have fallen willingly under the dominion of money and power. Like Christianity or communism, the scientific way of life has never been tried.

5.

To satisfy the March 4 dissenters, to break the military-industrial corporations and alter the priorities of the budget, would be to restructure the American economy almost to a revolutionary extent. But to meet the historical crisis of science at present, for science and technology to become prudent, ecological, and decentralized requires a change that is even more profound, a kind of religious transformation. Yet there is nothing untraditional in what I have proposed; prudence, ecology, and decentralization are indeed the high tradition of science and technology. Thus the closest analogy I can think of is the Protestant Reformation, a change of normal allegiance, liberation from the Whore of Babylon, return to the pure faith.

Science has long been the chief orthodoxy of modern times and has certainly been badly corrupted, but the deepest flaw of the affluent societies that has alienated the young is not, finally, their imperialism, economic injustice, or racism, bad as these are, but their nauseating phoniness, triviality, and wastefulness, the cultural and moral scandal that Luther found when he went to Rome in 1510. And precisely science, which should have been the wind of truth to clear the air, has polluted the air, helped to brainwash, and provided weapons for war. I doubt that most young people today have even heard of the ideal of the dedicated researcher, truculent and incorruptible, and unrewarded—for instance the "German scientist" that Sinclair Lewis described in

Arrowsmith. Such a figure is no longer believable. I don't mean of course, that he doesn't exist; there must be thousands of him, just as there were good priests in 1510.

The analogy to the Reformation is even more exact if we consider the school system, from educational toys and Head Start up through the universities. This system is manned by the biggest horde of monks since the time of Henry VIII. It is the biggest industry in the country. I have heard the estimate that 40 percent of the national product is in the Knowledge Business. It is mostly hocus-pocus. Yet the belief of parents in this institution is quite delusional and school diplomas are in fact the only entry to licensing and hiring in every kind of job. The abbots of this system are the chiefs of science, e.g., the National Science Foundation, who talk about reform but work to expand the school budgets, step up the curriculum, and inspire the endless catechism of tests.

These abuses are international, as the faith is. For instance, there is no essential difference between the military–industrial or the school systems, of the Soviet Union and the United States. There are important differences in way of life and standard of living, but the abuses of technology are very similar: pollution, excessive urbanization, destruction of the biosphere, weaponry, and disastrous foreign aid. Our protesters naturally single out our own country, and the United States is the most powerful country, but the corruption we are speaking of is not specifically American nor even capitalist; it is a disease of modern times.

But the analogy is to the Reformation, it is not to primitive Christianity or some other primitivism, the abandonment of technological civilization. There is indeed much talk about the doom of Western civilization, and a few Adamites actually do retire into the hills; but for the great mass of mankind, and myself, that's not where it's at. There is not the slightest interruption to the universalizing of Western civilization, including most of its delusions, into the so-called Third World. (If the atom bombs go off, however?)

Naturally the exquisitely interesting question is whether or not this Reformation will occur, how to make it occur, against the entrenched worldwide system of corrupt power that is continually aggrandizing itself. I don't know. In my analogy I have deliberately been choosing the date 1510, Luther in Rome, rather than 1517 when, in the popular story, he nailed his Theses to the cathedral door. There are everywhere contradictory signs and dilemmas. The new professional and technological class is more and more entangled in the work, statuses, and rewards of the system, and yet this same class, often the very same people, are more and more protestant. On the other hand, the dissident young, who are unequivocally for radical change, are so alienated from occupation, function, knowledge, or even concern, that they often seem to be simply irrelevant to the underlying issues of modern times. The monks keep "improving" the schools and getting bigger budgets to do so, yet it is clear that high schools will be burned down, twelve-year-olds will play truant in droves, and the taxpayers are already asking what goes on and voting down the bonds.

The interlocking of technologies and all other institutions makes it almost impossible to reform policy in any part; yet this very interlocking that renders people powerless, including the decision-makers, creates a remarkable resonance and chain-reaction if any determined group, or even determined individual, exerts force. In the face of overwhelmingly collective operations like the space exploration, the average man must feel that local or grassroots efforts are worthless, there is no science but Big Science, and no administration but the State. And yet there is a powerful surge of localism, populism, and community action, as if people were determined to be free even if it makes no sense. A mighty empire is stood off by a band of peasants, and *neither* can win—this is even more remarkable than if David beats Goliath; it means that neither principle is historically adequate. In my opinion, these dilemmas and impasses show that we are on the eve of a transformation of conscience.

Epilogue

Science originated with man's curiosity about his environment. Technology, the product of science, developed out of man's need and desire to live comfortably and compatibly with his surroundings. Yet modern science and technology seem to be completely out of line with this aim. We have created a reality removed from, and at odds with, nature—even with man's own nature. This development is eloquently summed up by Louis Mumford:

> Modern man . . . now approaches the last act of his tragedy, and I could not, even if I would, conceal its finality or its horror. We have lived to witness the joining, in intimate partnership, of the automaton and the id, the id rising from the lower depths of the unconscious and the automaton, the machine-like thinker and the man-like machine, wholly detached from outer life, maintaining functions and human reactions, descending from the heights of conscious thought. The first force has proved more brutal, when released from the whole personality, than the most savage of beasts; the other force, so impervious to human emotions, human anxieties, human purposes, so committed to answering only the limited range of questions for which its apparatus was originally loaded, that it lacks the saving intelligence to turn off its own compulsive mechanism, even though it is pushing science as well as civilization to its own doom.
> —*In the Name of Socialist Humanism,*
> Erich Fromm, ed. (New York: Doubleday, 1954).

It is currently in great fashion to accept this tragedy as a natural consequence of man's nature. Such passive acquiescence comes in the form of biological theories which matter-of-factly draw sweeping analogies between the ritualistic aggressive behavior exhibited in biological societies and the psychological behavior practiced in political–economic human society, and arrive at the conclusion that war is "natural" (e.g., Konrad Lorenz, Robert Ardry). It also comes in the form of the grotesquely optimistic followers of the behavioristic social sciences who are

267

busily engaged in engineering the smooth-running, computer-controlled society. Those who profess and participate in these theories and practices take no account of the autonomous human ego; they presume that it is a fiction of religion or psychology, or that it is obsolete in this day and age—or that it has been trampled and destroyed by modern society.

The important point is not to what extent the autonomous ego has been destroyed, but that it is the ego, revolting against the manipulated society, that is the hope for mankind; it is his creativity and his humanism. It is the obligation of all who have maintained their humanity to work and struggle to instill humanness back into science and into the society at large.

EDUCATION

Public education is of utmost importance in this area, for many of the vital decisions concerning the uses of science are made, or could be made, by the public. So education in this area must involve not only traditional types of classes but public forums, books and pamphlets, even public demonstrations. The humanistic scientist can be extremely vital in informing the public on the technical aspects concerning important social decisions. A good example of this kind of activity was the high degree of participation by scientists in informing the public about the pros and cons of ABM. And the Scientists' Institute for Public Information, which publishes the excellent periodical *Environment,* was established for just the purpose of making information of a technical nature available to the public.

Not only is specific technical information needed in the society, but scientists must also begin to discuss the general implications of social concepts of technical origin. For example, modern ecology tells us that man cannot afford to consider himself the king of the earth with free reign to manipulate the natural resources of the biosphere. What, then, should we say about such an accepted value as private property (or even state property): Does an individual or bureaucracy have the right to lay claim to a portion of the ecological system, the product of five billion years of physical and biological evolution, and use it in any way he or it wants, even if such use may have profound and disastrous consequences for millions of people living and for untold future generations? This is not an idle question, for just such situations are discussed specifically by many of the contributors in this book.

SAVING SCIENCE

A great deal is wrong with modern science. It is funded by governmental agencies interested only in military applications or fast and spectacular results; science is overspecialized and its approach to problems is too often atomistic instead of integrating; scientists too often want to work only with glamorous problems, ignoring the real problems of the society; and scientific societies are often polite monopolies on knowledge, effectively withholding important information from the public.

Only a humanistic science can fulfill its original promise, to create a technology that makes it possible for man to live in compatibility with his environment and his fellow man. This is a fundamental problem for man, for of all species, he is the only one that is not "reabsorbed" into the natural system. That is, his is not a purely biological society, but consists additionally of social and economic structures. If the structure of his society requires a science and technology that fly in the face of nature, then man is doomed. He must use his knowledge to construct a life-style of "natural artificiality," in which his technological developments become integral and consistent parts of the natural world. Man must learn to perceive the world as a dynamic system which contains him, not as a static object subject to external examination and manipulation. Otherwise, scientific knowledge will potentiate the destruction of mankind and the entire life system.

How is this philosophical concept to be translated into concrete action by scientists and citizens? The contributors of this volume have pointed out many activities which are worth summarizing.

Much can be done to reform science, and more is being done as scientists become aware of the dilemma we are facing.

There are several national and international organizations for social responsibility in science, and many scientists are working to reform the traditional societies. The problem of reforming the funding structure of science is a much more difficult one. Progress in this area will probably come about only when large numbers of scientists can make a convincing argument to the public that it is not wise to have military agencies sponsor research on health and education, or for health agencies to blacklist scientists for "security" reasons.

When Congress passed the Mansfield amendment (Section 203) to the Military Procurement Act, it cleared up the ambiguous situation of science research funding by the military. The amendment reads: "None of the funds authorized to be appropriated by this act may be used to carry out any research project or study unless such project or study has a direct and apparent relationship to a specific military function or operation." Clearly, conscientious scientists can no longer accept money from the DOD for the support of "basic" or "humanitarian" research.

The individual scientist may sincerely feel that his work is humanitarian, but the Defense Department maintains technical advisors to make sure that all research results in optimal military use. The Department of Defense will assure any scientist, who cares to inquire about the Mansfield amendment, of the military applicability of his research, though the details will often remain "classified."

MAKING SCIENCE COMPETENT

Because of its recent mechanistic, antihuman orientation, much of science is presently incompetent in dealing with many of the most pressing technical problems that face us. The boundaries which separate specialized fields from each other, and which separate science from the public, must be broken down. Many fields which have gone utterly neglected must be explored. Scientists must not be afraid to come to technological conclusions which may be at odds with major economic and political forces. A start in these directions has been made due to the increased interest in ecological problems in recent years. But the bulk of the task remains ahead.

THE YOUNG SCIENTIST

This book is addressed, in large part, to young scientists and science students. It is the young scientist who is most aware of the failure of science and most willing to do something about it. But there should be no illusions about the difficulty of the task. The image of an elementary-particle physicist who spends his spare time studying environmental problems is a profound illusion. The most realistic outlook for the idealistic young scientist today is unemployment. According to the March 1969 issue of *Physics Today,* 29.5 percent of the physicists awarded Ph.D. degrees in June 1968 received no job offer, and 32.6 percent received only one offer.

There should be no illusion that massive amounts of money will come pouring in for the study of technical–social problems. In contrast to the eight-billion-dollar DOD research budget it authorized for 1969, Congress later (in Senate Bill 1075) allocated only half a million dollars for ecological research, and that not until 1971.

The most probable expectation of a young scientist with a social conscience is an 18-hour day. He will have to find a job as a technician or high-school teacher in order to make a living, and spend the rest of the time doing self-supported research of social value. He will have to convince the public of the value of such work after the fact. Such is not an easy life, but it is the legacy of the social relations of science and society over the last 30 years.

A MATTER OF COMMITMENT

It is not possible to recommend the specific direction the individual scientist, or nonscientist, should take in dealing with the technological problems that face us. The important principle to keep in mind is that we wish to humanize our existence. With this in mind, and with the knowledge that all of us who see this need are obligated to work for it in some way, the individual must choose the range of activities, the field of study, where he can make his efforts most fully felt. We are cursed, but also blessed, to be living at the time of human evolution when our efforts may save mankind from final destruction.

M. B.

Topical
Bibliography

CHEMICAL AND BIOLOGICAL WARFARE

Airborne Microbes, Seventeenth Symposium, Society for General Microbiology, Imperial College, London, 1967.

Bernhard, R., "Biological Warfare: The Deadly Aerosol," *Scientific Research*, Jan. 22, 1968.

Brodine, V., "The Secret Weapons," *Environment*, Vol. 11, No. 5, June 1969.

California (State) University School of Public Health, Naval Biological Laboratory, Technical Progress Reports, 1953–1969.

"CBW: What's Being Done in Vietnam?", *Scientific Research*, Nov. 11, 1968.

"Chemical and Biological Warfare," *Scientist and Citizen*, Vol. 9, No. 7, Aug.–Sept., 1967.

"Chemical, Biological, Radiological Warfare," background paper prepared by the Committee for World Development and World Disarmanent, July 1965.

Clarke, R., "Biological Warfare," *Science Journal*, Nov. 1966.

Clarke, R., *The Silent Weapons*, New York, 1968.

Cook, R. E., W. Haseltine, and A. W. Galston, "Deliberate Destruction of the Environment: What Have We Done to Vietnam?", in *The New Republic*, Jan. 10, 1970.

Duffett, John (ed.), *Against the Crime of Silence*, 1968.

Harvey, G. R., and J. D. Mann, "Picloram in Vietnam," *Scientist and Citizen*, Sept. 1968.

Heden, C.–G., "Defenses against Biological Warfare," *Annual Review of Microbiology*, Vol. 21, 1967.

Hersh, S. M., *Chemical and Biological Warfare: America's Hidden Arsenal*, Bobbs-Merrill, New York, 1968.

Langer, E., "Chemical and Biological Warfare (I): The Research Program," *Science*, Vol. 155, Jan. 13, 1967.

————, "Chemical and Biological Warfare (II): The Weapons and the Politics," *Science*, Vol. 155, Jan. 20, 1967.

————, "Chemical and Biological Weapons: Once Over Lightly on Capitol Hill," *Science*, May 26, 1967.

Leopold, A. C.: "Defoliation," *Bioscience*, Vol. 18, 1968.

McCarthy, R., *The Ultimate Folly*, New York, 1969.

McDermott, W. (ed.), "Conference on Airborne Infection," *Bacteriological Reviews*, Vol. 25, No. 3, 1961.

Michaels, D., and R. Krickus, "Chemical and Biological Warfare," Newsletter of the Council for Correspondence, April, 1963.

Midwest Research Institute, *Assessment of Ecological Effects of Extensive or Repeated Use of Herbicides,* Defense Documentation Center.

Neilands, J. et. al., *Chemical Warfare in Indochina,* New York, 1971.

Rose, S. (ed.), *CBW, Chemical and Biological Warfare,* Boston, 1968.

Rosebury, T., "Medical Ethics and Biological Warfare," *Perspectives in Biology and Medicine,* VI, 1963.

Rothschild, J. H., *Tomorrow's Weapons,* New York, 1964.

Second International Conference on Aerobiology (Airborne Infection), *Bacteriological Review,* Vol. 30, 1966.

Sidel, V. W., and R. M. Goldwyn, "Chemical and Biological Weapons —a Primer," *New England Journal of Medicine,* Vol. 274, Jan. 6, 1966.

Takman, J. (ed.), *Napalm: An International Symposium.*

Tompkins, J. S., *The Weapons of World War III,* Garden City, 1966.

Tschirley, F. H., "Defoliation in Vietnam," *Science,* Feb. 21, 1969.

United Nations General Assembly, Report of the Secretary-General, "Chemical and Bacteriological (Biological) Weapons and the Effects of their Possible Use," July 1, 1969.

U.S. Congress, House of Representatives, "Banning Poison Gas and Germ Warfare: Should the United States Agree?" *Congressional Record*—Extensions of Remarks, May 21, 1969, Rep. Robert W. Kastenmeier, E 4207–4220.

U.S. Congress, House of Representatives, Committee on Foreign Affairs, "International Implications of Dumping Poisonous Gas and Waste into Oceans," May 8, 13, 15, 1969. Hearings before Subcommittee on International Organizations and Movements.

U.S. Congress, Senate Committee on Labor and Public Welfare, "Chemical and Biological Weapons: Some Possible Approaches for Lessening the Threat and Danger," Ninety-first Congress, First Session, 1969.

U.S. Department of the Army TM 3–216, "Military Biology and Biological Warfare Agents," Washington, D.C., 1956.

"Viet Report," New York, Jan., 1968.

Young, L. S., D. S. Bicknell, B. G. Archer, J. M. Clinton, L. G. Leavens, J. C. Feeley, and P. S. Brachman, "Tularemia Epidemic: Vermont, 1968," *The New England Journal of Medicine,* Vol. 280, No. 23, June 5, 1969.

Zinsser, H., *Rats, Lice and History,* New York, 1935.

CHEMICAL POLLUTION

Carson, R. L., *Silent Spring*, Boston, 1962.

"Chemicals Used in Food Processing," 1965 National Research Council, Publ. No. 1274, Washington, D.C.

Commoner, B., "Lake Erie, Aging or Ill?", *Scientist and Citizen* (now *Environment*), 10 (10), 1968.

Conway, G. R., "Pests Follow the Chemicals in the Cocoa of Malaysia," *Natural History*, 78(2), 1969.

Dahlsten, D. L., R. Garcia, J. E. Prine, and R. Hunt, "Insect Problems in Forest Recreation Areas," *California Agriculture*, July 1969.

———, and G. M. Thomas, "A Nucleopolyhedrosis Virus in Populations of the Douglas Fir Tussock Moth, *Hemerocampa pseudotsugata*, in California," *Journal of Invertebrate Pathology*, March 1969.

DeBach, P. (ed.), *Biological Control of Insect Pests and Weeds*, New York, 1964.

Egler, F. E., "Pesticides in Our Ecosystem," *American Scientist*, March 1964.

———, "Pesticides in Our Ecosystem: Communication II," *Bioscience*, Nov. 1964.

Geier, P. W., "Management of Insect Pests," *Annual Review of Entomology*, 1966.

Hickey, J. J., and D. W. Anderson, "Chlorinated Hydrocarbons and Eggshell Changes in Raptorial and Fish-eating Birds," *Science*, 1968.

Jukes, T. H., "People and Pesticides," *American Scientists*, Sept. 1963.

Leopold, A., *A Sand County Almanac*, New York, 1949.

Lindquist, A. W., and E. F. Knipling, "Recent Advances in Veterinary Entomology," *Annual Review of Entomology*, 1957.

McKee, J. E., and H. W. Wolf (eds.), "Water Quality Criteria," 2nd ed., State Water Quality Control Board, Resources Agency of California, publication No. 3–A.

McLean, L. A., "Pesticides and the Environment," *Bioscience*, 17 (9), 1967.

Peakall, D. B., "Pesticide-Induced Enzyme Breakdown of Steroids in Birds," *Nature*, 216, 1967.

Pfadt, R. E., *Fundamentals of Applied Entomology*, New York, 1962.

Ratcliffe, D. A., "Decrease in Eggshell Weight in Certain Birds of Prey," *Nature*, 215, 1967.

Risebrough, R. W., "Chlorinated Hydrocarbons in Marine Ecosystems," in M. W. Miller and G. G. Berg (eds.) *Chemical Fallout*, Springfield, 1969.

Rudd, R. L., *Pesticides and the Living Landscape*, Madison, Wis., 1964.

Smith, R. F., "Consideration of the Cotton Insect Problems in Guatemala," 1969.
———, and R. van den Bosch, "Integrated Control," in W. W. Kilgore and R. L. Doutt (eds.), *Pest Control: Biological, Physical and Selected Chemical Methods,* New York, 1967.
Whitten, J. L., *That We May Live,* N. J., 1966.
Woodwell, G. M., "Toxic Substances and Ecological Cycles," *Scientific American,* 216 (3), offprint No. 1066, 1967.
Wurster, C. F., "DDT Goes to Trial in Wisconsin," *Bioscience,* 19 (9), 1969.

ECOLOGY

Billings, *Plants and the Ecosystem,* Belmont, 1964.
Boochin, M., *Ecology and Revolutionary Thought,* New York, 1969.
Bronson, W., *How to Kill a Golden State,* New York, 1968.
Buchsbaum, R. and M., *Basic Ecology,* Boxwood, 1957.
"CBNS Notes," Center for the study of Natural Systems, St. Louis.
Cloud, P., *Resources and Man,* San Francisco, 1969.
Commoner, B., *Science and Survival,* New York, 1966.
Dasmann, R., *Destruction of California,* New York, 1969.
"Ecology," Ecology Action, Berkeley.
"Environment," CBNS, St. Louis.
Goldman, M., *Controlling Pollution,* New York, 1967.
Karmandy, E., *Concepts of Ecology,* Englewood Cliffs, 1969.
McHarg, I., *Design with Nature,* New York, 1969.
Odum, E., *Ecology,* New York, 1969.
Osborn, F., *Our Plundered Planet,* New York, 1948.
Ramparts magazine, May 1970.
"Restoring the Quality of Our Environment," Washington, D.C., 1965.
Scientists' Institute for Public Information, *Ecology Handbooks,* St. Louis, 1970.
Shepard, P., *The Subversive Science,* Boston, 1969.
Slater, R., D. Kitt, D. Widelock, and P. Kangas, *The Earth Belongs to the People* (pamphlet), San Francisco, 1970.
Storer, J., *The Web of Life,* New York, 1968.
Wagner, P., *Human Use of the Earth,* New York, 1960.

THE WORLD FOOD PROBLEM

Borgstrom, G., *The Hungry Planet,* New York, London, 1967.
de Castro, J., *The Black Book of Hunger,* Boston, 1967.
———, *The Geography of Hunger,* Boston, 1952.

Feeney, R. E., "Biochemical Studies of Cold-Adapted Antarctic Fishes," *Scientific American,* 1969.

"Food and Fiber for the Future," report of the National Advisory Commission on Food and Fiber, Superintendent of Documents, Washington, D.C., 1967.

Hardin, C. M., "For Humanity, New Hope," in C. M. Hardin, *Overcoming World Hunger,* New York, 1969.

"Hunger, U.S.A.," a report by the Citizens' Board of Inquiry into Hunger and Malnutrition in the United States, Boston, 1968.

International Atomic Energy Agency, "Desalination of Water Using Conventional and Nuclear Energy," Tech, Rep. Ser. 24, 1964.

Lowe, C. H., Jr., *The Desert, Life* Nature Library, 1961.

May, J. M., "Nutrition, Science, and Man's Food," *Food, Science, and Society,* The Nutrition Foundation, Inc., New York, 1969.

Notestein, F. W., "Population Growth and Its Control," in C. M. Hardin, *Overcoming World Hunger,* New York, 1969.

Paarlberg, D., "Food for more people and better nutrition," in C. M. Hardin, *Overcoming World Hunger,* New York, 1969.

Pawley, W. M., "Possibilities of Increasing World Food Production," FFMC Basic Study, No. 10, Rome, 1963.

Rasmussen, C. L., "Man and His Food, 2000 A.D.," *Food Technology,* May 23, 1969.

Revelle, R., "In the Shape of a Loaf of Bread," *War on Hunger,* report of Agency of International Development, Vol. 2, Washington, D.C., 1968.

Second International Congress of Antarctic Ecology, Cambridge, England, 1968.

"The World Food Problem," report of the President's Science Advisory Committee, Vol. 1, May 1967.

Young, G., *Dry Land and a Hungry World,* Trans. N. Y. Acad. Sci., Series II, Vol. 31, No. 2, 1969.

GENETIC MANIPULATION

British Medical Bulletin, Vol. 17, No. 3, Sept. 1961:
    Carter, C. O., "Inheritance of Congenital Pyloric Stenosis."
    Holzel, A., "Galactosemia."
    Lehman, H., E. Silk, and J. Liddell, "Pseudocholinesterase."

Meade, J. E., *Biological Aspects of Social Problems,* New York, 1965. Mather, K., "Medicine and Natural Selection in Man." Roberts, J. A., "Some Practical Applications."

Roberts, J. A., *An Introduction to Medical Genetics,* London, 1967.

Stern, C., *Principles of Human Genetics,* San Francisco, 1960.

Taylor, G., *The Biological Time Bomb,* New York, 1968.

Wolstenholme, G., *Man and His Future,* A CIBA Foundation Volume, Boston, 1963.

MISUSE OF AGRICULTURAL LAND

Bogue, D. J., "Metropolitan Growth and the Conversion of Land to Non-agricultural Uses," Scripps Foundation for Research, Oxford, Ohio, 1956.

Bronson, W., "How to Kill a Golden State," New York, 1968.

"California Soil and Water Conservation Needs Inventory," the California Conservation Needs Committee, Nov. 1961.

Geyer, R. E., "The Agricultural Sciences," *Bioscience*, May 1965.

House and Home Magazine, Aug. 1960.

"Land Conversions in California," USDA Soil Conservation Service.

MALNUTRITION

Apley, J.: "An Ecology of Childhood," *Lancet*, 2:1–4, 1964.

Brewer, T., "The American Medical Association: Fact and Fiction," *Herald of Health*, Feb. 1969.

———, "Political Effects of the Material Basis of Human Thought," *American Behavioral Scientist*, 9:9–14, June 1966.

Cannon, W. B., *The Wisdom of the Body*, New York, 1939.

de Castro, Josue, *The Black Book of Hunger*, Boston, 1967.

———, *The Geography of Hunger*, Boston, 1952.

Christakis, G., "City Survey: Seventy-five Percent of Youth on Poor Diet," *Hospital Tribune*, Aug. 26, 1968.

Fahy, A. and C. Muschenheim,"Third National Conference on American Indian Health," *Journal of the American Medical Association*, 194:1093–1096, Dec. 6, 1965.

Mayer, J., "The Nutrional Status of American Negroes," *Nutrition Reviews*, 23:161–164, June, 1965.

Ramazzini, B., *Diseases of Workers*, New York, 1964.

Riese, H., *Heal the Hurt Child*, Chicago, 1962.

U.S. Public Health Service, "The Health Consequences of Smoking," *A Public Health Service Review*, Washington, D.C.

"What Are You Doing about Smoking?", *Annals of Internal Medicine*, 69:163–165, July 1968.

MEDICINE

Carter, R., *The Doctor Business*, New York, 1958.

Drew, E., "The Health Syndicate," *The Atlantic*, Dec. 1967.

Gross, M., *The Doctors*, New York, 1966.

"Health Pac," Health Pac, New York.

"Health Rights News," Medical Committee for Human Rights, New York.

Hutton, W., *The Drug Price Scandal*, Boston, 1967.

Mintz, M., "FDA and Panalba," *Science*, Aug. 29, 1969.

Mintz, M., *The Therapeutic Nightmare*, Boston, 1965.

Ralston, R. (ed.), "Sources," Blue Cross, Chicago.

Rensberg, C. and B. Rensberg, "Why You Really Can't Get Good Medical Care," *Good Housekeeping*, Feb. 1970.

Talalay, P. (ed.), *Drugs in Our Society*, Baltimore, 1964.

The Body Politic, Medical Committee for Human Rights, San Francisco, Calif.

Tucker, R., *The Case for Socialized Medicine*.

NUCLEAR WEAPONS AND PEACEFUL USES OF ATOMIC ENERGY

Brown, A., *ABM: Yes or No?*, New York, 1968.

Bulletin of the Atomic Scientists.

Calder, N., *Unless Peace Comes*, New York, 1968.

Court–Brown, W. M., and R. Doll, "Mortality from Cancer and Other Causes after Radiotherapy for Ankylosing Spondylitis," *Brit. Med. J.* 2, 1327–1332, 1965.

Davis, N., *Lawrence and Oppenheimer*, New York, 1969.

Draper, G. J., and A. M. Stewart, "Decline in U.S. Childhood Leukemia Mortality," *Lancet*, Dec. 20, 1969, p. 1356.

"The Evaluation of Risks from Radiation," publication No. 8 of the International Commission on Radiological Protection.

Kahn, H., *On Thermonuclear War*, New York, 1969.

Lapp, R., *The Weapons Culture*, New York, 1968.

Lewis, E. B., "Leukemia and Ionizing Radiation," *Science 125*, 965–972, 1957.

Maki, H., T. Ishimaru, H. Kato, and T. Wakabayashi, "Carcinogenesis in Atomic Bomb Survivors," *Technical Report 24-68*, Atomic Bomb Casualty Commission, Nov. 14, 1968.

"Radiosensitivity and Spatial Distribution of Dose," publication No. 14 of the International Commission on Radiological Protection, London, 1969.

Rathjens, A., "The Dynamics of the Arms Race," *Scientific American*, April 1969.

Smyth, H. D., *Atomic Energy for Military Purposes*, Princeton, 1945.

Stewart, A., and G. W. Kneale, "Changes in the Cancer Risk Associated with Obstetric Radiography," *Lancet, 1*, 104–107, 1968.

———, J. Webb, and D. Hewitt, "A Survey of Childhood Malignancies," *Brit. Med. J. 1*, 1945–1508, 1958.

Szilard, L., *The Voice of Dolphins*, New York, 1961.

Teller, E., and A. Brown, *The Legacy of Hiroshima*, New York, 1962.

Weisner, J. (ed.), *An Evaluation of the Decision to Deploy ABM*, New York, 1969.

——"Tamplin—Gofman, Pauling, and the AEC," *Science and Public Affairs, Bulletin of the Atomic Scientists,* Sept. 1970.

POPULATION

Baran, P., *Political Economy of Growth,* New York, 1967.
Bogue, D. J., *Population of the United States,* Glencoe, 1959.
Bookchin, M., *The Population Myth,* New York, 1970.
Borgstrum, G., *The Hungry Planet,* New York, 1965.
——, *Too Many,* New York, 1969.
Commoner, B., interview in *The Earth Times,* June 1970.
Erlich, P., *The Population Bomb,* New York, 1968.
Forester, H. Von. P. M. Mer, and L. W. Amiot, "Doomsday: Friday, 13 November, A. D. 2026," *Science,* Nov. 1960.
Hardin, G., *Nature and Man's Fate,* New York, 1959.
——, *Population, Evolution and Birth Control,* San Francisco, 1969.
Luten, D., "California Revolution I," *The Nation,* Jan. 30, 1967.
——, "How Dense Can People Be?", *Sierra Club Bulletin,* Dec. 1963.
——, "Numbers Against Wilderness," *Sierra Club Bulletin,* Dec. 1964.
Meek, R. L., *Marx and Engels on the Population Bomb,* New York, 1970.
Paddock, W., *Famine 1975,* Boston, 1968.

SCIENCE, THE UNIVERSITY, AND THE GOVERNMENT

Dupree, A. H., *Science in the Federal Government,* Cambridge, 1957.
Fulbright, W. J., *Playboy Interview,* July 1968.
——, Senate speech, Dec. 13, 1967.
Gilpin, R., and C. Wright (eds.), *Scientists and National Policy Making,* New York, 1964.
Gredzins, M., and E. Rabinowitch, *The Atomic Age,* New York, 1963.
Greenberg, D. S., *The Politics of Pure Science,* New York, 1968.
——, "Social Sciences: Expanded Role Urged for Defense Department," *Science,* March 7, 1969, Vol. 163, No. 3871.
Klare, M., *The University–Military Complex: A Directory and Related Documents,* New York, 1968.
Long, F. A., "Support of Scientific Research and Education in Our Universities," *Science,* March 7, 1969, Vol. 163, No. 3871.
Langer, E., "Themis: DOD Plan to Spread the Wealth Raises Questions in Academe," *Science,* April 7, 1967.
Orlans, H., "The Impact of Federal Funds on Higher Education," Brookings Research Report No. 5, Oct. 1962.
Rickover, H., Testimony to Senate Foreign Relations Committee, May

28, July 19, 1968, on Senate Resolution 110, July 11, 17, 18, 1967, part 3.
Ridgeway, J., *The Closed Corporation*, New York, 1968.
Schooler, D., *Science, Scientists, and Public Policy*, New York, 1971.
Snow, C. P., *Science and Government*, Cambridge, Mass., 1961.
————, *The Two Cultures: And a Second Look*, Cambridge, Mass., 1964.

* * *

American Civil Liberties Union statement concerning the University and Contract Research, Nov. 24, 1959.
"The Case of Stephen Smale," *Notices* of American Math Society, Oct. 1967, and Jan., Feb. 1968.
"Conflicts between Federal Research Programs and the National Goals for Higher Education," Committee on Government Operations, Eighty-ninth Congress, First Session, June, 1965.
"Defense Department-Sponsored Foreign Affairs Research," hearings before the Committee on Foreign Relations, United States Senate, Ninetieth Congress, Second Session, part 2, May 1968.
Eighteenth Report by the Committee on Government Operations, Eighty-ninth Congress, First Session, House Report No. 1158, Oct. 1965.
"Federal Support of Basic Research in Institutions of Higher Learning," National Academy of Sciences, Washington, D.C. 1964.
Memorandum of the AAUP, Rochester University Chapter, concerning the $8,819,000 contract with the Center for Naval Analyses, similar to IDA. The memo is dated May 9, 1968.
"A Review of Current Problems in Contractual Procedures Affecting Relationships between the Department of Defense and Educational Institutions," Ad Hoc Committee of Research and Development Board, Oct. 1952.
Statistical Abstracts of the United States, Washington, D.C., 1970.
Thirty-second Report by the Committee on Government Operations, Eighty-fifth Congress, Second Session, House Report No. 2552, Aug. 1958.
"The Volpin Case: The Confinement of a Russian Mathematician," *Notices* of AMS, June 1968.

THE SOCIAL ROLE OF THE SCIENTIST

Bernal, J. D., *Science in History*, New York, 1965.
Boulding, K. E., *The Meaning of the Twentieth Century*, New York, 1969.
Bronowski, J., *Science and Human Values*, New York, 1965.
Ellul, J., *Technological Society*, New York, 1964.

Fromm, E., *The Revolution of Hope,* New York, 1968.

Hardin, G. (ed.), *Science, Conflict, and Society,* San Francisco, 1969.

Klaw, S., *The New Brahmin,* New York, 1968.

Mesthene, E., (ed.), *Technology and Social Change,* New York, 1967.

Nieburg, H. L., *In the Name of Science,* Chicago, 1966.

Platt, J. R., "Scientific Knowledge and Social Values," *The Excitement of Science,* Boston, 1962.

Price, D., *The Scientific Estate,* Oxford, 1968.

Rotblat, J., *Science and World Affairs: History of the Pugwash Conference,* London, 1962.

Sakharev, A., *Progress, Co-Existence, and Intellectual Freedom,* Cambridge, 1969.

Sarkman, H., *Computers, System Science, and Evolving Society,* New York, 1967.

Wald, G., "A Generation in Search of a Future" (pamphlet), Cambridge, 1969.

Walker, C. R., ed. *Technology, Industry, and Man,* New York, 1968.

Vickers, G., *Value Systems and Social Process,* New York, 1968.

VITAL PERIODICALS

Most scientific journals occasionally carry news and comments concerning the social consequences of science and technology. The best magazines in this respect are:

Environment
Population Bulletin
Science
Scientific American
SSRS Newsletter
The Bulletin of the Atomic Scientists